"It is about movement. *Praying for Freedom* invites us into the movement of the Ignatian *Spiritual Exercises*, into becoming swept up and responsive to the overabundance of God's grace, into turning toward the sacramentality of all bodies, and into unlearning white supremacy, a holy unlearning. Dare to move."

— Nancy Pineda-Madrid, T. Marie Chilton Chair of Catholic Theology, Loyola Marymount University

"To answer the question posed by Jesuits and, by extension, all who are touched by Ignatian spirituality, 'Why are we not more deeply changed by the *Spiritual Exercises*?' is also to confront the painful issue of racism in America. What emerges through the poignant and prayerful essays offered in this volume is hope and a broadened perspective. Together, the collection demonstrates that the heritage of racially-charged violence, negligence, and human suffering that so often give way to indifference and paralysis do not have the final word in our discourse and imagination. Compassionate solidarity grounded in Christian and Ignatian tradition uncover paths of transformative possibilities."

— Joseph Lagan, director, Ignatian Spirituality Program, University Mission, Regis University

"*Praying for Freedom* translates Ignatian spirituality as a warm embrace that liberates us from the shackles of racism so that we can fall in love with all of humanity. As we actively engage with the *Spiritual Exercises*, we begin to see differently, hear differently, and move differently in community. Let freedom ring as we encounter these all-encompassing exercises in love!"

— Lori Stanley, executive director of Loyola Institute for Spirituality

Praying for Freedom

Racism and Ignatian Spirituality in America

Edited by
Laurie Cassidy

LITURGICAL PRESS
ACADEMIC

Collegeville, Minnesota
litpress.org

Cover art by Fabian Debora. This painting, *Falling Star 2009*, is of my daughter and I as we are both the falling stars in our community of Boyle Heights where this image of Father and Daughter symbolizes safety, protection, and most importantly change and transformation which helps pave the way for our new generations to come. fabiandebora.com.

1   2   3   4   5   6   7   8   9

Library of Congress Cataloging-in-Publication Data

Names: Cassidy, Laurie M., editor.
Title: Praying for freedom : racism and Ignatian spirituality in America / edited by Laurie Cassidy.
Description: Collegeville, Minnesota : Liturgical Press Academic, [2024] | Summary: "Why do the Spiritual Exercises not change us as deeply as we hope? This is the question that was raised at the general congregation of the Jesuits about Ignatius's Spiritual Exercises and the question the contributors to this book explore and attempt to answer in the context of ongoing racial injustice in the United States. Contributors explore this question by examining how "color-blindness racism" determines our interpretation of the Spiritual Exercises in the United States"—Provided by publisher.
Identifiers: LCCN 2023042018 (print) | LCCN 2023042019 (ebook) | ISBN 9780814667910 (trade paperback) | ISBN 9780814667927 (epub) | ISBN 9798400801273 (pdf)
Subjects: LCSH: Ignatius, of Loyola, Saint, 1491-1556. Exercitia spiritualia. | Race discrimination—Religious aspects—Catholic Church. | Racism—Religious aspects—Catholic Church. | Race discrimination—United States. | Racism—United States. | United States—Religion.
Classification: LCC BX2179.L8 P68 2024 (print) | LCC BX2179.L8 (ebook) | DDC 261.8/32—dc23/eng/20231122
LC record available at https://lccn.loc.gov/2023042018
LC ebook record available at https://lccn.loc.gov/2023042019

With Deepest Gratitude

to all

Our Ignatian Ancestors

especially the

Jesuits   *Women Religious*   *Lay People*

Inspired by Vatican II

whose intelligence, passion for justice, and creativity

makes this work possible

Contents

PART I
Presuppositions

PART II
The Spiritual Exercises

PART III
Contemplating God's Laboring and Loving in the World

Acknowledgments

This collection was made possible by many "friends of God and prophets." The idea for this volume grew out of an inspiring conversation at Seattle University with Lucas Sharma, SJ, in 2018. His insight and encouragement were foundational to the development of this project. Ongoing conversations with Catherine Punsalan-Manlimos, PhD, were critical to clarifying the vision of this book. Patrick St. Jean, SJ's prolific writing on race and Ignatian spirituality has pushed forward our national conversation, and he was generous in contributing to this volume. I am indebted to Fabian Debora for allowing his artwork to grace the cover; it is a blessing to this volume. Damien Costello, PhD, was gracious enough to introduce me to Maka Black Elk, making possible his contribution. With perfect timing Kristin Heyer, PhD, recommended Armando Guerrero Estrada, PhD, as a contributor, and Armando's collaboration with Paulina Delgadillo is a gift to this book. Jeff LaBelle, SJ, energized this project through his conversations with me about spirituality and Critical Race Theory. I am grateful to John Schwantes, SJ, for his faithful friendship and willingness to be continually consulted on all things Ignatian; he supported this work at every turn. My dear friend Vera Alston prayed for all the contributors in this book, and so did Tony Mazurkiewicz. Their prayer was a precious gift that enabled the completion of this project. I deeply appreciate Hans Christoffersen at Liturgical Press. Mary Carol Kendzia and Stephanie Lancour's meticulous editing accompanied by Michelle Verkuilen and Tara Durheim's committed marketing are invaluable. Their vision, professionalism, and kindness are unmatched. Alex Mikulich, PhD, was, as always, a comrade and a generous conversation partner throughout this project. Finally, John Sabo's humor, calm, and loving companionship make all the difference on the journey.

Introduction

Praying for Freedom

Laurie Cassidy

What does it mean to "pray for freedom"? Ignatius of Loyola understood freedom as a person being available and responsive to God. Freedom is a fundamental disposition of Christ's companions envisioned in Ignatian spirituality.[1] To pray for this graced disposition in America is not simple or straightforward because the word "freedom" conjures deeply contested visions and contradictory realities that are imprinted upon our national psyche.[2] We sing, "My country

---

[1] "[T]his freedom, is a yearning inside a man(sic) to say 'Yes' to God as God moves him interiorly. It is a desire to sell all that one has to buy the field, or to get the pearl of great price." See John English, *Spiritual Freedom: From the Experience of the Exercises to the Art of Spiritual Direction* (Guelph, Ontario: Loyola House, 1973), 53. English explains that such freedom is prayed for and is a result of knowing one is loved by God. From an Ignatian perspective, only knowing the depth of God's love creates the conditions of possibility for genuine freedom. See also Eileen Burke-Sullivan and Kevin Burke, SJ, *The Ignatian Tradition* (Collegeville, MN: Liturgical Press, 2009), xxxiii–xxxiv.

[2] "No one would deny that today freedom stands unchallenged as the supreme value of the Western world." Orlando Patterson, *Freedom: Freedom in the Making of Western Culture* (New York: Basic Books, 1991), ix. Also see Anneleine De Dijin, *Freedom: An Unruly History* (Cambridge, MA: Harvard University Press, 2020). Probing how the Ignatian understanding of freedom functions in relationship to the broader history of this idea is critical both for Ignatian scholarship and in pastoral ministry and spiritual direction in America, but regrettably is beyond the scope of this introduction.

'tis of thee, sweet land of liberty" but for whom does "freedom ring"?[3] How does our collective history of white supremacy impact our understanding of and prayer for freedom? At the birth of the United States the Constitution spelled out freedom for its citizens, while this freedom was ratified into law by slave-owning founding fathers. In the words of Frederick Douglass, "What to the Slave is the Fourth of July?"[4] Even today, Lady Liberty stands in New York Harbor, inviting "huddled masses yearning to be breathe free,"[5] while at the southern border of our country we have constructed a wall to prevent access.[6] In America, the very word, "freedom" evokes the best and worst of America. We carry these contradictions, and the whole history of "freedom" in America within us when we pray, whether we are conscious of this or not. Inspired by Ignatius, how can prayer for freedom today "break the crippling spell cast by the dominant culture" in order to embody genuine availability and authentic responsiveness to God at this moment in American history?[7] This is the central question the contributors grapple with in this volume.

The artwork gracing the cover of *Praying for Freedom* was chosen because it is an imaginative way into reflecting on the diverse dimensions of freedom within Ignatian spirituality that we are exploring in this book. The freedom described by Ignatius is often hijacked by

[3] Martin Luther King Jr. spoke of his dream for freedom to ring for all people, everywhere in America. "If America is to be a great nation, this must become true." See "I Have a Dream" speech at Stanford University's Martin Luther King, Jr. Research and Education Institute at https://kinginstitute.stanford.edu/news/freedoms-ring -i-have-dream-speech (accessed May 6, 2023).

[4] To read the full address of Douglass at the Corinthian Hall in Rochester, New York, in 1852 see Frederick Douglass, *The Portable Frederick Douglass* (New York: Penguin Books, 2016), 195.

[5] These words from the poem "The New Colossus" by Emma Lazarus are inscribed on the bronze plaque at the base of the Statue of Liberty. See Małgorzata Szejnert, *Ellis Island: A People's History*, trans. Sean Gaspar (Minneapolis: Scribe Publications, 2009); Gregory Eiselein, *Emma Lazarus: Selected Poems and Other Writings* (Peterborough, Ontario: Broadview Press, 2002).

[6] Jean Guerrero, "A Trump-like Border Wall Is about to Be Built—unless Biden Stops It," *Los Angeles Times* (February 27, 2023), https://www.latimes.com/opinion /story/2023-02-27/border-wall-united-states-mexico-biden-trump-immigration (accessed May 3, 2023).

[7] This quotation comes from M. Shawn Copeland, *Knowing Christ Crucified: The Witness of African American Religious Experience* (Maryknoll, NY: Orbis Books, 2018), 58.

the toxic individualism of white supremacy and reduced to simply an inner disposition, realized on retreat or in prayer. To "spiritualize" Ignatius's wisdom is to divorce its transformative potential from everyday life and relationships. In contrast, Fabian Debora's artwork invites us to explore freedom on multiple levels. Like Ignatius's conversion experience, Debora went through a graced transformation, turning away from a life of drug addiction and gang violence to a new life of creativity, commitment, compassion, and hope. He describes his painting *Falling Stars* as a vision of hope for his daughter, who is carrying his heart. With arms outstretched, Debora protects her from his past in the fenced off neighborhood behind him, "ensuring her safety and innocence."[8] Debora's freedom from addiction and self-destruction created conditions of freedom for his daughter. His freedom is not only an inner disposition, but is embodied, intergenerational, and communal. This image illustrates what M. Shawn Copeland describes as "enfleshing freedom."[9] Copeland retrieves the "dark hidden wisdom" of her enslaved ancestors who in desiring freedom wanted not only an inner space to think, feel, imagine, and long for what was stolen from them, but desired to redeem their own bodies, families, and futures from chattel slavery.

> The freedom for which enslaved people prayed proved impatient of political or social or spiritual or religious distinctions; rather, the freedom for which the enslaved people longed, struggled, fought, and died was holistic—at once, political *and* social, psychic *and* spiritual, metaphysical *and* ontological, this worldly *and* otherworldly.[10]

This dark and hidden wisdom is counter to the wisdom of the world—particularly in the ethos of the individualism of white supremacy in America—and suggests that when we ask for the grace of freedom, what God desires for us is infinitely more than we can

---

[8] Sylvia Mendoza, "Homeboy Industries: The Salvation of Artist Fabian Debora," *accessHealth*, https://accesshealthnews.com/homeboy-industries-the-salvation-of-artist-fabian-debora/ (accessed May 8, 2023).

[9] M. Shawn Copeland, *Enfleshing Freedom: Body, Race, and Being* (Minneapolis: Fortress Press, 2010).

[10] Copeland, *Knowing Christ Crucified*, 58.

ever hope for or imagine (cf. Eph 3:20). Debora's image and M. Shawn Copeland's words expand the horizon of freedom. We are called to enflesh freedom because "Jesus of Nazareth is the paradigm of enfleshing freedom; he *is* freedom enfleshed."[11]

Debora's image also raises the question of our freedom to find God in all things. How can we recognize the face of God in this man and his daughter? David Fleming, SJ, explains that one of the lasting gifts of the Spiritual Exercises is seeing the face of God in our lives.[12] Seeing the face of God in our lives may not only involve freedom from distorted images from our own personal histories, but also freedom from the distorted inherited narratives of white supremacy. For example, the man in this image on the cover was born in El Paso and lives in Boyle Heights in Los Angeles, he has brown skin, tattoos, and black hair gathered into a ponytail—can we contemplate the Risen Christ in his face? Doesn't Debora's life story from death to new life reveal the paschal mystery on this land? As we gaze into the eyes of his daughter, do we see the yearning and joy of Christ as she holds the small, vulnerable Sacred Heart summoning us to have a new heart and a new spirit within us?

These reflections on Fabian Debora's image should not be viewed as a "multicultural" excursus.[13] These reflections illustrate two fundamental elements of interpreting Ignatian spirituality in *Praying for Freedom: Racism and Ignatian Spirituality in America*. First, the starting point for this volume is how our living on this particular land, which some call Turtle Island, with our specific history of colonization and enslavement, and within our present circumstances enables interpret-

---

[11] Copeland, *Enfleshing Freedom*, 53; emphasis in original. This theological description of Jesus of Nazareth as freedom enfleshed echoes the name of Jesus, "Creator Sets Free," which is used in Terry Wildman's *First Nation: An Indigenous Translation of the New Testament* (Downers Grove, IL: InterVarsity Press, 2021).

[12] David Fleming, SJ, *Like the Lightning: The Dynamics of the Ignatian Exercises* (St. Louis, MO: Institute of Jesuit Sources, 2004), 63.

[13] The importance of the arts within Jesuit spirituality and Ignatian pedagogy cannot be overstated. See John O'Malley, SJ, and Gauvin Alexander Bailey, *The Jesuits and the Arts, 1540–1773* (Philadelphia: St. Joseph's University Press, 2005); Clement McNaspy, SJ, "Art in Jesuit Life," *Studies in the Spirituality of Jesuits* 5, no. 3 (April 1973). See also Burke-Sullivan and Burke, *Ignatian Tradition*, 99–120. In their section titled "Imagination," the authors give a philosophical and theological understanding of the critical role arts play in the Ignatian perspective on imagination.

ing Ignatian spirituality, which confronts and resists white supremacy. When Pope Francis delivered his apology to Indigenous school survivors at the former site of the Ermineskin Indian Residential School, he said, "These are lands that speak to us; they enable us to remember."[14] During this penitential pilgrimage Pope Francis often spoke of the connections between land, memory, and the resistance to indifference. This starting point situates our personal "graced histories" in collective histories of this land.[15] Recognizing our own stories as inextricably linked to the history of America is not just knowing new historical data, but rather is a form of authentic memory, which "is not a type or degree of knowledge, but a relationship to what is known."[16] This volume's contributors in diverse ways skillfully demonstrate how the connection of land and memory enable a contemporary appropriation of Ignatian spirituality in American.[17]

Second, this volume centers the experience of people of color in America in order to more deeply understand the paschal mystery on this land. As a methodological move, this centering is to hear people of color as subjects of their own religious experience of Ignatian spirituality.[18] Our being subjects of religious experience is a fundamental assumption of how to grow in authentic spiritual

[14] "Read the Full Text of Pope Francis' Apology to Residential School Survivors," *National Post* (July 25, 2022), https://nationalpost.com/news/canada/deplorable -evil-full-text-of-the-popes-residential-school-apology (accessed May 12, 2023).

[15] John English, SJ, created the term "graced histories." For an overview of evolution of English's wisdom regarding graced history in Ignatian spirituality see a 1998 interview of English by Jim Bowler, SJ, at https://orientations.jesuits.ca/intro_eng .html (accessed May 22, 2023).

[16] M. Shawn Copeland, "Chattel Slavery as Dangerous Memory," in *Tradition and the Normativity of History*, ed. Lieven Boeve and Terrence Merrigan, with C. Dickinson (Leuven, Belgium: Peeters, 2013), 169.

[17] "Everything in US history is about the land—who oversaw it and cultivated it, fished its waters, maintained its wildlife; who invaded it and stole it; how it became a commodity . . ." Roxanne Dunbar-Ortiz, *An Indigenous Peoples' History of the United States* (Boston: Beacon Press, 2014), 1.

[18] For more on this point see Joseph Brown, SJ, *To Stand on the Rock: Meditations on Black Catholic Identity* (Eugene, OR: Wipf and Stock, 1998), 11–12. This centering on people of color as subjects of faith experience is responsive to what is described by Kelly Schmidt and Billy Critchley-Menor, SJ, in "To Jesuits, Black Americans Were Objects of Ministry, Not Agents of Their Own Faith," *Daily Theology* (October 28, 2020), https://dailytheology.org/2020/10/28/to-jesuits-black-americans-were -objects-of-ministry-not-agents-of-their-own-faith/.

consciousness in making the Spiritual Exercises.[19] Also, to privilege the experience of people of color resists any move to interpret Ignatian spirituality by moving "up and away" rather than "down and among."[20] As Bryan Massingale observes, "Almost every social justice challenge that faces us in the United States is entangled with or exacerbated by racism against persons of color . . ."[21] And this social, political, and cultural reality of racism has profound theological and spiritual implications. In the words of James Cone, the "cross and the lynching tree interpret each other." Cone explains,

> The cross and the lynching tree interpret each other . . . need each other: the lynching tree can liberate the false pieties of well-meaning Christians . . . The cross needs the lynching tree to remind Americans of the reality of suffering—to keep the cross from becoming a symbol of abstract, sentimental piety . . . We are faced with a clear challenge: as Latin American liberation theologian Jon Sobrino has put it, "to take the crucified people down from the cross."[22]

White supremacy in America violently pursues the desecration of all bodies that are not white. To place the crucified body of Jesus alongside the lynched bodies of African American women and men, and the mutilated bodies of Cheyenne and Arapahoe families at the Sand Creek massacre, as well as the ongoing intergenerational trauma of Japanese Americans from internment is to "reinforce the sacramentality of the body"—*all bodies* in America.[23]

All the contributors testify to what it means to contemplate the paschal mystery unfolding on this land.[24] They push forward a collec-

---

[19] See an excellent overview on this point by Katherine Dyckman, SNJM, Mary Gavin, SNJM, and Elizabeth Liebert, SNJM, *The Spiritual Exercises Reclaimed: Uncovering Liberating Possibilities for Women* (Mahwah, NJ: Paulist Press, 2001), 4–6.

[20] Norman Wirzba, *Agrarian Spirit: Cultivating Faith, Community and the Land* (Notre Dame, IN: Notre Dame University Press, 2022), 50.

[21] Bryan N. Massingale, "Racism Is a Sickness of the Soul: Can Jesuit Spirituality Help Us Heal?," *America* (November 20, 2017).

[22] James Cone, *The Cross and the Lynching Tree* (Maryknoll, NY: Orbis Books, 2011), 161.

[23] This image of Jesus's suffering body alongside the suffering bodies in history is from Copeland, *Enfleshing Freedom*, 124.

[24] Cone and Copeland's theology resonates with the theology of Ignacio Ellacuría, SJ, and his notion of "historical soteriology." Jesus's life, death, and resurrection not

tive interpretation of the insight of Gilles Cusson, SJ, that the Exercises invite us to contemplate, experience, consent to, integrate, and participate in Christ's saving work.

> It means, further to consent with one's whole being to being personally integrated into the paschal mystery, to pass into the life which Christ has destined for us, and to accept a more conscious participation in the building up of his Kingdom, which is *the total Body of Christ* in process of being built up.[25]

The authors in this book are intuitively probing the importance of Cusson's insight for our lives—collectively—on this land and reveal how and where this mystery of saving Love is being embodied.

Racism and Ignatian Spirituality in America

Praying for Freedom: Racism and Ignatian Spirituality in America is inspired by a haunting question raised by Jesuits in the General Congregation 36. The Jesuits ask, "The question that confronts the Society today is why the *Exercises* do not change us as deeply as we would hope."[26] All of us who love and are engaged in Ignatian spirituality must ask ourselves this same question. Moreover, Jesuits reflect more

---

only shed light on our reality, but our reality also enriches how we understand revelation. As Michael Lee explains, "Ellacuría emphasizes the complementary assertion that the contemporary situation enriches and makes present the fullness of revelation as well." See Michael Lee, *Transforming Realities: Christian Discipleship in the Soteriology of Ignacio Ellacuría* (PhD dissertation, Notre Dame University, 2005); Michael Lee, *Bearing the Weight of Salvation: The Soteriology of Ignacio Ellacuría* (New York: Crossroad, 2009); Kevin Burke, SJ, *The Ground Beneath the Cross: The Theology of Ignacio Ellacuría* (Washington, DC: Georgetown University Press, 2004). See Andrew Prevot, "Hearing the Cries of the Crucified Peoples: The Prayerful Witness of Ignacio Ellacuría and James Cone," in *Witnessing: Prophesy, Politics, and Wisdom*, ed. Maria Clara Bingemer and Peter Casarella (Maryknoll, NY: Orbis Books, 2014), 45–59.

[25] Gilles Cusson, SJ, *The Spiritual Exercises Made in Everyday Life: A Method and Biblical Interpretation*, trans. Mary Angela Roduit, RC, and George Ganss, SJ (St. Louis, MO: Institute of Jesuit Sources, 1989), 111; emphasis added. Cusson is insistent that it is insufficient to simply contemplate the paschal mystery. For Cusson we must consent and experientially participate in this mystery in our own histories and specific concrete circumstances to understand how God's saving action is at work. This consent and participation are critical to discernment and election.

[26] General Congregation 36, no. 18, https://jesuits.eu/images/docs/GC_36 _Documents.pdf (accessed July 31, 2023).

deeply by inquiring into, "What elements in our lives, works, or life-styles hinder our ability to let God's gracious mercy transform us?"[27]

All across the United States Jesuits and their collaborators have been inspired into action by the challenging words of GC 36 in relationship to white supremacy. For example, Jesuits are courageously confessing that slave holding is an ignominious legacy of their presence in America.[28] In addition, there are ongoing processes of reconciliation and restorative justice between Indigenous communities and the Society of Jesus in relationship to the legacies of colonization.[29] There is also a growing body of scholarship that addresses the Jesuits and racism in America.[30] In grassroots groups from New England to the West Coast people have been gathering, working, and creatively envisioning new ways of praying the Spiritual Exercises

[27] GC 36, no. 18.

[28] See the "Slavery, History, Memory and Reconciliation Project" sponsored by the Jesuits of the United States. The stated purpose of this project is "a transformative process of truth-telling, reconciliation, and healing, that in conversation with the descendants of people held in bondage, acknowledges historical harms, seeks to repair relationships, and works within our communities to address the legacies of slavery that persist in the form of racial inequalities today," at https://www.jesuits.org/our-work/shmr/ (accessed May 6, 2023). See also *Georgetown University's Slavery, Memory and Reconciliation Initiative* at http://slaveryarchive.georgetown.edu/ (accessed May 6, 2023). This initiative at Georgetown University involves financial reparations, reparative justice with decedents, public history, and memorialization, as well as research. For an excellent overview of the Society of Jesus and slaveholding in America see Adam Rothman, "The Jesuits and Slavery," *Journal of Jesuit Studies* 8, no. 1 (2021): 1–10, https://doi.org/10.1163/22141332-0801P001 (accessed May 6, 2023).

[29] See Maka Black Elk and William Critchley-Menor, SJ, "Atoning for Sins against Indigenous People Begins with Confronting the Past. Red Cloud Indian School is Showing the Way," *America* (October 8, 2021), https://www.americamagazine.org/politics-society/2021/10/08/indigenous-peoples-day-orange-shirt-culture-jesuits-boarding-school (accessed December 26, 2022).

[30] For example, R. Bentley Anderson, "Black, White, and Catholic: Southern Jesuits Confront the Race Question, 1952," *Catholic Historical Review* 91, no. 3 (July 2005): 484–505; Ken Homan, SJ, "The Complicated History of American Jesuits and Racial Justice," *Daily Theology* (October 20, 2020), https://dailytheology.org/2020/10/20/the-complicated-history-of-american-jesuits-and-racial-justice/; Kelly Schmidt and Billy Critchley-Menor, SJ, "To Jesuits, Black Americans Were Objects of Ministry, Not Agents of Their Own Faith," *Daily Theology* (October 28, 2020), https://dailytheology.org/2020/10/28/to-jesuits-black-americans-were-objects-of-ministry-not-agents-of-their-own-faith/; Justin Poche, "How Southern Jesuits Handled Racism in the Past," *Conversations on Jesuit Higher Education* 51, no. 6 (2017), http://epublications.marquette.edu/conversations/vol51/iss1/6.

in order to unlearn white supremacy. For example, in response to the death of George Floyd, the United States Province staff initiated *Parish Journey for Racial Justice and Equity*.[31] Jesuits around the United States created and are actively engaged in the Jesuit Antiracism Sodality (JARS).[32] The Ignatian Solidarity Network is continually developing resources bridging Ignatian spirituality and racism.[33] And CORE (Jesuits West's Collaborative Organizing for Racial Equity) weaves together Ignatian spirituality and community organizing to embody personal and social transformation.[34] Holy Trinity Church, a Jesuit parish in Washington, DC has developed an innovative Ignatian retreat, "Setting Captives Free: Racism and God's Liberating Grace." This six-week retreat invites, "participants to 'center' on their complicity with racist structures and be open to being 'decentered' on oneself by God's transforming and reconciling grace."[35]

The work of this volume is related to these initiatives of confronting racism, yet its purpose is distinct. All the authors in this volume are confronting racism, and are also unveiling how whiteness functions in interpreting Ignatian spirituality. I return to the question posed by the Jesuits in their General Congregation 36, "What elements in our lives, works, or lifestyles hinder our ability to let God's gracious mercy transform us?"[36] This book explores this question by probing how "color-blindness racism" determines the "normative" interpretation of the Spiritual Exercises in America. Sociologist Eduardo Bonilla-Silva created the term "color-blind racism."[37] He demonstrates that this form of racism is the dominant racial ideology and

---

[31] See Chloe Becker, "Jesuit Parishes Journey Toward Racial Justice and Equity" (May 11, 2021), https://ignatiansolidarity.net/blog/2021/05/11/jesuit-parishes-journey-toward-racial-justice-equity/.

[32] For a sample of JARS' work see https://www.jesuitsmidwest.org/jars-jesuit-antiracism-sodality/.

[33] The Ignatian Solidarity Network offers a variety of resources; for one example, see Maddie Murphy, "An Examen for White Allies" (December 12, 2018), at https://ignatiansolidarity.net/blog/2018/12/12/an-examen-for-white-allies/ (accessed May 30, 2023).

[34] See https://www.jesuitswestcore.org/about.

[35] For more on this retreat see https://trinity.org/ignatian-spirituality/setting-captives-free (accessed May 30, 2023).

[36] General Congregation 36, no. 18.

[37] Eduardo Bonilla-Silva, *Racism Without Racists: Color-Blind Racism and the Persistence of Racial Inequality in America* (New York: Rowman & Littlefield, 2018), xiv.

is how the majority of white people "think, talk and even feel about racial matters . . ."[38] Bonilla-Silva explains that living in American society we are *all* affected by racialization: no one can escape this socialization.[39] How this color-blindness functions is through its being invisible to white people and its operations are "subtle, institutional, and apparently nonracial."[40] Color-blind racism keeps the mechanics of whiteness invisible, which radically "hinders our ability to let God's gracious mercy transform us."

For white people this color-blind racism prevents us from seeing ourselves. We white folks are socialized *not to see* race as something *we have*. Like a landscape painting, racism can be interpreted as "out-there," adversely impacting people of color, and this distancing strategy is how whiteness remains invisible to us but is reproduced in our everyday life.[41] But if we are white the vast majority of us, "cannot answer the question 'How has race shaped your life?'"[42] let alone how our faith has been formed by being white.[43] Contrary to our (mis)perception, white supremacy is the very architectural framework of our nation; we live in "the house built on race."[44] As philosopher Charles Mill explains, "whites will generally be unable to understand the world they themselves have made."[45] Being white

---

[38] Bonilla-Silva, *Racism Without Racists*, xiv.

[39] M. Shawn Copeland details the dangers of "color-blind" racism in hiding white supremacy from being viewed and preventing it from being dislodged (Copeland, *Enfleshing Freedom*, 66–73).

[40] Bonilla-Silva, *Racism Without Racists*, 3.

[41] Joe Feagin, *The White Racial Frame: Centuries of Racial Framing and Counter Framing*, 2nd ed. (New York: Routledge, 2013), 11.

[42] Robin DiAngelo, *What Does It Mean to Be White? Developing White Racial Literacy* (New York: Peter Lang, 2016), 193.

[43] See Alex Mikulich, *Unlearning White Supremacy: A Spirituality of Radical Liberation* (Maryknoll, NY: Orbis Books, 2022); Maureen O'Connell, *Undoing the Knots: Five Generations of American Catholic Anti-Blackness* (Boston: Beacon Press, 2021).

[44] M. Shawn Copeland, "Racism and the Vocation of the Christian Theologian," *Spiritus* 2 (2002): 25. This metaphor of America as a house built on race is found in the work of Joe Feagin. He explains that this metaphor is critical to understanding that white supremacy is not an "add on" to the structure of our country but the very foundation. This framing of the house is not only a systemic reality but is also our worldview (Feagin, *White Racial Frame*, x).

[45] Charles Mills, *The Racial Contract* (Ithaca, NY: Cornell University Press, 1997), 18–19.

involves internalizing a frame of reference—for us—that is unquestioned, invisible, and unnamed.[46]

Color-blind racism impacts our interpretation of the Spiritual Exercises like a pair of reading glasses. We read the text without even knowing we read with glasses. Color-blind interpretations of the Spiritual Exercises are perceived to be racially neutral because the text does not mention race. Throughout the essays in this volume contributors point to how unexamined assumptions act as normative interpretation. To make whiteness visible in interpreting Ignatian spirituality is critical because the pervasiveness and subtlety of white supremacy is often invisible to those of us who are white. For example, unfortunately, the nationwide initiatives listed above can be misinterpreted and marginalized as being a social justice "addendum" or an anti-racist postscript to making "the real, authentic, and genuine" Spiritual Exercises. For white people, to participate in these initiatives can be seen an altruistic choice because racism is not essentially "my/our problem."

Exploring how we interpret Ignatian spirituality is in itself a prayer for freedom. The question of GC 36, "What elements in our lives, works, or lifestyles hinder our ability to let God's gracious mercy transform us?" can be a graced opening into our work of interpretation. As a classic, Ignatius's life and writing have an excess of meaning, which transcends his specific sixteenth-century European context.[47] David Tracy has argued that each generation has a responsibility to engage in the risks of interpreting classic texts in order for this surplus of meaning to emerge, and for the potential of the classic to be realized within the limits of our particular horizon. The sherd of white supremacist violence confronts American society as an urgent challenge for us to discover the liberating potential of the Spiritual Exercises for our twenty-first-century context. Confronting this color-blindness allows the wisdom of the Spiritual Exercises—and more importantly God's transforming power—to be discovered in new and life-giving ways.

---

[46] Bryan Massingale, *Racial Justice and the Catholic* Church (Maryknoll, NY: Orbis Books, 2010), 22.

[47] David Tracy, *The Analogical Imagination: Christian Theology and Culture of Pluralism* (New York: Herder & Herder, 1998).

Taking up this task of reinterpreting the Spiritual Exercises takes on an urgency as we see the rising tide of white nationalism and its lethal violence in America.[48] Researcher Robert P. Jones gathered data that lays out a profoundly disturbing picture of our situation, "the more racist attitudes a person holds, the more likely he or she is to be identified as a white Christian."[49] For those of us who are engaged in Ignatian spirituality Jones' research requires our soul searching. For those of us who are white, growing up in America and being surrounded by images of God in white formed our faith and way of life.[50] We must help each other acknowledge, "The white liberal and the white supremacist share the same root postulates. They are different in degree not kind."[51] This is a hard pill to swallow, but how

---

[48] See Catholic News Service, "Fr. Bryan Massingale: White Nationalism Is the Greatest Threat to Peace Today," *National Catholic Reporter* (August 5, 2021), https://www.ncronline.org/news/justice/fr-bryan-massingale-white-nationalism-greatest-threat-peace-today (accessed February 21, 2023); Carter Heyward, *The 7 Deadly Sins of White Christian Nationalism: A Call to Action* (Lanham, MD: Rowman & Littlefield, 2022); Pamela Cooper-White, *The Psychology of Christian Nationalism: Why People Are Drawn In and How to Talk Across the Divide* (Minneapolis: Fortress Press, 2022); Anthea Butler, *White Evangelical Racism: The Politics of Morality in America* (Chapel Hill, NC: The University of North Carolina Press, 2021); Kyle Edward Haden, *Embodied Idolatry: A Critique of Christian Nationalism* (Lanham, MD: Rowman & Littlefield, 2020); Obery M. Hendricks Jr., *Christians Against Christianity: How Right-Wing Evangelicals Are Destroying Our Faith and Our Nation* (Boston: Beacon Press, 2021).

[49] This quotation of Robert P. Jones is taken from Michael Luo, "American Christianity's White-Supremacy Problem: History, Theology, and Culture All Contribute to the Racist Attitudes Embedded in the White Church," *The New Yorker* (September 2, 2020), at newyorker.com (last accessed November 3, 2021). See Robert P. Jones, *White Too Long: The Legacy of White Supremacy in American Christianity* (New York: Simon and Schuster, 2020).

[50] Recent social psychological studies reveal how white images of God determine who is believed to be powerful in society, even when people do not believe in God. See Melissa De Witte, "Who People Believe Rules in Heaven Influences Their Beliefs about Who Rules on Earth, Stanford Scholars Find," *Stanford/News* (January 31, 2020), https://news.stanford.edu/press-releases/2020/01/31/consequences-perng-god-white-man/ (accessed November 11, 2021). For more detail on this study see S. O. Roberts, K. Weisman, J. D. Lane, A. Williams, N. P. Camp, M. Wang, M. Robison, K. Sanchez, and C. Griffiths, "God as a White Man: A Psychological Barrier to Conceptualizing Black People and Women as Leadership Worthy," *Journal of Personality and Social Psychology* 119, no. 6 (2020): 1290–1315.

[51] These words of Lerone Bennett are cited in Shannon Sullivan, *Good White People: The Problem with Middle-Class White Anti-Racism* (Albany: SUNY Press, 2014), 1.

do the Exercises enable us to *dis*identify with the white nationalism when we "grow from the same tree of white dominance"?[52]

The contributors to this volume intelligently, creatively, and courageously take up this task of interpreting Ignatian spirituality in the face of this rising tide of white nationalism. This book does not propose to answer all questions raised in reinterpreting the Spiritual Exercises but is rather one part of the process unfolding across this country in which liberating interpretations are arising. A hope of this volume is to create space for more collective, public, and national conversations. Amid this unfolding graced process these authors are bringing to bear their gifts as spiritual directors, community organizers, theologians, and educators. The essays are deeply informed by psychology, history, settler colonial theory, Ignatian pedagogy, restorative justice, and anti-racist activism. But the foundation of all the essays is love for Ignatian spirituality, and a faith in God's passionate desire for human transformation.

Structure and Plan

Praying for Freedom is organized in three parts resonating with the dynamic of the Spiritual Exercises. "Movement is the stuff of the Exercises; it indicates direction, marks progress or regression and reveals true preferences."[53] Reading these essays should not merely be an academic exercise, but an opportunity to pray with the interior movements that arise while reading. The volume lends itself to this prayerful reflection in the variety of genres, voices, and even in the differing length of the essays.

> The first section opens with Ignatius' presupposition in the *Spiritual Exercises*. . . . it should be presupposed that every good Christian ought to be more eager to put a good interpretation on a neighbor's statement than to condemn it. Further, if one cannot interpret it favorably, one should ask how the other means it . . .

---

[52] Sullivan, *Good White People*, 4.

[53] Katherine Dyckman, SNJM, Mary Gavin, SNJM, and Elizabeth Liebert, SNJM, *The Spiritual Exercises Reclaimed: Uncovering Liberating Possibilities for Women* (Mahwah, NJ: Paulist Press, 2001), 56.

and seek out every appropriate means through which, by under-standing the statement in a good way, it may be saved.[54]

Practicing this wisdom in conversations about race in America is a struggle. Ignatius's wisdom invites us to presuppose the good inten-tions of others, and to engage others in conversation to grow in mu-tual understanding. Katherine Dyckman, Mary Gavin, and Elizabeth Liebert point out that this requires generosity involving significant time and effort.[55] To begin with Ignatius's presupposition is an invita-tion in how to engage the text, and also how to use the text to talk with each other as we pray for freedom.

In part 1, Andrew Prevot, Ken Homan, SJ, and Alex Mikulich face squarely the problems and possibilities of praying the Spiritual Exer-cises on this land right under our feet.

Andrew Prevot describes racism as a soul sickness, not only for white people—but for all people living in America. Out of his own experience of both praying and teaching the Spiritual Exercises he asks the central question of this volume; on this land with the legacy of slavery and colonization, why have the followers of Ignatius been unwilling or unable to fight racism? Exploring the entire dynamic, Prevot demonstrates how the Spiritual Exercises could and should strengthen us for the struggle against racial injustice. He states that God has and is giving us everything we need for this struggle, and our responsibility is to actively engage these abundant gifts—and to do so without delay.

Ken Homan, SJ, writes out of his own experience of praying the Spiritual Exercises. Reflecting on his prayer and ministerial experi-ence he articulates three strategies that white people use to deflect and to minimize the historical realities of Jesuit slave-holding: "it was commonplace," "the good we did," and "we are trapped by this discussion." Homan explores these deflections in relationship to the graces of the First Week of the Spiritual Exercises. He believes our resistance and fear of facing history thwarts the experience of God's mercy. His essay raises larger questions regarding other strategies of deflection operative in exploring the realities of white supremacy in the past and also in the present.

---

[54] Dyckman, Gavin, Liebert, *Spiritual Exercises Reclaimed*, 61.
[55] Dyckman, Gavin, Liebert, 61.

Alex Mikulich leads us more deeply into the questions raised by Prevot and Homan by exploring the Ignatian practice of "Composition of Place." He argues that this practice intends to facilitate prayer that creates a bridge between our faith and our concrete historical circumstances. Such prayer risks becoming abstract. To confront this risk, Mikulich describes how we must engage in embodied questioning of the internalized assumptions of, what he names as "modernity/colonization in-nature." Mikulich demonstrates that Composition of Place positions us to experience the connections of white supremacy and ecological destruction on this land in order to participate in God's work of intergenerational healing and repair.

The second part begins with Ignatius's words setting forth the purpose of the Spiritual Exercises, "To overcome oneself, and to order one's life, without reaching a decision through some disordered affection."[56] Each of the contributors probe specific prayer experiences and reinterpret key elements within the Spiritual Exercises that demonstrate Ignatius's purpose in relationship to our life together on this land.

Beginning with the Principle and Foundation, Hung Pham, SJ, historically situates an understanding of indifference. He contends that we confuse Ignatian indifference with disinterest, or apathy. Pham demonstrates that Ignatian indifference is a grace of the praying the Principle and Foundation. This grace enabled early Jesuits to take seriously and learn from cultural difference as they went into mission around the world. By careful reflection on Ignatius's story Pham establishes that Ignatius's conversion was a process in which he was displaced from his center, and he became recentered in Christ. Pham demonstrates that this decentering/recentering of Ignatius gave him the freedom to deal creatively and respectfully with the very real differences in the gathering of the early Jesuits. Pham concludes that indifference is a product of conversion, and like Ignatius, it decenters us. Indifference enables freedom in relationship to one's own prejudices and biases, which creates the possibility of love because we can begin to encounter others as they are—loved by God.

Jeannine Hill Fletcher offers a detailed vision of praying the First Week, which takes seriously our participation in institutional racism.

---

[56] *Ignatius of Loyola: Spiritual Exercises and Selected Works*, ed. George Ganss, SJ (Mahwah, NJ: Paulist Press, 1991), no. 21, p. 129.

Institutional racism is what is considered normative, in custom, law, church, and education; it is our very way of life. To pray the First Week through this understanding of racism gets at the depths of our sinfulness as the architecture of our country. Hill Fletcher argues that opening ourselves to this level of graced transformation in praying the First Week may enable us to participate in collective healing and restorative justice for creating new patterns of living together in America.

Christopher Pramuk explores Ignatius's direction in the First Week for us to speak to Christ, "suspended on the cross before you, and converse with him."[57] Pramuk invites us to speak with the Crucified Christ, by placing alongside his suffering the bodies of Trayvon Martin, Elijah McClain, Sandra Bland, and George Floyd. For Pramuk, this invitation interrupts American society's push to forget the crucified people on this land and therefore also refuses to make Christ's passion into an abstraction. Pramuk reveals that to feel shame and confusion in such prayer and to be given the gift of tears is a sign of reconnection to our kinship with one another and the healing of our humanity.

Maureen O'Connell invites us to explore the meditation on the Two Standards in order to become aware of how insidious white supremacy is in conditioning our choices. O'Connell suggests that racism and white supremacy revolve around the question of identity. Praying with the Two Standards invites us to reflect upon the source of our identity. White supremacy can subvert anti-racism into a charitable industriousness, which makes this activity performative rather than transformative. O'Connell proposes we imagine resting under the standard of Christ, in contrast to the restless idolatry of the standard of white supremacy. To rest under the standard of Christ makes possible our being genuinely present to God's activity in people and in our relationships as the locus of anti-racism.

Armando Guerrero Estrada and Paulina Delgadillo invite us to explore Ignatius's Second Week contemplations on the "Presentation in the Temple" and the "Obedience of the Child Jesus to His Parents" through the lens of undocumented and migrant youth and young adults. If we have the courage to pray through this lens will we see

---

[57] *Ignatius of Loyola*, no. 53, p. 138.

el niño Jesus? Estrada and Delgadillo write from their own locations as two Jesuit-educated and undocumented/DACAmented, Mexican-born theologians. They read and pray Luke 2:41-52 alongside and from the perspective of undocumented youth. To pray this Lukan text alongside this reality is to recognize that like Jesus, migrant youth and young adults are *agents* in the unfolding history of the Catholic Church in America—and that history is now. Contemplating *el niño Jesus* calls for a solidarity born from the realization that until migrant and undocumented youth are safe, protected, and free none of us is free.

María Teresa Morgan demonstrates "historical soteriology" in her own experience as a child of Operation Pedro Pan. Morgan illustrates the power of Scripture in revealing meaning in our lives and how our lives can deepen our understanding and experience of revelation. In discovering the story of Mephibosheth in the second book of Samuel, Morgan found a way into experiencing God's providence in her own painful journey of exile. Morgan explains that using the Ignatian prayer of imagination and memory rescued her story and reframed her life in the death and resurrection of Christ. Rather than denying the pain of exile from Cuba, this reframing in Christ engendered in Morgan compassion for all people who are lost, despised, and ignored at the borders and margins of our society.

Marilyn Nash demonstrates the importance of understanding our embodied historical context when making decisions. Discernment is a critical practice for Ignatius. Nash points out that self-knowledge and contextual awareness are considered fundamental to genuine discernment, but what if we are ignorant of the culture of whiteness as our lens and ignorant of the historical context of the very land on which we live? Through storytelling and concrete example, Nash invites us into exploring how what we are ignorant of can disable our ability to discern.

Patrick Saint-Jean, SJ, confronts color-blind racism and debunks it through a dialogue between Ignatius of Loyola and Frantz Fanon. For Ignatius and Fanon bodies matter. The human body enables knowledge of reality. Moreover, bodies carry meaning in the world and enable human beings to be seen. In this conversation between Ignatius and Fanon, Saint-Jean reveals the theological and social danger of color-blind racism. Color-blind racism participates in the denial of the Incarnation and also erases embodied identity. Saint-Jean demonstrates that by denying embodied identity color-blind racism deforms bodies into a surface to be written upon by others. He shows us that Ignatian spirituality offers a way into right seeing, which is a struggle—but one in which we not only discover the genuine reality of others but also of God.

The third part begins with Ignatius's words, "Love ought to manifest itself more in deeds than by words," which introduces the Contemplation to Attain Love.[58] In this section the contributors invite us to contemplate the love they describe, and also, their writing inspires us to love in deeds and not just by words.

Matthew Cressler invites us to explore how Ignatian retreats are a part of our formation into white American Catholicism. Drawing upon his own experience, he observes that in over twenty years of making an Ignatian weekend retreat he was never asked to reflect upon racism, or on his racial identity. Cressler states that in order to understand how the Spiritual Exercises form us we must examine the ideas, the institutions, the relationships, and social forces that structure our experience of the Exercises. He explores how religion, specifically Catholicism in America, is part of our formation into whiteness. Cressler demonstrates that in order for us to experience the liberating potential of Ignatian spirituality we must interrogate how it has been a mechanism of principalities and powers of white supremacy in America.

In June of 2022 the Jesuit Antiracism Sodality (JARS) hosted a retreat, "The God of Us All: Praying with Black Spirituality" at Bay St. Louis in Mississippi. There the retreatants gathered at the first seminary in America open to Black men preparing for priesthood. Justin White and Elise Gower attended the retreat and share their experiences in the form of an Ignatian examen. White admits he came into the retreat with unacknowledged desolation. However, as the retreat unfolded, he discovered this was the first Ignatian retreat space where he could bring his whole fully functioning Black self. White describes how being in Mississippi, singing and praying the spirituals, and remembering civil rights history created conditions for healing and for desiring church to be a space for all to be fully functioning

---

[58] *Ignatius of Loyola*, no. 230, p. 176.

selves in relation to it. Gower admits to anticipating an "anti-racism" experience, but the retreat was a time of discovering the depth to which she still imagined God as white. The retreat was not an intellectual exercise but an embodied reception of God's presence and activity in a new way. For Gower, the retreat experience redefined anti-racism for white people as transformed consciousness that makes us open to participating in God's work.

Maka Black Elk has the last word. Black Elk's contribution is intentionally placed last as a litmus test regarding the validity of our work of reinterpreting the Spiritual Exercises. To begin our reinterpretation with the land under our feet necessitates hearing the voices of the Indigenous people, whose land we have colonized. Does our work make us willing and capable of participating in the work of truth, healing, and reconciliation? For Black Elk, truth, healing, and reconciliation are a process akin to Ignatius's prayers in the First Week. The process involves fearlessly facing the truth of intergenerational trauma of Indigenous people through close scrutiny of institutional and communal history. For Black Elk healing is a personal journey; one needs to desire to heal, one has to believe it is possible, and one needs to know one is deserving of healing. Black Elk asks all of us to ask these questions in order to participate in genuine reconciliation. We never ask these questions alone; Black Elk declares God's love is at the center of these questions. Let us follow Black Elk's lead to end our prayer, with the Lakota words, *Mitakuye Oyasin*, meaning "all our relations." New patterns of right relationships with all our relations will demonstrate the legitimacy of our collective interpretations of Ignatian spirituality on this land.

As you read these essays, I ask you dear reader to return to the image on the cover by Fabian Debora. The flaming red sky of Debora's image is reminiscent of how Ignatius of Loyola often ended his letters to the early Jesuits going off to missions, *"Ite, inflammate omnia"*—"go set the world on fire." Ignatius "wanted everyone to be set afire with passion for the Kingdom of God."[59] Contemplate this painting as a

---

[59] See Jim Manney's essay, "God Set the World on Fire," at https://www.ignatian spirituality.com/go-set-the-world-on-fire/ (accessed May 8, 2023). Manney notes that Ignatius's phrase is reminiscent of the tongues of fire descending on those gathered at Pentecost.

challenge to discover that there are places and people in the world that are *already* on fire with God's passionate love. Pope Francis has said we live in a profound "change in epochs" that affects all human beings and creation.[60] *Falling Stars* powerfully illustrates that the grace arising during this epochal change is at the fence lines, border lands, and liminal spaces that exist within us, and in our society on this land. It is at these places we may contemplate and discover God's desire for us to be free.

[60] Hannah Brockhaus, "Pope Francis Reorganized Diocese of Rome in the Face of 'Epochal Change,'" *Catholic News Agency* (January 7, 2023), https://www.catholic newsagency.com/news/253284/pope-francis-reorganizes-diocese-of-rome-in-face -of-epochal-change# (accessed May 8, 2023).

PART I

Presuppositions

. . . it should be presupposed that every good Christian ought to be more eager to put a good interpretation on a neighbor's statement than to condemn it. Further, if one cannot interpret it favorably, one should ask how the other means it . . . and seek out every appropriate means through which, by understanding the statement in a good way, it may be saved.

Ignatius of Loyola: Spiritual Exercises and Selected Works,
ed. George Ganss, SJ (Mahwah, NJ: Paulist Press, 1991),
no. 22, p. 61.

1

Training the Soul

A Black Catholic Journey through the Spiritual Exercises

Andrew Prevot

It is now common to think of racism not merely as a prejudiced mindset of a hateful individual but as a set of cultural and structural forces that violently govern bodies, and so it is.[1] Racism—indeed, the very idea of race—marks bodies with words that supposedly signify pigment, geography, and genealogy but which were invented for the purpose of assigning particular kinds of labor, social advantage, and fully recognized humanity to some and not others. These words, as if from a box of Crayola crayons, call bodies black, white, brown, yellow, and red. They color-code the distribution of pleasures, privileges, and rights on the one hand, and exploitations, traumas, and premature deaths on the other. To perceive this injustice, it suffices to study what has happened to bodies that are so marked.

To understand and resist the full magnitude of this injustice, however, it is necessary to recognize its effects on the *souls* of Black folk,

---

[1] Bryan Massingale, *Racial Justice and the Catholic Church* (Maryknoll, NY: Orbis Books, 2010), 13–15 and 74–78; and M. Shawn Copeland, *Knowing Christ Crucified: The Witness of African American Religious Experience* (Maryknoll, NY: Orbis Books, 2018), 61–80.

white folk, and everyone in between.[2] Our souls—those mysterious centers of thought, emotion, and decision that our bodies sustain—are not spared the harms of a racist system of social control. Our capacities to understand, feel, and choose have all been compromised. This sinful system affects our cognition by filling our minds with falsehoods about others and ourselves and by weakening our ability to think creatively beyond the racial scripts in which we have been formed. It affects our emotional sensitivity by triggering painful feelings such as anxiety, shame, and anger and by hardening our hearts to the sufferings of others. It affects our wills by encouraging choices that violate the common good and by making us behave like pawns in a sadistic game. Racialization distorts the soul's basic capacities for knowledge, affect, and volition, and it does this across the racial spectrum.

Although such soul-damage spreads widely, leaving hardly anyone unscathed, its effects vary significantly by race.[3] A white person who unconsciously accepted the racist cultural message that Black people are worthless would be morally corrupted by this falsehood, and this would be a real loss, but a Black person who succumbed to this lie would be inwardly crushed by it. Their sense of self would be torn asunder. The anxiety, shame, and anger that a white person may feel in an honest conversation about white supremacy may be difficult to bear, but it is not the same as the anxiety, shame, and anger that a Black person endures when their very humanity is denied by virtually the whole political, cultural, and religious establishment. Acquiring the inner freedom to act boldly for the sake of a better world can help a white person live into the truest version of them-

---

[2] W. E. B. Du Bois, *The Souls of Black Folk* (New York: Simon & Schuster, 2005); Michele Elam, *The Souls of Mixed Folk: Race, Politics, and Aesthetics in the New Millennium* (Stanford, CA: Stanford University Press, 2011); Frantz Fanon, *Black Skin, White Masks*, trans. Richard Philcox (New York: Grove, 2008), 89–119; Phillis Isabella Sheppard, *Self, Culture, and Others in Womanist Practical Theology* (New York: Palgrave Macmillan, 2011), 23–39; and Andrew Prevot, "Sources of a Black Self? Ethics of Authenticity in an Era of Anti-Blackness," in *Anti-Blackness and Christian Ethics*, ed. Vincent W. Lloyd and Andrew Prevot (Maryknoll, NY: Orbis Books, 2017), 77–95.

[3] Laurie Cassidy, "Contemplative Prayer and the Impasse of White Supremacy," in *Desire, Darkness, and Hope: Theology in a Time of Impasse*, ed. Laurie Cassidy and M. Shawn Copeland (Collegeville, MN: Liturgical Press, 2021), 103–29; and Massingale, *Racial Justice*, 19–24.

selves, as it can for everybody. However, for a Black person to be free in this sense means something especially poignant when set against the background of their community's bitter history of unfreedom.

I do not want to draw the lines too sharply in my analysis, however. Although our souls are not raceless transparencies but rather sponges that soak up the messy stuff of our racial worlds, many things are true of our souls insofar as they are human and not only insofar as they are racially divided. Moreover, the struggle against racism must be a shared struggle if it has any hope of victory. For these reasons, although I offer a Black perspective on the Spiritual Exercises, I emphasize their contribution to the common human challenge to understand, feel, and choose rightly, which no one can evade. I am also mindful that each person's experience of the Spiritual Exercises is singular. God's movements are tailored to the inner and outer circumstances of each person. A racially conscious reception of Ignatian spirituality must not overlook these *universal* and *individual* dimensions, even as it acknowledges that Black and white souls carry different burdens.

In this essay, I do not insist that the Spiritual Exercises should be the only spiritual means of combatting racism or that they will necessarily be the most effective means for everyone. However, I do argue that those who participate (however formally or informally) in the spirituality they represent can use it to strengthen their souls for the fight against racism that we all must wage. This particular way to receive Ignatian spirituality ought to be incorporated into the ways it is generally taught and practiced, so that its socially transformative effects are not limited to a narrow few. In making this claim, I echo the arguments of other Black Catholic interpreters of the Spiritual Exercises such as LaReine-Marie Mosely, Bryan Massingale, and Patrick Saint-Jean.[4] In what follows, I share some of my own distinctive wrestling with this spiritual training program. Like feminist

---

[4] LaReine-Marie Mosely, "Negative Contrast Experience: An Ignatian Appraisal," *Horizons* 41 (2014): 74–95; Bryan N. Massingale, "Racism Is a Sickness of the Soul: Can Jesuit Spirituality Help Us Heal?," *America* (November 20, 2017); and Patrick Saint-Jean, SJ, *The Spiritual Work of Racial Justice: A Month of Meditations with Ignatius of Loyola* (Vestal, NY: Anamchara Books, 2021).

commentators Katherine Dyckman, Mary Garvin, and Elizabeth Liebert, I highlight its mixture of "problems and possibilities."[5]

My Experience of the Nineteenth Annotation

If you ask a Jesuit about the Spiritual Exercises, the first thing you will likely hear is that they are not a text to be read but something to be *experienced*. And rightly so. St. Ignatius of Loyola's volume called *The Spiritual Exercises* is a handbook for leaders of retreats. It offers a structure and set of best practices to help spiritual directors guide participants through a month-long, or in some cases year-long, series of activities that are meant to strengthen their souls, deepen their intimacy with God, and help them make important decisions about their lives. A few years ago, as a faculty member at Boston College, which is a Jesuit Catholic university, I had the opportunity to participate in such a retreat—to have "the experience," so to speak. I did the year-long version, outlined in a section of the text called the Nineteenth Annotation, which allows Ignatius's prescribed spiritual practices to be integrated into the rhythms of one's daily life.[6] I carved out pockets of time each week throughout the academic year to do the necessary prayers, meditations, contemplations, and examens and to meet with my spiritual director and a small faith-sharing group, who were members of my campus community doing the same retreat.

The best way I can describe this experience is to embrace Ignatius's analogical use of the word "exercise." Just as we train our bodies to function well by doing things such as walking and running, so too we must train our souls to be ready to discover and enact the will of God, in whatever circumstances we find ourselves.[7] My spiritual

[5] Katherine Dyckman, SNJM, Mary Gavin, SNJM, and Elizabeth Liebert, SNJM, *The Spiritual Exercises Reclaimed: Uncovering Liberating Possibilities for Women* (Mahwah, NJ: Paulist Press, 2001), 3–24. Although I focus more on race than gender here, I recognize with womanist scholars that these are interlocking realities. See Stacey M. Floyd-Thomas, ed., *Deeper Shades of Purple: Womanism in Religion and Society* (New York: New York University Press, 2006).

[6] Ignatius of Loyola, *The Spiritual Exercises of Saint Ignatius: A Translation and Commentary*, George E. Ganss, SJ (Chicago: Loyola Press, 1992), sec. 19, 27.

[7] Ignatius, *Spiritual Exercises*, sec. 1.3, 21.

director tried to get me to stop intellectualizing the process, which was my tendency as an academic. He wanted me to "let my imagination run wild," as he put it, and to spend more time with the emotions—the movements in the heart—that these exercises were generating for me.

Although this was very good advice for my personal spiritual journey, I continued then—and I continue now—to find value not only in experiencing the Spiritual Exercises but also in thinking critically about them and how they have been used and received. My goal as a theologian is to maintain an interactive unity of prayer and thought. In my scholarship, I have studied the influence of Ignatian spirituality on theologians working in Europe (e.g., Erich Przywara, Karl Rahner, Hans Urs von Balthasar, Henri de Lubac, and Michel de Certeau) and Latin America (e.g., Ignacio Ellacuría, Jon Sobrino, Segundo Galilea, and Dean Brackley). I have discussed contested questions such as the meaning of the "consolation without preceding cause" and the sociopolitical stakes of the Ignatian model of spiritual discernment.[8]

In my teaching, I regularly introduce undergraduate students to Ignatius through a combination of traditional and experiential pedagogy. After going over some key points in his life story,[9] I ask the students to journal about a difficult decision that is facing them. I explain some of his Rules for the Discernment of Spirits and then lead the class in a meditation (often the Meditation on the Two Standards).[10] Finally, I facilitate a conversation about how this sort of exercise may or may not help them decide what to do.

---

[8] Andrew Prevot, *Thinking Prayer: Theology and Spirituality amid the Crises of Modernity* (Notre Dame, IN: Notre Dame University Press, 2015), chaps. 2 and 5; Andrew Prevot, *The Mysticism of Ordinary Life: Theology, Philosophy, and Feminism* (Oxford: Oxford University Press, 2023), chaps. 1–3; Andrew Prevot, "Henri de Lubac (1896–1991) and Contemporary Mystical Theology," in *A Companion to Jesuit Mysticism*, ed. Robert A. Maryks (Leiden, Netherlands: Brill, 2017), 279–309; and Andrew Prevot, "Ignatian Spirituality, Political Effectiveness, and Spiritual Discernment: Dean Brackley's Account of Liberation Theology," *Political Theology* 18, no. 4 (2017): 309–24.

[9] Ignatius of Loyola, *A Pilgrim's Journey: The Autobiography of Ignatius of Loyola*, trans. Joseph N. Tylenda, SJ (San Francisco: Ignatius Press, 2001).

[10] Ignatius, *Spiritual Exercises*, sec. 136–48 and 313–36, 65–67, and 121–28.

When I participated in the Nineteenth Annotation, the Movement for Black Lives was in its early stages.[11] Trayvon Martin was dead, but Michael Brown was still alive. Although the violence facing the Black community and the activism rising up from it occupied my mind nearly every day, my daily experience of the Spiritual Exercises seemed to occur at a remove from such pressing realities. At the time, I was doing research on the prayerful roots of Black theology—thinking especially about how James Cone drew on the songs that enslaved Black people composed, sung, and danced together in the wilderness.[12] While Ignatius's Exercises certainly strengthened me, I was not in the habit of applying them directly to the fight for racial justice. Instead, when seeking resources that could help me and others resist a resurgent white supremacy, I looked to the Black spirituals that Cone wrote about so movingly.

In subsequent years, I have started to ask what these two traditions of Christian spirituality have to do with one another. As a Black Catholic, this question was almost inevitable for me. But such a connection should not be sought only by Black Catholics. The pursuit of racial justice should form part of the common practice of the Spiritual Exercises for everyone, regardless of each person's race. Promoters of Ignatian spirituality and those who stand to benefit from it live in contexts (such as the United States) that are shaped by white supremacy and anti-Black racism. However, the racial injustice of the larger social context is not the only problem. There are also specific histories of Jesuit involvement in the owning and selling of slaves and other violent actions toward persons of color, which raise challenging questions.[13] Why did the Spiritual Exercises fail to prevent such behavior? If these techniques succeed in preparing one to glorify God with one's life, why have their followers so often been unwilling or unable to fight racism or even to recognize it as an evil that is

---

[11] Olga M. Segura, *Birth of a Movement: Black Lives Matter and the Catholic Church* (Maryknoll, NY: Orbis Books, 2021), 1–22.

[12] James H. Cone, *The Spirituals and the Blues: An Interpretation* (Maryknoll, NY: Orbis Books, 2008); and Prevot, *Thinking Prayer*, chap. 6.

[13] Cyprian Davis, OSB, *The History of Black Catholics in the United States* (New York: Crossroad, 1990), 35–37; and Laura E. Masur, "Plantation as Mission: American Indians, Enslaved Africans, and Jesuit Missionaries in Maryland," *Journal of Jesuit Studies* 8 (2021): 385–407.

hateful to God? Although I do not have answers to all of these questions, I hope that my reflections as a Black Catholic journeying through the Spiritual Exercises will help reveal why they could and *should* strengthen our racially wounded souls for a shared struggle against racial injustice.

The Principle and Foundation

The text of the Spiritual Exercises begins with a single-page section meant to give one a basic orientation. At the start of this section, which is called The Principle and Foundation, Ignatius writes that "human beings are created to praise, reverence, and serve God our Lord."[14] *Human beings*. From the first line, I have to ask if I am included. Does my body make it less likely for some retreatants who hear this word "human" to picture a person like me? Already, though, I am speculating about what others think about me, and this is not the purpose for which I, a human being, was made. I agree with Ignatius that I am meant to praise, reverence, and serve God our Lord. Although this list of self-surrendering activities gives me pause, its divine focal point reassures me. That my created purpose should be to serve and glorify another pokes at old wounds. That I owe such deference exclusively to God applies a healing balm. I am meant to be no human being's slave.

Ignatius goes on to explain, "The other things on the face of the earth are created for the human beings, to help them in the pursuit of the end for which they are created."[15] Again, a doubt creeps into my mind: am I a person or a thing that is meant to be used? Drawing such a sharp ontological dividing line between humans and other instrumentalized creatures seems dangerous to me. As a Black person, it seems far too easy to slip from one side of this line to the other, depending on who is doing the sorting, and to end up with my dignity denied. Moreover, when I see, hear, and touch the things around me, they do not seem to be mere tools of human self-actualization. Like Daniel Castillo, I am concerned that the Principle and Foundation may inadvertently suggest an anthropocentric perspective that

[14] Ignatius, *Spiritual Exercises*, sec. 23.2, 32.
[15] Ignatius, sec. 23.3, 32.

reduces the meaning of animals, plants, seas, and skies to their utility for human ends. One front in the battle against racism is the struggle for environmental justice. This struggle requires care for our common home and all its inhabitants, along with resistance to what Pope Francis calls the "technocratic paradigm." It means treating things not as disposable objects but as fellow creatures.[16]

Let me turn now to Ignatius's famous doctrine of *indiferençia*. To attain the end for which we were created, he says that "it is necessary to make ourselves indifferent to all created things," adding that "we ought not to seek health rather than sickness, wealth rather than poverty, honor rather than dishonor, a long life rather than a short one, and so on."[17] What he means is that we should not put our individual cares ahead of the primary work of doing God's will. I agree with Ignatius on this point.

Yet I confess that I am not indifferent to the wretched conditions of inaccessible health care, widespread impoverishment, and social stigmatization that plague poor Black neighborhoods. It would be callous and absurd to ask a community not to care about such hardships when they have been specifically allotted to them because of their race. In solidarity with other Black people, I demand a spirituality that talks positively (thus not indifferently) about their search for life-sustaining material goods and that regards the equitable distribution of such goods as a moral, political, and religious imperative. At this early point in the Spiritual Exercises, it is not yet clear whether they are equipped to satisfy this demand.

Even so, I believe Ignatius is correct to insist that these sorts of goods are incapable of completely satisfying any human being, regardless of racial background. The human soul needs more than material supports. It needs to give itself into God's hands. Though

---

[16] Daniel Castillo, "'To Praise, Reverence, and Serve': The Theological Anthropology of Pope Francis," in *The Theological and Ecological Vision of* Laudato Si': *Everything Is Connected*, ed. Vincent J. Miller (New York: Bloomsbury, 2017), 95–108, at 96; Pope Francis, *Laudato Si'*, On Care for Our Common Home (Vatican City: Libreria Editrice Vaticana, 2015), 101–14; Melanie Harris, *Ecowomanism: African American Women and Earth-Honoring Faiths* (Maryknoll, NY: Orbis Books, 2017); and James Cone, "Whose Earth Is It, Anyway?," in *Risks of Faith: The Emergence of a Black Theology of Liberation, 1968–1998* (Boston: Beacon Press, 2000), 138–45.

[17] Ignatius, *Spiritual Exercises*, sec. 23.5–23.6, 32.

not affiliated with Ignatius, my heroes in the Black Christian freedom struggle abandoned themselves to lives of reverent service, just as he would have advised them to do. I am thinking, for example, of the Black women, men, and children who braved fire hoses, police dogs, and overcrowded jail cells in Birmingham, Alabama, in the demonstrations that led to the 1964 Civil Rights Act.[18] They understood that if the situation required it, as it surely did, it would be right for them to risk their possessions, social standing, and even health for the sake of doing what God willed. Their transformative social impact depended on their actively acquired strength of soul—which is to say, their *indiferençia*. Brackley calls this virtue a freedom to love.[19]

The First Week

The First Week of the Spiritual Exercises is a period of honest self-examination. It is a time to take stock of one's personal faults and failings, while viewing oneself in the larger context of fallen humanity. It is an opportunity to ask questions that might spark conversion, such as "What have I done for Christ? What am I doing for Christ? What ought I to do for Christ?"[20] Contemporary interpretations of this week sometimes deemphasize the threat of punishment for sin and focus more positively on God's mercy.[21] In the original text, however, Ignatius does not mince words.

I have wrestled in particular with the fifth exercise of the First Week, which is the Meditation on Hell. It asks the retreatant to imagine this place of damnation in vivid detail, applying all five senses: looking at the burning bodies, hearing the screams, smelling the smoke and the rotting flesh, tasting one's tears and sadness, and feeling the flames on one's skin. The desire that is supposed to guide this horrifying exercise has to do with increasing one's motivation to

[18] David Aretha, *The Story of the Birmingham Civil Rights Movement in Photographs* (Berkeley Heights, NJ: Enslow Publishing, 2014).

[19] Dean Brackley, SJ, *The Call to Discernment in Troubled Times: New Perspectives on the Transformative Wisdom of Ignatius of Loyola* (New York: Crossroad, 2004), 10–13.

[20] Ignatius, *Spiritual Exercises*, sec. 53.2, 42.

[21] Kevin O'Brien, SJ, *The Ignatian Adventure: Experiencing the Spiritual Exercises of Saint Ignatius in Everyday Life* (Chicago: Loyola Press, 2011), 79.

do the right thing. Ignatius says, "If through my faults I should forget the love of the Eternal Lord, at least the fear of those pains will keep me from falling into sin."[22] This multisensory anticipation of hell is supposed to function as a deterrent.

I find this exercise useful for a different reason. It reveals our unsettling human capacity to visualize torture. It shows that the unthinkable is not unthinkable for us. The fact that we are capable of doing such a mental exercise is itself a sign of the evils that we may dream up for others and ourselves, and that some human beings have put into practice. As Ignatius intended, I do experience this exercise as a confrontation with sin but not mainly through a consideration of its eschatological consequences. Instead, this exercise primarily makes me confront the relative ease with which we are able to conjure up the cruelest possible scenarios. We should be troubled by how susceptible our minds are to such destructive ideations.

More concretely, this exercise makes me think of the hell of the slave ship: persons abducted, chained, beaten, raped, starved, crammed together in filth, some dead, some dying, some wanting to die, transported to a foreign territory in which they would be forced to work under the lash, in which they would be torn from their loved ones and children, in which they would be classified as objects meant only for others' gratification.[23] My mind wanders to the hell of the master's quarters, the hell of the cotton field, the hell of the lynch mob, the hell of gang violence, the hell of the prison cell, the hell of being treated each day like a worthless nothing.[24] These hells are real and historical. They have been made by human minds and human hands. This truly is a world dominated by sin, and we are all living in it, and no one is innocent.

---

[22] Ignatius, *Spiritual Exercises*, sec. 65.5, 46.

[23] Christina Sharpe, *In the Wake: On Blackness and Being* (Durham, NC: Duke University Press, 2016); Édouard Glissant, *Poetics of Relation*, trans. Betsy Wing (Ann Arbor, MI: University of Michigan Press, 1995), 5–7; and Willie James Jennings, *The Christian Imagination: Theology and the Origins of Race* (New Haven, CT: Yale University Press, 2010), 176.

[24] These hells, as I am calling them, have recently been represented in a soul-shaking, multisensory fashion by the Equal Justice Initiative in Montgomery, Alabama. For more information, see https://museumandmemorial.eji.org/.

The Second Week

In the Second Week, Ignatius instructs one to begin contemplating biblical mysteries such as the incarnation of the Word, the infancy of Jesus, and his earthly ministry. This week includes meditations that urge one to follow Christ as one's king and to live under his holy banner and not that of the devil, which is characterized by sinful attachments to wealth, honor, and pride. The point of this week is to begin moving out of a condition of sin toward a practice of discipleship. It involves a period of preparation for a choice about the particular state of life in which one will follow Jesus. Ignatius calls this "the Election."[25] He is specifically envisioning vocational choices for either married or celibate life, but one can use the exercises of this week as tools to help one make any number of decisions that may shape one's personal path.

It would be worthwhile for those experiencing the Second Week to use it as an occasion to decide what they are going to do concretely to become agents of change in the fight for racial justice. There are many ways to join the struggle, and one does not need to do them all, but there must be some way to use one's gifts to resist the overwhelming maelstrom of sin that is racism. If one hopes to make the right kinds of practical choices, even when it is costly to do so, one must develop a strong soul. For Ignatius, as we have seen, this means being "indifferent" in a particular sense. But more than that, it means knowing how to think rationally and imaginatively, how to interpret one's deepest emotions productively, and how to detect signs of the interior presence of God when they occur. These points correspond roughly to what Ignatius calls the "Three Times . . . for Making a Sound and Good Election."[26]

Ignatius advises the use of reason specifically when one has no immediate experience of God's intentions for one's life and when the practice of sorting through one's feelings has not yielded sufficient clarity. He calls this a "time of tranquility" and suggests that in such moments one should think carefully about the action one is weighing and about the goals that one has for it, and then "see to which side

---

[25] Ignatius, *Spiritual Exercises*, sec. 135 and 169–89, 64 and 74–80.
[26] Ignatius, sec. 175–77, 76.

reason more inclines." He also recommends using one's imaginative capacities to view the possible course of action from various angles that may be illuminating, asking questions such as how it relates to the love of God, what a righteous person would do in the same situation, and what one would like to have done when looking back at this moment from one's deathbed or from judgment day.

Perhaps more common than the time of tranquility is a time in which one's emotions are trying to tell one something important about the right thing to do. Ignatius's treatment of this time of election encourages us to increase our emotional intelligence. Generally speaking, he thinks we ought to do the things that bring us deep spiritual joy, make us feel more alive and at peace in ourselves, and strengthen our capacity for faith, hope, and love. He calls these inner feelings "consolations." But he warns that such consolations can be deceptive and sometimes involve evil desires and impulses. Therefore, it is important to study them "with great vigilance and attention," noticing if there is any sign of demonic misdirection in them, such as a mixed motive or a concession to sin. Conversely, experiences of "desolation" around a sinful action can be contrastive signs sent by God that are meant to turn one around and lead one in a positive direction. Discerning the movements in our souls requires introspective practice and the loving attention of others such as trusted friends and spiritual directors.[27]

Finally, in rare cases, Ignatius thinks God may move the soul so immediately, indubitably, and completely that it has little need for rational deliberation or prolonged emotional discernment. As one example of this time of election, Ignatius cites Saul's experience of Christ on the road to Damascus, which changes his heart and converts him into the Apostle Paul (Acts 9:1–19).[28] Ignatius also describes a particular type of consolation that is not connected with any concrete object but is like a river of divine joy washing over the soul and inundating it entirely. In his words: "It is the prerogative of the Creator alone to enter the soul, depart from it, and cause a motion in it which draws the whole person into love of His Divine Majesty." This is the

---

[27] Ignatius, sec. 176 and 313–36, 76 and 121–28.
[28] Ignatius, sec. 175, 76.

"consolation without preceding cause."[29] One should not count on such mystical experiences, but one should not rule them out either. They can and do happen. In the Black Christian tradition, the female preacher Jarena Lee had an experience of sanctification that seems similar to what Ignatius means by a consolation without preceding cause. She describes a moment of ecstasy that felt "like an ocean of light and bliss." This extraordinary event fortified Jarena Lee's resolve to preach the Gospel and serve God and neighbor through her ministry.[30]

Although the fact that God opposes racism should be clear with or without the Spiritual Exercises, the cognitive and affective tools employed during the Election period of the Second Week can help one decipher the individual choices that one is called to make in the divinely willed fight against racism. They can help one break through the false consciousness, emotional barriers, and spiritual inertia of one's racially damaged soul and arrive at personally tailored, anti-racist action plans for one's renewed life in Christ. The question is not whether to resist racism but *how* to do so. Our minds and hearts have work to do to answer this question well.

The Third and Fourth Weeks

The Third and Fourth Weeks of the Spiritual Exercises ask the spiritual trainee to plunge into the saving mysteries of Jesus's death and resurrection. These weeks bring one into contact with his suffering human flesh, which he shares with all the crucified and lynched peoples of the world, and with his glorified body, which gives hope that the violence of history will not have the final word. In the meditations of the Third Week, Ignatius wants us to feel the suffering of Jesus. To this end, he offers the following guidance: "I will try to foster an attitude of sorrow, suffering, and heartbreak, by calling often to memory the labors, fatigue, and sufferings which Christ our Lord suffered, from his birth up to whatever mystery of his Passion I am

[29] Ignatius, sec. 330, 126.

[30] Jarena Lee, *The Life and Religious Experience of Jarena Lee*, in *Sisters of the Spirit: Three Black Women's Autobiographies of the Nineteenth Century*, ed. William L. Andrews (Bloomington, IN: Indiana University Press, 1986), 25–48, at 34.

contemplating at the time."[31] The goal is to be with Jesus in his mortal anguish, to place oneself imaginatively and affectively in the scene.

Christopher Pramuk notes that Billie Holiday's 1939 recording of Abel Meeropol's "Strange Fruit" acts in a similar way. Like Ignatian meditations on the crucified Jesus, the lyrics and somber tones of Holiday's protest song draw those who listen to it into a scene of intense physical and psychological torment and invite them to connect emotionally.[32] Inspired by Holiday and other Black musicians, artists, and poets, Cone argues that the relationship between Christ on the cross and the Black body on the lynching tree is no mere analogy. Christ is present in and with the thousands of African Americans and other racially marginalized people who have been mutilated and murdered by white supremacists. Cone concludes, *"Every time a white mob lynched a black person, they lynched Jesus."*[33]

While the sorrowful meditations of the Third Week are designed to make us feel regret for our sins and gratitude for the awesome love that Christ shows by dying for us, reflecting on them in connection with the horrors of lynching puts me in touch with other emotions, such as righteous anger at the cruelty of such actions and fear of having my Black male body treated so violently. Although the Third Week ought to increase solidarity with the victims of history by forging deep emotional bonds with them, the word "solidarity" is perhaps too anemic to capture all that could and should take place in this part of the Spiritual Exercises. These meditations cultivate a flesh-and-spirit unity between the incarnate God, the lynched person, and myself to which no words are fully adequate.

Yet Ignatius is adamant that this violence is not the ultimate truth of things. The Fourth Week invites one to experience the joy of the resurrection. In addition to meditating on biblical verses related to this mystery and responding joyfully to them, Ignatius encourages retreatants to find happiness in their natural environments: "I will

---

[31] Ignatius, *Spiritual Exercises*, sec. 206.4, 84.

[32] Christopher Pramuk, "Beauty Limned in Violence: Experimenting with Protest Music in the Ignatian Classroom," in *Transforming Ourselves, Transforming the World: Justice in Jesuit Higher Education*, ed. Mary Beth Combs and Patricia Ruggiano Schmidt (New York: Fordham University Press, 2013), 15–29, at 20.

[33] James Cone, *The Cross and the Lynching Tree* (Maryknoll, NY: Orbis Books, 2011), 158; emphasis in original.

avail myself of light or the pleasant features of the seasons, such as the refreshing coolness in summer or the sun or heat in winter, as far as I think or conjecture that this will help me to rejoice in Christ my Creator and Redeemer."[34] Ignatius believes that God wants human beings to flourish and be glad.

Although the Third and Fourth Weeks highlight dramatic tensions between death and resurrection, they may also help participants sustain hope amid the seemingly mundane difficulties of everyday life. These difficulties may have to do with employment, relationships, families, or mental and physical well-being. Donelda Cook, an African American psychotherapist, explains how Ignatian spiritual practices helped one of her Black female clients navigate hardships and blockages in her life and reconnect with a feeling of joy in God's presence.[35] Ignatius affirms that the small crosses and triumphs of quotidian life may be opportunities to strengthen the soul and participate in a larger salvific process.

The Contemplation to Attain Love

The retreat concludes with a final exercise called The Contemplation to Attain Love. I would like to bring my own reflections to a close by commenting on this highly cherished feature of Ignatian spirituality. The first point of this contemplation instructs one to recall the many gifts one has received from God. Its goal is not merely to inspire gratitude but to motivate an extravagant return-gift of one's whole existence. Ignatius here offers his famous *Suscipe* prayer: "Take, Lord, and receive, all my liberty, my memory, my understanding, and my will—all that I have and possess. You, Lord, have given all that to me. I now give it back to You, O Lord. All of it is yours. Dispose of it according to your will."[36] This experience of divine-and-human mutuality presupposes freedom and strength on both sides. It presupposes that my soul has been nourished and enriched and that I

---

[34] Ignatius, *Spiritual Exercises*, sec. 228.4, 93.

[35] Donelda A. Cook, "Crossing Traditions: Ignatian Prayer with a Protestant African American Counseling Dyad," in *Casebook for a Spiritual Strategy in Counseling and Psychotherapy*, ed. P. S. Richards and A. E. Bergin (Washington, DC: American Psychological Association, 2004), 173–86.

[36] Ignatius, *Spiritual Exercises*, sec. 234.4, 95.

have the agential capacity necessary to surrender it fully to God's will. To the extent that racism damages and weakens our souls, it prevents us from enjoying this deeply consoling mystery, at least to the level we should.

The remaining parts of the exercise seek to raise our awareness about the active presence of God in all things. The world around us is no longer framed as a set of instruments for human use. It is described as a place teeming with divine life and initiative. God is "working in the heavens, elements, plants, fruits, cattle, and all the rest." God "dwells also in myself, giving me existence, life, sensation, and intelligence." My power, "justice, goodness, piety, mercy, and so forth" come from this divine source within me and within the whole of creation.[37] Looking around at the dismal state of human affairs and the pessimism that characterizes much public discourse, particularly about race, it may seem that we simply lack the virtues and gifts that we need to make a better world that would be more in keeping with God's loving designs. But Ignatius helps us recognize that this is not the case. Everything we need has already been given. The created order is radiant with divine blessings, both material and spiritual, external and internal. Everything we would require in order to live the right way is already at hand, including God's own personal nearness.

We have to take responsibility for receiving and activating the gifts that are being lavishly poured out upon us. We need to do this together and without delay. A racism-defeating abundance of love is within reach, if we but train ourselves to attain it and put this training into practice. Because some will refuse to do this work, there will undoubtedly be incidents of violence and even calamity, but all I can say, to echo St. Paul, is that where sin abounds, grace abounds all the more (see Romans 5:20). Such is the hope that I have gained from praying according to the principles outlined by St. Ignatius.

---

[37] Ignatius, sec. 235–37, 95.

2

Digging into Jesuit Slaveholding, Digging into the Exercises[1]

Ken Homan, SJ

I sat before the statue of Mary, awkwardly fidgeting and doing my best not to check my watch. *Pray about your sinfulness.* I wondered what I had gotten myself into and what good would come of these exercises. *Sit with Mary and ask to feel abhorrence for your sins. Perceive their disorder. Detest all that is vain.* I checked my watch, astounded that only eight minutes of the prescribed hour had gone by. At twenty years old, the First Week of Ignatius of Loyola's Spiritual Exercises was a daunting undertaking.[2] The First Week requires honesty, openness, trust, and humility in a way I had never before experienced. I completed that first attempt at the First Week as best I could; but it has taken me years of annual eight-day retreats to both trust and discover how essential the First Week is.

Ignatius breaks the Exercises into four "weeks" or movements: sin and trusting God's mercy; Jesus's mission; Jesus's passion and crucifixion; and Jesus's resurrection and God's enduring love. These Exercises are undertaken to free ourselves from attachments and open

---

[1] This essay originally appeared as an article in *Review for Religious* Online on October 12, 2021, and is reprinted with permission.

[2] For those unfamiliar with Ignatius's Spiritual Exercises, a good introduction is Michael Ivens, SJ, *Understanding the Spiritual Exercises* (Herefordshire, UK: Gracewing, 1998).

to God's call. In his commentary on the Exercises, Michael Ivens comments on the First Week: "Mercy, then, is the dominant theme of the First Week Meditations, but there can be no profound sense of God's mercy without a profound sense of one's sin."[3]

The experience of awkwardness, humility, and demand for openness returned to me in summer 2021. For two weeks, I joined an archeology team at St. Inigoes, Maryland, the site of one of our former Jesuit plantations. Each day, descendants of those families who we Jesuits had enslaved joined us on the dig. We worked together, speaking at length about the history, reality, and legacy of Jesuit slaveholding. We gathered the broken pieces of pottery, porcelain, pipe stems, bricks, and glass bottles. I listened to the stories, names, feelings, and experiences of those present, all while uncovering artifacts of the lives of those who worked at the plantations.

The time together forced me to ask: Have we American Jesuits honestly engaged with the First Week regarding our slaveholding? Have we had a profound sense of our sinfulness?

Impediments to Honesty

Openly discussing sin can be taboo. Years of over-emphasis, misuse, misapplication, and finger-pointing cause many to shirk engagement with the idea of sin, sometimes even rejecting it as a useful category. When I taught high school, a significant portion of my students saw discussions about sin as the prerogative of hypocritical authorities who chastised others but saw themselves as spotless. Many of my young adult Catholic peers feel constantly berated by church officials regarding sex and beliefs around marriage, ordination, and contraception. On the other hand, other young adult Catholic peers view regular confession as a thriving part of their prayer lives. Among my Jesuit peers, sin and confession are a simple, everyday part of prayer. Despite this, some sinful subjects still seem taboo. Jesuit slaveholding is one of them.

Conversations with my fellow Jesuits about slaveholding vary widely. Discussing racism and the legacy of slaveholding is acceptable in the academic sense. Most applaud the study and research undertaken to learn about the lives of the people we enslaved. When

---

[3] Ivens, *Understanding the Spiritual Exercises*, 44.

it comes to the legacy of slaveholding and systematic racism, how our schools and institutions continue to benefit from those legacies and what we owe individuals and communities in reconciliation, the conversations get murkier. Deflections lurk around each corner of the conversation.

Three deflections come up with some regularity.[4] These deflections seek to lessen the burden of confronting sin. They either downplay the sin's significance or try to historicize it in a way that reduces its brutality. I share the deflections here and address their shortcomings briefly thereafter.

It Was Commonplace

Slaveholding was increasingly widespread during the years the Jesuits established (and post-suppression[5] reestablished) themselves in the United States. As with other religious orders, we participated in the full range of slaveholding—buying, selling, renting, borrowing, punishing, and enslaving Black[6] people. When discussing slaveholding, it is common to hear, "Well, nobody was against it at the time: it was commonplace." There is a sense that we should not judge historical actors too harshly for appropriating what was then considered moral.

The Good We Did

When discussing slaveholding with my fellow Jesuits, many feel that the discussions of wrongdoing and sin prevent us from acknowledging the good that we did. Whether it was spreading the Gospel

---

[4] Curiously, they are the same deflections I hear from Jesuits and other Catholics regarding slaveholding, the sex abuse crisis, Native or First Nations residential schools, and sexism in the church.

[5] In 1773, following pressure from numerous European monarchs, Pope Clement XIV suppressed the Society of Jesus. Several kingdoms (most notably Russia), however, used a loophole to allow the Jesuits to continue ministering and working. In 1814, Pope Pius VII restored the Society. (See https://www.americamagazine.org /faith/2014/07/22/unlikely-story-how-jesuits-were-suppressed-and-then-restored.)

[6] I follow the common practice of capitalizing "Black" as is done with other ethnic identities and following the lead of the National Association of Black Journalists. See this explainer from the David Lanham for more: https://www.brookings.edu/blog /the-avenue/2020/06/16/a-public-letter-to-the-associated-press-listen-to-the-nation -and-capitalize-black/.

or teaching enslaved persons to read and write, there is a sense that emphasis on the sin of slaveholding diminishes a fuller picture. There is a desire for the historical context to affirm the path that we took.

We Are Trapped by This Discussion

We Jesuits are held to high standards by ourselves, our superiors, our communities, and the church alike. Indeed, the church as a whole is held to high standards, as seen by the rightful outrage of the sex abuse crisis. Some feel these standards can be a debilitating trap, that we are not allowed to be human, to struggle, or to question. When it comes to the legacy of slaveholding and our response, there's a temptation to throw one's hands up and frustratedly ask, "What *exactly* do you want me to do?"

Spiritually (and emotionally), these deflections often emerge from fear and attachments, two conditions Ignatius addresses in the First Week. Fear and attachments impede our ability to honestly wrestle with sin or the legacy of slaveholding. Authentically giving ourselves to the First Week, however, makes us freer and our commitment to justice more fruitful.

Bringing What Is Buried to the Light

In the First Week of the Exercises, Ignatius begins with the Principle and Foundation. It states, "[Human beings are] created to praise, reverence, and serve God our Lord, and by means of this to save [their] souls."[7] Ignatius goes on to urge indifference—not to "prefer health to sickness, riches to poverty, honor to dishonor, a longer life to a short life. The same holds for all other things."[8] In short, we are to use any possible tools, works, or situations to glorify God.

Sin stands in the way of that glorification.

Ignatius uses the rest of the First Week to help the retreatant honestly place their sins before God. The process is not meant to crush the retreatant under a sense of their own sinfulness. Rather, it is to be open and honest so to recognize the infinite mercy and goodness

---

[7] Louis J. Puhl, SJ, *The Spiritual Exercises of St. Ignatius: Based on Studies in the Language of the Autograph* (Chicago: Loyola University Press, 1951), 12.

[8] Puhl, *Spiritual Exercises*, 12.

of God. Ignatius meant for this recognition of God to go beyond the Jesuits or just those who completed the Exercises to extend to all persons, so that all might experience God's tremendous mercy.

That openness begins with a general confession. Ignatius states of the general confession, "During these Spiritual Exercises one reaches a deeper interior understanding of the reality and malice of one's sins than when one is not so concentrated on interior concerns." He points to the role of indifference. Freeing oneself from attachments allows the retreatant to recognize more fully the malevolence of sin. More importantly, it allows the retreatant to recognize the role of God's grace and mercy.

From there, Ignatius turns to the three exercises on sin. In the first, the retreatant asks for shame, confusion, tears, and suffering while praying about the sins of the fallen angels, Adam and Eve, and others in hell. The exercise ends with a colloquy in which the retreatant imagines Christ on the cross. In the second exercise, the retreatant imagines their sins being read off as in a court record, including the time, place, and accomplices. While there is a temptation to linger on the corruption and foulness that Ignatius prescribes, the true movement is toward the wonder at all of God's goodness and mercy. The third exercise is a colloquy, a three-part conversation. The retreatant goes from Mary, to God the Son, to God the Father asking to feel abhorrence for their sins. After repeating the third exercise, the retreatant concludes with a contemplation on hell—the people there, the smells, the feelings, and the horror of lost souls separated from God.

Upon first glance, these exercises seem to lay a tremendous burden on the retreatant: they ask someone to focus and meditate on the serious and traumatizing nature of sin, without succumbing to hopelessness. The end goal, however, is recognition of God's mercy and goodness. Having undertaken the Exercises and directed eight-day retreats, I can confidently say that retreatants who bear their sins to God feel a tremendous sense of freedom afterward. That freedom is *vital* for pursuing justice in a fuller, more authentic manner.

Pursuing that internal and external freedom is frequently difficult. We have many attachments and fears that prevent us from moving forward. I return here to those common deflections and how the First Week might help to move past them.

It Was Commonplace

Slaveholding was increasingly commonplace in the United States upon the Jesuits' arrival, and fully cemented at the time of our restoration. To say that nobody was against it, however, is completely false. Enslaved persons regularly fought back against their bondage in a variety of creative ways; to claim otherwise is to disregard the voices of enslaved persons both in the past and at present. Moreover, there were critics in the church hierarchy as well. In a tweet, Spanish scholar Catherine Addington, points out, "if there's one thing you learn from my twitter feed, let it be that 'you gotta judge them by the standards of their time' is easily done, because for every chronicle of colonial Spaniards' genocidal actions there's a contemporary who petitioned the Crown to punish their crimes."[9] The same can be said of slaveholding. There were many critics of slaveholding at the time, including in our own Jesuit hierarchy.

This historicization is key—it prevents us from diminishing the sinfulness, forcing the honesty that is pivotal to the First Week. Ignatius suggests in the first exercise that we consider the mortal sin of someone who has gone to hell. As I consider Jesuits and slaveholding, I am forced to ask myself—are there Jesuits in hell because of our slaveholding? I wonder if any of my Jesuit forebearers are like the rich man in Luke 16, desperately wanting to warn our present company. Being honest about the sinfulness of our slaveholding helps us to heed the prophets, to listen more attentively regarding racial justice in our own time.

The Good We Did

No doubt, Jesuits in North America have done a tremendous amount of good. However, Ignatius's teaching in the First Week shows that such good in no way absolves an individual or community from grappling with their sin and the harm they have caused, of which Jesuits are also guilty. If we want to move forward with the Exercises in a full and fruitful way, we must be deeply, shamefully, and painfully sorrowful. That sorrow, however, is not our stopping point.

---

[9] Catherine Addington, PhD, Twitter post, June 18, 2019, 2:33 p.m., https://twitter .com/catherineofalx/status/1141081519903186972.

Ignatius makes it abundantly clear that honesty about our sinfulness allows us to truly appreciate the Principle and Foundation and appreciate God's mercy. When we deflect or try to skip ahead, we are in fact shortchanging the goodness and grace God lays before us.

We Are Trapped by This Discussion

The dynamics of the First Week are precisely designed to avoid being trapped by an overwhelming sense of sin. If a deep sense of sin is all that comes from the First Week, the exercise has not been successfully completed. The freedom gained allows us to correctly discern, without attachment, the true and just course of action that God wills for us, including how to handle our sinful history.

The First Week helps to free us from our attachments, fears, and what Ignatius describes as vanity. For myself personally, much of that vanity is about my image as a Jesuit. I want us to be known as the religious order that works tirelessly for justice, that prays deeply, and gives of ourselves to the poor and oppressed. Yet I sometimes attach to that image rather than God who calls us to be those things.

An Ongoing Examen

During the dig, descendants of those families we enslaved regularly pushed me to confront the sins of our historic and present Jesuits alike. We spent hours working alongside each other. While the dig itself was important work, the conversations bore a greater impact on me. Descendants offered several observations and questions that have stood out in my prayer:

Why are you the only Jesuit here listening to us?

Is this something Jesuits talk about regularly, or do you avoid it like other uncomfortable topics?

Is this something you all learn about? Or is it only you making this effort?

I'm upset that you're the first Jesuit who has made an effort to talk to me.

Are you actually going to do something about this, or is this dig just an experience?

I'm just very angry.

It's just so moving to be in the places my ancestors were, to hear their story, to learn about it. But I'm so hurt that it's taken this long to facilitate a conversation.

Do you all know what you have done to my family?

These questions and comments gave me pause, forcing me to stop and ask if I had really reckoned with the sins of my own Jesuit brethren; or if I had truly wrestled with the legacy of slaveholding that helped build the Society of Jesus in America. I can honestly say that I am in the infancy of that process. The descendants and the dig itself have offered me a prophetic witness and invitation to dig further into Ignatian spirituality. The shattered and scattered pieces of pottery we found on the dig reminded me of the lives we Jesuits likewise shattered and scattered.

As we Jesuits dig further into our slaveholding history, it is equally important that we dig further into the Exercises, particularly the First Week. We might ask ourselves about our present-day attachments and fears. What prevents us from reckoning with our past and pursuing justice for the sins for which our company is responsible? Are we willing, especially with our institutions, to give and not to count the cost? To fight and not to heed the wounds?

3

The Composition of Place in Ignatian Spirituality

Repositioning a Historical-Ecological Encounter with Jesus in the Context of Modernity/Coloniality

Alex Mikulich

"The lynching tree is the cross in America."

James Cone[1]

The Spiritual Exercises "historicize the word of God as they turn to historical, personal, and situational signs so that word might be discovered in the concrete."

Ignacio Ellacuría[2]

"Contemporary African Americans cannot fully enjoy self-certified biophilia if their status in the social sphere remains compromised . . . our future in our current life support system is predicated on our ability to strengthen interconnected ecosocial security."

Kimberly Ruffin[3]

---

[1] James H. Cone, *The Cross and the Lynching Tree* (Maryknoll, NY: Orbis Books, 2011), 158.

[2] J. Matthew Ashley, "Ignacio Ellacuría and the *Spiritual Exercises* of Ignatius Loyola," *Theological Studies* 61 (2000): 16–39, here 26. Ashley cites Ignacio Ellacuría, "Lectura latinoamericana de los *Ejercicios Espirituales* de San Ignacio," *Revista latinoamericana de teología* 23 (1991): 111–47, here 113.

[3] Kimberly Ruffin, "Biophilia on Purpose: A Declaration to Become an Ecosocial Citizen," *Intervalla* 3 (2015): 44–48, here 47.

How do we pray for freedom as a community of faith gathered around the cross of Jesus Christ within white supremacist US imperial rule in modernity/coloniality? How do we engage the Spiritual Exercises of St. Ignatius of Loyola as a way of co-creating God's love to "enflesh freedom"[4] so that all human and non-human kin may thrive in our historical context of "modernity-in-nature"?[5] These questions grapple with the epistemological assumptions we tend to take for granted and that undergird our entire way of living in the US American context. We are all engulfed in a cultural matrix of domination that is so intent on killing Black and Indigenous peoples and the Earth in the name of infinite economic growth that Pope Francis laments a downward "spiral of self-destruction."[6]

A critical assumption of St. Ignatius in his Spiritual Exercises is that God encounters persons in their concrete historical circumstances. Ignatius invites a "Composition of Place" at the start of the first meditation as a way of preparing people for an encounter with God. While many commentators focus attention on the "imaginative gaze" Ignatius invites in the first meditation, few concentrate on the how and why of the actual Composition of Place. I contend that an effective Composition of Place, that is, one that facilitates critical reflection on faith within the concrete historical circumstances of our time and place, demands *embodied* questioning of the epistemological assumptions of modernity/coloniality-in-nature.[7] A failure to bodily question the epistemological assumptions of modernity/coloniality, I argue, risks abstraction or dislocation from the concrete historical and ecological circumstances in which people seek God.

My argument proceeds in four sections. First, I suggest a composition of our time and place that interconnects death-dealing colonization of Black spaces and bodies and destruction of the Earth itself. Second, I offer a brief historical overview of the ways that various

---

[4] M. Shawn Copeland, *Enfleshing Freedom: Body, Race, and Being* (Minneapolis: Fortress Press, 2010).

[5] Jason W. Moore, *Capitalism in the Web of Life: Ecology and the Accumulation of Capital* (New York: Verso Press, 2015), 4.

[6] Pope Francis, *Laudato Si'*, On Care for Our Common Home (Vatican City: Libreria Editrice Vaticana, 2015), 163.

[7] My riff on Jason W. Moore's insight underscores how the oppressive side of modernity includes colonization of Black spaces and bodies and the earth itself.

commentators have interpreted the Composition of Place in the Spiritual Exercises that concludes with a call for Ignacio Ellacuría's historicization of the Composition of Place and a "mysticism of the historical event." Third, returning to a composition of our time and place, I suggest a way we might "reposition" white settler engagement with the Spiritual Exercises that might ultimately lead to a mysticism of the historical-ecological event. Finally, I suggest three concrete practices retreat centers and directors practically utilize to begin a process of repositioning a Composition of Place for today. A mysticism of the historical-ecological event invites a shared struggle for racial and ecological justice in the one-earth, one-life, and one-love in which the Exercises draw all of us into ongoing re-creation with God.

A Composition of Our Time and Place

My chapter grapples with the question raised by Jesuits in their General Congregation 36: "The question that haunts the society today is why the Exercises do not change us as deeply as we would hope."[8] A reconsideration of the Composition of Place is one way that the entire "Ignatian Family," especially in the North American context, might "appropriate ever more fully the gift of the Exercises."[9] We US white settlers need an updated composition of our time and place that interrelates the interpenetrating crises of anti-Black white supremacy and ecological devastation.

The Earth and its peoples are literally crying out for life. As a planet, we are now living beyond ecological boundaries for climate change, biodiversity loss, land conversion, and nitrogen and phosphorus loading, according to a planetary boundaries framework.[10] These crises remain unabated, in part, because we white settler Americans consume a "happy story" about economic growthism in our socialization, media, and education systems even as this so-called

---

[8] General Congregation 36, decree 1, no. 18, available online at https://jesuits.eu/images/docs/GC_36_Documents.pdf.

[9] GC 36, dec. 1, no. 18.

[10] W. Steffan, K. Richardson, and J. Rockstrom et al., "Planetary Boundaries: Guiding Human Development in a Changing Planet," *Science* 347, no. 6223 (February 2015): 1–10.

"free market" impoverishes billions of people and destroys the planet. We white American settlers conveniently forget that the economic rise of the West and the United States depended upon enslavement of African and American Indigenous peoples, expropriating both labor and capital, and dispossessing them of lands and abundant resources. This legacy of racial, economic, and ecological oppression continues today in modernity/coloniality-in-nature. For example, rich nations, such as the US, rely on a large net appropriation of resources from the global South, including all forms of aid. Far from "developing" the South, the global North is plundering the global South. Economic drain from the global South is "worth over $10 trillion per year, in Northern prices," while the South's losses "outstrip their aid receipts by a factor of 30."[11] Nevertheless, we North American white settlers, who object to wearing a cloth mask to stem a pandemic, tend not to question an economic way of life that creates "ill health from pollution, diabetes, and obesity, and so on."[12]

It is precisely this economic and cultural way of life that perpetuates police and vigilante violence against Black people at rates nearly the same as that of lynching just a century ago.[13] It is precisely this modern system that colonizes Black, LatinX, and Indigenous space and bodies through the school to prison pipeline, hyper-incarceration,[14] and by fostering a political economy of segregation through a combination of racially structured banking, real estate, and governmental policies that "hastens physical decline in urban neighborhoods [and] forever incentivizes their perpetuation."[15]

[11] Jason Hickel, Christian Dorninger, Hanspeter Wieland, and Intan Suwandi, "Imperialist Appropriation in the World Economy: Drain from the Global South through Unequal Exchange, 1990–2015," *Global Environmental Change* 73 (March 2022): 1–13.

[12] Jason Hickel, *Less Is More: How Degrowth Will Save the World* (London: Windmill Books, 2021), 175.

[13] Isabel Wilkerson, "Mike Brown's Shooting and Jim Crow Lynchings Have Too Much in Common: It's Time for Americans to Own Up," *The Guardian*, August 25, 2014.

[14] Alex Mikulich, Laurie Cassidy, and Margaret Pfeil, *The Scandal of White Complicity in U.S. Hyper-Incarceration: A Nonviolent Spirituality of White Resistance* (New York: Palgrave Macmillan, 2013).

[15] Keeanga-Yamahtta Taylor, *Race for Profit: How Banks and the Real Estate Industry Undermined Black Home Ownership* (Chapel Hill, NC: University of North Carolina Press, 2019), 11.

The predominantly Western, white-settler Christianity where the Spiritual Exercises are offered in the US context, tends to assume a *normative single consciousness* whereby our presence is modern, natural, and right. In an essay exposing the problem of that single consciousness, Bryan Massingale asks a piercing question: "Why is it that so many white religious and spiritual formation programs have failed to produce the vanguard of contemplative white persons with a consciousness freed from the soul sickness of White supremacy?"[16]

Predominantly white contemplative centers and spiritual formation programs that offer the Spiritual Exercises are not exempt from this question. The implication of the question is not merely that we have *not* become a vanguard released from the soul sickness of anti-Black supremacy, but that our predominant mode of being, that tends to accept the terms of a single, dominant consciousness—that of modernity/coloniality-in-nature—reifies the oppressive side of Western modernity. For example, when I procured training in the Spiritual Exercises of St. Ignatius at a suburban Catholic retreat center, I was simultaneously serving as a lay pastoral associate at a Black Catholic parish in San Francisco. When I invited members of the parish to take advantage of the retreats offered by the suburban retreat center, I began to realize that even if the center addressed issues of geographical and financial inaccessibility, there was little interest among parish members to go there. My white male ignorance blinded me to a deeper problem for white retreat centers. As Dr. Angela Rose Black explains, contemplative and mindfulness centers "were just an extension of the racial aggression and isolation I felt at-large, except worse."[17] When she would enter a predominantly white space "*already* fatigued by racial aggression" and attempt practices that might aid in "diffusing some of the burden I carried . . . I had to navigate the complexities of feeling unwelcomed while curiously hyper-focused on; unseen yet aggressively overdirected by White

---

[16] Bryan N. Massingale, "Toward a Spirituality for Racial Justice: The Transformation of Consciousness and the 'Souls of White Folks,'" in *Desire, Darkness, and Hope: Theology in a Time of Impasse*, ed. Laurie M. Cassidy and M. Shawn Copeland (Collegeville, MN: Liturgical Press, 2021), 345.

[17] "Disrupting Systemic Whiteness in the Mindfulness Movement," interview with Dr. Angela Rose Black in *Mindful: Healthy Mind, Healthy Life* (December 2017), https://www.mindful.org/disrupting-systemic-whiteness-mindfulness-movement/.

practitioners and teachers."[18] How many Ignatian retreat centers actually "center people of color, including their trauma, gifts, experiences, ancestral traditions, and activism"?[19] Perhaps this is why there is a broader movement of people of color moving beyond dominant white Christianity "to chart their own spiritual initiatives."[20] Predominantly white Ignatian contemplative centers will need to address their own white ignorance before creating programs "resonant with historically oppressed and marginalized people of color who experienced the transgenerational impact of collective traumas such as genocide, slavery, and colonization as well as the dehumanizing soul-assaults of ongoing racism and intersectional oppression."[21]

As white settler Americans, the single normative consciousness assumed by modernity educates us into ignorance of the histories of colonialism and slavery, which cultural anthropologist Walter Mignolo calls the "darker side of Western modernity," or the "colonial matrix of power."[22] As I reflect upon on my training in the Spiritual Exercises of St. Ignatius at a Catholic retreat center, even though the program included an orientation to social justice, the program never questioned the assumptions of modernity as a relentless achievement of progress, development, modernization, and democracy. The program never addressed our predominantly white suburban context or internalized superiority much less consider the needs of peoples who have experienced transgenerational traumas from slavery, genocide, and enduring anti-Black violence. Christian theology and spirituality, especially as it is practiced in predominantly white contemplative centers and social justice institutes in the United States, even when individual practitioners may be critical of aspects of our contemporary world—tend not to question the rules of the game set by modernity/coloniality-in-nature. In other words, even with some

---

[18] Black, "Disrupting Whiteness."

[19] Deborah Jian Lee, "Christians of Color Are Rejecting Colonial Christianity and Reclaiming Ancestral Spiritualities," *Religion Dispatches* (January 10, 2018), https://religiondispatches.org/christians-of-color-are-rejecting-colonial-christianity-and-reclaiming-ancestral-spiritualities/.

[20] Jian Lee, "Christians of Color."

[21] Shelly P. Harrell, "Soulfulness as an Orientation to Contemplative Practice: Culture, Liberation, and Mindful Awareness," *The Journal of Contemplative Inquiry* 5, no. 1 (2018): 9–40, here 9.

[22] Walter Mignolo, *The Darker Side of Western Modernity: Global Futures, Decolonial Options* (Durham, NC: Duke University Press, 2011).

theologies of liberation, the problem is that even "in the disputes between (neo) liberalism and (neo) Marxism, both sides of the coin belong to the same bank: the disputes are entrenched within the same rules of the game, where the contenders defend different positions but do not question the terms of the conversation."[23] These unquestioned assumptions are the problem.

While Western modernity celebrates itself through a rhetoric of incessant progress, secular salvation, and newness, its "underside," or "hidden agenda" reveals the *dispensability* (or expendability) *of human life*," as Western economic practices and "knowledge justified racism and the inferiority of human lives that were naturally considered dispensable."[24] The Colonial Matrix of Power (or coloniality), referred to above, is the logic or framework of colonial domination that "generates, reproduces, modifies, and maintains" interconnected, historical hierarchies of race, class, labor, gender/sex, heterosexuality/homosexuality, spiritual/religious, aesthetic, epistemic, and linguistic categories, and classifies them as natural and right. The CMP constructs the "modern subject" as "the idea of Man," i.e., the white, male, heterosexual, Christian who "became the model for the Human and for Humanity."[25]

The Composition of Place in the Spiritual Exercises

At the very start of the first meditation in the SE,[26] St. Ignatius invites a preparatory prayer "to ask God for the grace that all my intentions, actions, and operations may be ordered purely to the service and praise of his Divine Majesty." Ignatius recommends this prayer before all the remaining prayer periods as a way of placing himself before God in the entirety of his mental and physical activities.[27] He then advises that one making the exercises should "see the place" and he calls this prelude or preliminary the "composition":

---

[23] Mignolo, *Darker Side*, 92.

[24] Mignolo, 6.

[25] Mignolo, 17–19.

[26] I will refer to the Spiritual Exercises with the shortened "SE" or "Exercises" from here on.

[27] *Ignatius of Loyola: Spiritual Exercises and Selected Works*, ed. George Ganss, SJ (Mahwah, NJ: Paulist Press, 1991), see note 29 to the Spiritual Exercises, 396–97.

The First Prelude is a composition made by imagining the place. Here we should take notice of the following. When a contemplation or meditation is about something that can be gazed on, for example, a contemplation of Christ our Lord, who is visible, the composition consists of seeing in imagination the physical place where that which I want to contemplate is taking place. By physical place I mean, for instance, a temple or a mountain where Jesus Christ or Our Lady happens to be, in accordance with the topic I desire to contemplate.

When a contemplation or meditation is about something abstract and invisible, as in the present case about the sins, the composition will be to see in imagination and to consider my soul as imprisoned in this corruptible body, and my whole compound self as an exile in this valley of tears among brute animals. I mean, my whole self as composed of soul and body.

Most commentators focus on the imaginative gaze as a warning to the person making the exercises that this is not about fantasizing; rather, it is to focus on something that is real, explains Nicolas Standaert, a professor of Sinology at the University of Leuven and an expert on the Jesuit missions to China.[28] Standaert and other commentators explicate how the Older Directories don't have very much to say about the Composition of Place.[29] Even when they did say something positive, it usually included a warning against the composition.

Standaert explains that many modern commentators tend to be constrained about the composition as well. For example, the entry "Composition de lieu" in the *Dictionaire de spiritualité* draws upon commentators who "warn those engaged in meditation not to tire themselves over the composition" and that for experienced souls this preliminary could be disregarded entirely.[30] Indeed, when I was trained in the Spiritual Exercises in a Jesuit divinity school, one of the course's main texts only stated that one should seek "a setting that is real to what you are pondering" and "let your imagination

---

[28] Nicolas Standaert, "The Composition of Place: Creating Space for An Encounter," *The Way* 46, no. 1 (January 2007): 7–20, 8.

[29] See also Juliano Ribeiro Almeida, " 'The Composition of Place' and the 'Application of the Senses' in Ignatian Prayer," *The Downside Review* (2019): 1–12.

[30] Almeida, "Composition of Place," 12.

give you some way of looking at the reality" of a passage of Scripture.[31] The course text did not offer any other reflection on the composition.

In contrast to early and modern commentators who tended to be more constrained, Jeronimo Nadal (1507-1580) offers a much more expansive vision of the composition. Nadal's magnum opus, *Annotations and Meditations on the Gospels*, Standaert explains, dedicates extensive attention both to composition and visualization. Juan Polanco believed that Nadal "had been blessed with a true understanding of what Ignatius" intended.[32] Nadal's *Annotations* utilized a series of gospel images to assist a process of prayer that is "an appropriate elucidation to accompany" the exercises.[33] The goal of the composition, understood in Nadal's elucidation, is facilitating a dialogue between the gospel passage and the retreatant. One composes a place to make room for another—"room for somebody different from myself."[34] The composition, then, becomes a starting point for an encounter between two narratives; that of the gospel and a person's life. The exercises do not invite the person to simply project their own experience upon the gospel story; rather, "by quietly standing alongside 'the places, the persons, the objects and the events' we are invited to place ourselves in a certain situation and be moved by it, and undertake a pilgrimage."[35] The pilgrimage invited by the Exercises "relocates" us as persons in relationship "with the person in whom God gives himself—Jesus of Nazareth."[36]

The dynamics of the exercises, beginning with the *composito loci*, "allows us to knit together the context in which we move" and that of the gospel story in which "Jesus becomes present to us here and now." That knitting together and ongoing interconnection may lead to "a further relocation" that is not merely "mental or personal repositioning" but a "'relocation-become-flesh'" in the personal lives of people who welcome Jesus's presence and ongoing transformation

[31] Marian Cowan, CSJ, and John Carroll Futrell, SJ, *The Spiritual Exercises of St. Ignatius of Loyola: A Handbook for Directors* (Cambridge, MA: Jesuit Educational Center for Human Development, 1982), 57.

[32] Standaert, "Composition of Place," 12.

[33] Standaert, 12.

[34] Standaert, 14.

[35] Standaert, 16.

[36] Standaert, 17.

of who we are in the world. Ultimately, Standaert argues that the composition, understood within the entirety of the exercises, is a "way to take resurrection faith seriously as something to be made flesh. But at the same time it is the revelation of a way of human living rooted in reality."[37] The composition opens up a "repositioning" that is essential to a personal encounter with Jesus where a life of reverence, service, and love transforms the world.

Professor of philosophy and theology Juliano Ribeiro Almeida suggests that it "is precisely the Composition of Place and the Application of the Senses which give the exercitant the opportunity to recollect him or herself in a deep level . . . [and] at the same time, in a way deeply committed with the change of reality, by means of an incarnate contemplation of the mysteries of faith."[38] In this encounter with Jesus, the retreatant develops capacity to "update the Gospel in a stronger way."[39] By updating the Gospel, Almeida means that "human beings attain closeness to God, not by reaching out to the beyond, but somehow by participating in history—a history which is also God's. We require thus a spiritual theology that builds systematically on the basic principle of God's irrevocable self-commitment to creation."[40] Similarly, Howard Gray, SJ, emphasizes God's self-commitment to creation within an encounter of "mutual donation." Freedom for Ignatius, Gray writes, "is the power to donate, not simply to act."[41]

While Standaert, Almeida, and Gray offer helpful hermeneutical approaches to the Exercises, however, they tend not to discuss any reading of the "signs of the times" or the actual composition of historical context *in which they reflect* upon the spiritual and theological issues at stake. I find this lacuna stunning in the wake of Vatican II's call to take responsibility for "reading the signs of the times and of

---

[37] Standaert, 19.

[38] Almeida, "Composition of Place," 1–12, here 10.

[39] Almeida, 10.

[40] Almeida, quoting Philip Endean, "The Ignatian Prayer of the Senses," *The Heythrop Journal* 31 (1990): 391–418, here 398.

[41] Howard Gray, SJ, "Soul Education: An Ignatian Priority," in George W. Traub, SJ, *A Jesuit Education Reader* (Chicago: Loyola Press, 2008), 205.

interpreting them in the light of the Gospel" as integral to the task of solidarity.[42]

Drawing upon Ignacio Ellacuría's engagement with the *Spiritual Exercises* in the Latin American context, J. Matthew Ashley perceives how the Exercises reveal a deeper structure of the Composition of Place that can be understood as the "mysticism of the historical event."[43] The "mysticism of the historical event" fully interrelates both the historical reality of the person making the exercises and God's co-creative action in our lives. Ellacuría finds hermeneutical accounts lacking, that is, approaches "that take human knowing to consist in grasping the meaning of things" do not engage how human being and knowing engages reality.[44] For example, as compelling as his interpretation may be, Standaert primarily relies upon a hermeneutical approach to the exercises that does not take up how a spiritual director or retreatant would actually engage a historical reading of the "signs of the times" in their composition. In contrast, Ellacuría develops a more nuanced understanding of human knowing as a process that interweaves three dimensions of engaging reality.

Ellacuría elucidates the first task or dimension of intelligence as recognizing the gravity of reality. The Composition of Place helps to facilitate a historical encounter that realizes "'the weight of reality, which implies being in touch with the reality of things (and not merely being before the idea of things . . .),'" which is "'exactly the opposite of being thing-like and inert.'"[45] In other words, the composition invites an active, dynamic encounter with reality in each person's historical time and place. Second, an active encounter with reality means "'shouldering the weight of reality,' which manifests the integral part in human intelligence" by taking up reality as it is, not as we might wish it to be, and apprehending what reality demands of us.[46] Last, and certainly not least, Ellacuría illuminates a third task

---

[42] Vatican II, *Gaudium et Spes* 4, in Austin Flannery, ed., *Vatican Council II: Constitutions, Decrees, Declarations; The Basic Sixteen Documents* (Collegeville, MN: Liturgical Press, 2014), 163–282.

[43] J. Matthew Ashley, "Ignacio Ellacuría and the *Spiritual Exercises* of Ignatius Loyola," *Theological Studies* 61 (2000): 16–39, here 39.

[44] Ashley, "Ignacio Ellacuría," 34.

[45] Ashley, 34.

[46] Ashley, 35.

of intelligence that involves "'taking charge of the weight of reality,'" which is "the praxis-dimension of knowing" that means that "human intelligence is only fully actualized to the extent that it is involved in the dynamic processes" of reality itself. Ultimately, "it is a historical contextualization insofar as the context is not nature, but history—the realm of human freedom and responsibility, the realm of praxis."[47] This split between nature and history, as I discuss below, is fatal both for colonized bodies and the earth itself. Ellacuría's approach to the SE, however, reveals both how social-historical reality *changes us* and how *we change reality*.

Ellacuría integrates this dynamic and directional way of human knowing (epistemology) with a critical reading of the signs of times (through critical social theory) as a way "persons can critically contextualize" through their composition in the exercises "their understanding of God's saving love and work in their own historical situation."[48] He underscores three ways the Exercises offer a theological place for historical contextualization. First, the person's desire for a personal encounter with God's will is "already a principle of historicization."[49] The goal of the Exercises does not concern information about God but encountering "God's will and responding to it here and now."[50] Furthermore, and importantly, the Exercises facilitate an encounter that is not exclusively individualistic; rather, for Ellacuría it meant thinking with the Church at Medellín (the Latin American bishops meeting to continue the work of Vatican II in Medellín, 1968) in a way that allows God's will "to confront the Latin American Church and transform it."[51] Second, Ellacuría emphasizes that the Exercises "'historicize the word of God insofar as they turn to historical, personal and situational signs so that word might be discovered in the concrete.'"[52] One example of this historicization within the Exercises is the Rules for the Discernment of Spirits that discerns God's will by "a reading and diagnosis of one's external circumstances and internal disposition."[53] Another example is con-

---

[47] Ashley, 24.
[48] Ashley, 25.
[49] Ashley, 25.
[50] Ashley, 25.
[51] Ashley, 25.
[52] Ashley, 26.
[53] Ashley, 26.

templating the Incarnation as God's loving response to a historically and socially imagined world "dying and going down to hell" (no. 106). The Meditation on the Two Standards invites an encounter with the historical reality in which "the will of the enemy of our nature and of Christ" are at work in concrete historical places of the towns, cities, nations, and individual states of life.[54]

These examples point to an ongoing encounter throughout the Exercises. The person brings her situation into play in the colloquies that end the contemplations throughout the Exercises. The way the retreatant composes their place, thus, is not just one moment early in the Exercises; rather, composing one's social-historical place concerns an ongoing process of conforming one's own life and history "to the will of God, by means of a more radical love for and imitation of Jesus' humanity and his 'history.' "[55] The composition, then, far from being an isolated and passing comment by Ignatius, involves a deeper theological structure and dynamic of encountering God's will. The deeper theological structure of the Exercises facilitate an encounter with God's will through composing one's "place" at the crossroads of three histories: (1) one's individual history, (2) the broader social and historical reality in which one is embedded, and (3) salvation history with its "definitive moment in Jesus' history."[56]

Ultimately, the Exercises facilitate an encounter in which God is present not primarily in any words, theology, or dogma but rather "enfleshed in a historically realized human life."[57] Simultaneously, the Exercises draw people into a living discipleship that "continues what Jesus was" and I would add who Jesus is with and for us in the present.[58] Discipleship is not about any "ahistorical ideal"; rather, it is "effecting a historical continuation" that Ellacuría named a " 'progressive historicization'—governed by 'the Spirit of Christ who animates those who follow him.' "[59]

Lastly, returning to the main point of my chapter, the progressive historicization that Ellacuría recommends involves a *critical* historical

---

[54] Ashley, 26, note 33.

[55] Ashley, 26.

[56] Ashley, 26.

[57] Ashley, 29.

[58] Ashley, 29. Although Ashley describes Jesus's action in the past tense, I think the present tense more accurately describes Ellacuría's intent.

[59] Ashley, 29.

contextualization: "*'Demonstrating the impact of certain concepts within a particular context is what is understood here as their historicization. Hence, historicization is a principle of de-ideologization.'*"[60] For example, Ellacuría demonstrated how the defense of private property as a basic human right in El Salvador actually "serves to disguise and legitimize a system that attacks human dignity in general, and for the majority of its people denies in practice the right to own property."[61] Ashley draws out three integral aspects of Ellacuría's historicization. First, it interrogates how a concept is utilized within a historical context. Thus, for example, Ellacuría perceived how the values of human rights in general and private property specifically stood in urgent need of historical contextualization. El Salvadorans were denied basic human rights and the right to property. Second, for Ellacuría this contextualization happens in the realm of history, not nature, that is, the realm of praxis—taking responsibility for freedom in our space and time. Third, historicization demands a critical process, like a hermeneutics of suspicion, to unveil how concepts like human rights are used to conceal or distort the truth.[62]

Recomposing Our Place:
Toward a Mysticism of the Historical-Ecological Event

I believe that we North American white settlers need to "reposition," recontextualize, and newly historicize how we approach the Composition of Place. Given the interwoven threats of anti-Black supremacy and ecological destruction, our Composition of Place needs an integration of these interdependent struggles for racial and ecological justice. In the spirit of Ignatius, if we are to find God in all things, that means that we can no longer split history from nature. This split between nature and history is as unnecessary and consequential as the divisions that J. Matthew Ashley laments between theory and praxis and spirituality and theology.[63] Comprehending the theological and moral issues at stake, Pope Francis wrote that the

[60] Ashley, 24; emphasis in original.
[61] Ashley, 24.
[62] Ashley, 24.
[63] Ashley, 17.

"acceptance of our bodies as God's gift is vital for welcoming and accepting the entire world as a gift from the Father and our common home, whereas thinking that we enjoy absolute power over our own bodies turns, often subtly, into thinking that we enjoy absolute power over creation."[64]

We need—as contemplatives—a historical contextualization of the composition that accounts for the insight of "cultural neuroscience, which holds that culture, socioecological environment, and mind mutually constitute each other and are co-sustaining."[65] We need to be able to grasp "the intimacy, porosity, and permeability of humans and human organizations within the web of life."[66] Human histories and their environments

> are not independent but interpenetrated at every level, from the body to the biosphere. Perhaps most of all, it means relations that seemingly occur purely between humans—say, culture, or political power—are already *bundled* with the rest of nature, flowing inside, outside, and through human bodies and histories. . . . In this, human history is understood as an "unbroken circle" of being, knowing, and doing.

Recall Ellacuría's insight that we need to demonstrate that the *"impact of certain concepts within a particular context is what is understood here as their historicization.* Hence, historicization is a principle of de-ideologization."[67] A critical first step for a white settler composition of our time will need to historicize, that is de-ideologize, and decolonize the split between Nature and Society that is the "originary dualism" of modernity/coloniality-in-nature.[68] This originary dualism, Pope Francis laments, is a technique of possession that has "made it easy to accept the idea of infinite or unlimited growth," which is "based on the lie that there is an infinite supply of the earth's goods and this leads to the planet being squeezed dry beyond every limit."[69]

---

[64] Pope Francis, *Laudato Si'* 155.

[65] Harrell, "Soulfulness," 9–40, here 11–12.

[66] Moore, *Capitalism in the Web*, 7.

[67] Ashley, "Ignacio Ellacuría," 24.

[68] Moore, *Capitalism in the Web*, 48.

[69] Francis, *Laudato Si'* 106.

World-ecologists express a similar critique to that of Pope Francis. Ecologists Raj Patel and Jason Moore explain that European ruling classes viewed most human beings, including "women, people of color, Indigenous peoples—as extended, not thinking beings."[70] It is upon this division of mind and body, nature and society, that Descartes argued that "we" Europeans must become "the masters and possessors of nature."[71] Dualism was utilized to justify not only colonization of land but the bodies of the colonized themselves.[72]

Historicizing and de-ideologizing this dualism, deployed over the past 500 years, I suggest, may help us understand why we white Catholics foster ignorance of the crucified peoples of the Americas, including James Cone's insight that the "lynching tree is the cross in America."[73] Dualism is a way that white people, within modernity/ coloniality-in-nature, cultivate "strategic ignorance"[74] of the multitudinous ways we crucify Black, Indigenous and peoples of color, and the Earth. When Cone writes that "one can lynch a person without a rope or tree,"[75] I believe his insight demands that we white folks historicize and de-ideologize the originary dualism of modernity/ coloniality-in-nature as a way of confronting our complicity in white supremacist violence.

Consider Christina Sharpe's reflection in her book *In the Wake: On Blackness and Being*. Sharpe leads readers to imagine the historical, hydrological wake of an Atlantic slave ship in order to recall enslaved peoples who were deliberately drowned in the Middle Passage. People who drowned during the Atlantic crossing still endure through "residence time," the amount of time it takes for a substance to enter the ocean and then leave it. A colleague who is a marine geographer explains to Sharpe that human blood is salty, and that

---

[70] Raj Patel and Jason Moore, *A History of the World in Seven Cheap Things: A Guide to Capitalism, Nature, and the Future of the Planet* (Oakland, CA: University of California Press, 2017), 52.

[71] Patel and Moore cite René Descartes, *Philosophical Writings: Volume I*, trans. John Cottingham, Robert Stroothoff, and Dugald Murdoch (Cambridge, UK: Cambridge University Press, 1985), 142–43.

[72] Hickel, *Less Is More*, 76.

[73] Cone, *Cross and the Lynching Tree*, 158.

[74] Jennifer Mueller, "Advancing a Sociology of Ignorance in the Study of Racism and Racial Not-Knowing," *Sociology Compass* (May 2018): 5.

[75] Cone, *Cross and the Lynching Tree*, 163.

sodium has a residence time of 260 million years.[76] She asks: "And what happens to the energy produced in the waters? It continues cycling like atoms in residence time. We, Black People, exist in the residence time of the wake, a time in which 'everything is now. It is all now.'"[77]

"Living in the wake of slavery," Sharpe writes, ". . . is living the afterlife of *partus sequitur ventrem* (that which is brought forth follows the womb) in which the Black child inherits the non-status, the non/being of the mother."[78] The historical inheritance of non-being and non-status as human "is everywhere apparent in the ongoing criminalization of Black women and children."[79] This inheritance also includes "the gratuitous violence of stop and frisk and Operation Clean Halls," mind-boggling rates of incarceration, and "the immanence of death as a 'predictable and constitutive aspect of *this* democracy.'"[80]

No less important for practitioners of the Exercises is understanding how dualism has obscured the *giftedness* of Africans in diaspora, including their adaptiveness and capacity to cultivate their own love of nature, biophilia, which enabled their survival through enslavement.[81] The condition of the possibility of white settlers perceiving the *gifts* of Black folk depends, in part, upon a repositioning of our Composition of Place. Such a repositioning is prerequisite to prepare ourselves to perceive our mutual relatedness and belonging in God's creation. This repositioning is necessary to create conditions of the possibility of retrieving African ecological traditions that form a critical piece of becoming "ecosocial" citizens who cultivate "civic participation informed by the interconnectedness of ecological and social worlds."[82] Kimberly Ruffin draws upon the ecological blues poetry of Jayne Cortez (1934–2012), among many other African

---

[76] Christina Sharpe, *In the Wake: On Blackness and Being* (Durham, NC: Duke University Press, 2016), 41.

[77] Sharpe, *In the Wake*, 198. Here Sharpe quotes Toni Morrison, *Beloved* (New York: Plume, 1987), 198.

[78] Sharpe, 15.

[79] Sharpe, 15.

[80] Sharpe, 15; emphasis in original.

[81] Kimberly Ruffin, "Biophilia on Purpose: A Declaration to Become a Ecosocial Citizen," *Intervalla* 3 (2015): 44–48, here 45.

[82] Ruffin, "Biophilia on Purpose," 45.

American artists, poets, musicians, and slave narratives, as ways of thinking and working through ecological crises. Cortez viscerally articulates our physical entanglements with landscapes we have rendered surreal since the slave trade. For example, in her "I got the blue-ooze," Cortez laments, "I got the toxic-waste dump in my back-yard blue-ooze" and "I got the dead house dead earth blue-ooze." Urging readers and listeners to sit with Cortez's images and sounds as a way of embracing ecological emergencies of our day, Ruffin reflects:

> Disruptive, memorable and unexpected images in angry tones push the reader/listener to expand their ecological consciousness and think with an epistemological orientation that is not stunted by the alienation of modern daily living. Those who are in eco-logical crisis may find in Cortez's poetry artful acknowledgement and advocacy. Those sheltered from crisis may find their buffer eroding from her acidic vision.[83]

Recomposing Place: Three Practices

The Ignatian family in the North American context of modernity/coloniality-in-nature needs a shared repositioning of the Composition of Place that honestly confronts the dual crises of anti-Black white supremacy and ecological destruction. Returning to Bryan Massingale's incisive question at the beginning of this chapter, "why is it that so many white religious and spiritual formation programs have failed to produce the vanguard of contemplative white persons with a consciousness freed from the soul sickness of White supremacy?" I suggest a practical set of decolonial exercises for retreat centers and spiritual directors to initiate a process of critical inquiry that creates conditions for the possibility of transforming and liberating consciousness.

First, retreat centers can begin by learning, and acknowledging, if they have not already, the history of Indigenous (as in First Peoples) ancestors who lived on the land where the retreat center is located. Developing a formal and ritual way of acknowledging original in-

---

[83] Kimberly Ruffin, *Black on Earth: African American Eco-Literary Traditions* (Athens, GA: University of Georgia Press, 2010), 150.

habitants who lived and may be buried beneath the ground of retreat centers is a critical first step for initiating an anti-racist and decolonial Composition of Place. Land acknowledgement can work in tandem with meeting and learning from First Peoples who may live nearby. Land acknowledgement is a critical first step toward processes of decolonization.

Second, Crossroad's Anti-Racism Ministry, which trained Pax Christi USA's anti-racism team, typically begins its program by immersing participants in the history of racial oppression and resistance to oppression. Retreat centers can utilize a variation of this exercise by creating a timeline of histories of oppression and resistance by marking dates and key events on a wall of paper in a classroom. The Crossroad's historical exercise typically begins in 1492, the year in which Columbus "discovers" the "New World" and the "Doctrine of Discovery" establishes colonialism.[84] Undoubtedly, "under this legal cover for theft," Euro-American "wars of conquest and settler colonialism devastated Indigenous nations and communities, ripping their territories away from them and transforming land into private property, real estate."[85] I extend this historical timeline, which Crossroads calls the "Wall of History," to include the role the Renaissance papacy played in the early fifteenth century and the Great Events of 1444 that inaugurated the African slave trade.[86] The Roman Catholic papacy and Church bears undeniable responsibility both in the African slave trade and in the theft and destruction of Indigenous peoples and lands throughout the Americas. Retreat centers have a moral and spiritual responsibility to prepare their own Composition of Place in relationship to this history.

Third, another practical process that facilitates a Composition of Place is ethnoautobiography. Ethnoautobiography begins with the fundamental question "who am I?" but is not oriented to one's name, profession, or accomplishments; rather, it invites a creative process

---

[84] Joseph Barndt, *Understanding and Dismantling Racism: The Twenty-First Century Challenge to White America* (Minneapolis: Fortress Press, 2007), 15. Barndt is founder of the Crossroad's Anti-Racism Ministry in Chicago, Illinois.

[85] Roxanne Dunbar-Ortiz, *An Indigenous Peoples' History of the United States* (Boston: Beacon Press, 2014), 198.

[86] Alex Mikulich, *Unlearning White Supremacy: A Spirituality for Racial Liberation* (Maryknoll, NY: Orbis Books, 2022), chap. 3, "The Roman Catholic Origins of Coloniality."

that may include mapping[87] and multiple forms of artwork to discern the "long body" of one's Indigenous ancestors going back seven generations that includes all human and non-human pasts of our embodied being.[88] Ethnoautobiography facilitates a shift from an autonomous, independent, Western, Educated, Industrialized, Rich, Democratic (WEIRD) view of the self to an interdependent, social, and ecological sense of self that is embedded in place, stories, ritual, spirit, and human and non-human ancestors.[89]

This shift from an egocentric to expansive self is partially inaugurated by "shadow work" for people socialized into WEIRD culture to expose the oppressive, dominating, colonizing, genocidal, sexist, and racist dimensions of our past and present ways of being. For example, in his poem "I Am a White Man," Jürgen Werner Kremer acknowledges how he "does not walk alone, something walks with me," a cultural shadow, white superiority, that is "boxed into a box that forgets its name."[90] In terms of an Ignatian Composition of Place, acknowledging our collective shadow is a critical first step to develop the courage to examine personally and communally the racial and ecologically oppressive dimensions of Western, North American culture.

This chapter and the process of ethnoautobiography invites shadow work in an Ignatian Composition of Place, as a way to prepare to become present to, and understand the reality of, the Meditation on the Two Standards.[91] Ethnoautobiography invites an ongoing process of questioning and exposing the hidden past of modernity-in-nature and understanding how its oppressive side has divided people of faith from Christ and Christ's presence within the whole of creation.

---

[87] For alternative forms of mapping see Lisa Brooks, *The Common Pot: The Recovery of Native Space in the Northeast* (Minneapolis: University of Minnesota Press, 2008), " A Note on Maps" and "Introduction: A Map to the Common Pot." See also Dionne Brand, *A Map to the Door of No Return: Notes to Belonging* (Toronto: Vintage Canada, 2001).

[88] Jürgen Werner Kremer and R. Jackson-Paton, *Ethnoautobiography: Stories and Practices for Unlearning Whiteness, Decolonization, and Uncovering Ethnicities* (Sebastopol, CA: ReVision, 2014).

[89] Kremer and Jackson-Paton, *Ethnoautobiography*, 44.

[90] Kremer and Jackson-Paton, 58.

[91] *Spiritual Exercises*, Second Week, Meditation on the Two Standards, 136–48.

Ethnoautobiography is a way to perceive the limits of Western individualism and its dualisms. As we become aware of the multiple ways that Western modernity has divided us against ourselves, one another, and nature, we can also begin to learn to lament what we have lost, that is, lament loss of connection to our ancestors and the local ecologies in which we are rooted (or not). For example, although I remember some of the stories that my Bylorussian grandparents shared about their life in Bylorusse, I now regret that I cannot name the village where they lived and so I do not know where to go to retrieve this dimension of my past. My family criticized the Bylorussian "old country" as backward and so we dismissed the wisdom of my grandparents way of life. My family's dismissal of the "old country" reveals Western individualism erasing this important connection to our past. This disconnection also means I do not know generations who preceded my grandparents, including Indigenous ancestors and how they related to their local ecologies.

As we retrieve and remember communal and collective pasts and lament particular losses, we open the possibility of engaging new ways of understanding who we are in relationship with multiple cultures, life-worlds, and ecologies. We begin to create conditions of the possibility of imagining and recreating how we live in relationship with and for all human and non-human kin.

A process of land acknowledgment, developing histories of oppression and resistance in local contexts, and ethnoautobiography each offer practical ways to initiate a repositioning in the practice of a Composition of Place. Through such repositioning we may yet engage a mysticism of the historical-ecological event that heals intergenerational traumas of slavery, genocide, and ecological destruction. Perhaps, then, we will fully prepare ourselves to live the Contemplation to Attain Love and pray with Ignatius: "Take Lord, and receive all my liberty, my memory, my understanding, and all my will—all that I have and possess."[92]

---

[92] See the full Contemplation to Attain Love in the Exercises, 230–37.

PART II

The Spiritual Exercises

To overcome oneself, and to order one's life, without reaching a decision through some disordered affection.

Ignatius of Loyola: Spiritual Exercises and Selected Works, ed. George Ganss, SJ (Mahwah, NJ: Paulist Press, 1991), no. 21, p. 129.

4

From Self-Centered to Other-Centered

Ignatian Indifference on Racial Differences

Hung T. Pham, SJ

The concept of Ignatian indifference could be easily misconstrued, and thus be misleading. According to the *Oxford Illustrated American Dictionary*, the word "indifference" is defined as "1. lack of interest or attention. 2. unimportance (*a matter of indifference*). 3. neutrality."[1] The term as defined in the Oxford dictionary conveys a sense of apathy of the person in dealing with any subject matter at hand. Such a lethargic attitude was far from Ignatius's experience, and thus his intention, in dealing with issues of racial difference. The *Tesoro de Covarrubias*, a sixteenth-century Spanish dictionary, offers us a closer read into what Ignatius likely intended by the term "indifferent." Therein, the term is defined as "all that which of its own nature, neither good nor bad, and takes quality in the use and in intention for which it works" (*es todo aquello que de su naturaleza, ni es bueno ni malo, y toma calidad del uso, y de la intención del que obra*). The Spanish definition seems to free one from any prenotion or prejudice without taking into account the quality and intention for which the term is applied. Even so, such an understanding remains problematic in leaving open or even unasked the question of whose decision or

---

[1] *DK Oxford Illustrated American Dictionary* (Oxford: Oxford University Press, 2000), 412.

evaluation will be counted, and thus prioritized. Failing to specify such basic questions of agency could lead to interpretations and applications that are culturally biased, which have been proven to be harmful at best and detrimental at worst.

In the Ignatian tradition, being indifferent remains an essential part of the architectural Principle and Foundation that has accompanied generations of Jesuits to deal with cultural differences in such a way that was mutually life-giving for themselves and for the people with whom they ministered. Jesuits like Peter Claver serving African Americans in Colombia at the end of the sixteenth century; those working among the Guarani of the Paraguay Reduction in the seventeenth century; Mateo Ricci laboring and conversing in the imperial court of China; or more recently Pedro Arrupe caring for the Japanese during the aftermath of the atomic bomb in Hiroshima and Nagasaki serve as exemplary witnesses to how the grace of indifference is practiced. Rediscovering the meaning of indifference in the Ignatian tradition, which these Jesuits embodied, could provide rich insights into the ongoing discussion and debate about the racial differences that exist in the world today.

Inspired by the Ignatian rules of discernment, the rules of perceiving (*sentir*), knowing (*conocer*), then moving to applying,[2] this article studies Ignatius's personal experience to further explain the concept of indifference, so as to better apply it. Concretely, this in-depth study looks at the role of racial differences played in Ignatius's conversion from a self-centered individual into an active member of a multiracial apostolic community. Drawing from Ignatius's personal experience and his conversion, the knowledge of Ignatian indifference will be further explicated. Finally, for those who wrestle with the reality of racial differences in our world today, the grace of Ignatian indifference could help them to reach a point of balance where respect and reverence for people of all different races are cherished, thus fostered, and where collaboration and mutuality are prioritized and thus promoted in the effort of building a better community for all.

---

[2] *The Spiritual Exercises of Saint Ignatius of Loyola*, 313. The rules of perceiving (*sentir*), knowing (*conocer*), then accepting or ejecting (*aceptar o ejectar*).

Ignatius's Personal Experience with Racial Differences

Though Ignatius of Loyola encountered racial differences at a very young age, his conversion from a self-centered individual to a member of a multicultural apostolic community involved a long process of wrestling with issues of racial differences. It began with Ignatius's great-grandfather, Don Juan Pérez de Loyola, and seven of his sons. At the battle of Beotiar in 1321, the Loyolas had defeated the French and the Navarrese, and thus earned high honor from the Castilian Crown. However, when Don Juan Pérez rebelled against the king and was defeated in 1456, he was exiled to fight against the Moors in Andalusia. Upon returning to Loyola after three years in exile, at the order of the Crown, he reconstructed the Loyolas' fortress (*casa torre*) into a home by adding another story on top and fashioned it in the Moorish style (*estilo mudejar*) that he had come to appreciate in Andalusia. It was in this half Basque, half Moorish home that Íñigo de Loyola was born and raised. Until this day, the Loyola Castle remains "one of the oldest and most typical examples of the arabesque styles in Guipúzcoa [Ignatius's home region]"[3] and stands as an example of racial integration in the House of Loyola as well as in the region.

Íñigo was not only raised in a "biracial" home, architectually speaking, but he was also brought up in a racially diverse environment. As Guipúzcoa came under the protection of the Castilian kings, the Basque-Castilian mixed culture (*vasco-castellano*) became more prevalent in the Basque country and introduced the Loyola family to various language usage and cultural customs. Like other Guipúzcoan nobles, "the family of Saint Ignatius was undoubtedly bilingual: Basque-speaking because of the social context, and Spanish-speaking because of their belonging to the nobility and being in constant communication with their kings as well as in trips to the rest of Spain, and its European and American dominions."[4] Cultural and racial differences remained an important part of the formation of Íñigo's identity.

<hr />

[3] Pedro Leturia, *El gentilhombre Iñigo Lopez de Loyola* (Barcelona: Editorial Labor, 1941), 19–20.

[4] Gabriel Maria Verd, "De Íñigo a Ignacio: El cambio de nombre en San Ignacio de Loyola," *Archivum Historicum Societatis Iesu* 60 (1991): 113–60, 121.

Furthermore, because of the Loyolas' connection to the Castilian Crown, Íñigo was exposed not only to new languages and customs, but also to people of different races through the experiences of his siblings. Íñigo's oldest brother, Juan Pérez, joined the army of the Castilian and Aragonese Crowns and fought against the Kingdom of Naples. His second oldest brother, Martín García—whose wife took Íñigo under her care after they were married—fought in the wars against the Navarre and France, and consequently won the favor of the Aragonese King Ferdinand and Castilian Queen Isabella. His third brother, Beltrán, fought and died in Naples. Another of Íñigo's brothers, Ochoa Pérez, offered his service to Juana of Castile in the Low Countries and in Spain. Yet another, Hernando, left for the New World and died among Native Americans. Only one of Íñigo's brothers, Pedro López, who followed an ecclesiastical career, eventually took over the House of Loyola's patronage of the church in Azpeitia and remained at home.[5] So, for the first fifteen years of his life, Íñigo was very much aware of the racial differences surrounding his family relationship and environment.

More than the experience of his brothers, Íñigo personally experienced racial conflicts and ethnic rivalries during his training in Arévalo. When his father, Don Beltrán de Oñaz Íñigo, died, the fifteen-year-old Íñigo was sent to Arévalo,[6] a town south of Guipúzcoa, to the household of a family friend, Don Juan Velázquez de Cuéllar.[7]

---

[5] Ricardo García-Villoslada, *San Ignacio de Loyola* (Biblioteca Autores Cristianos, 1986), 50–55. Also see R. García Mateo, "El mundo caballeresco en la vida de Ignacio de Loyola," *Archivum historicum Societatis Iesu* 60 (1991).

[6] Arévalo is a town in the diocese of Ávila. It was considered one of the old towns of the Celtic *arévacos* people. The word was thought to be an Arabic assimilation from the Hebraic root of the word, *arrebal* or *arrabal*, designating the expanding suburbs of a big town. S. Covarrubias Horozco, *Tesoro de la lengua castellana o española* (1611) (Madrid: Castalia, 1995), 204; Í. Arranz, "Arévalo," *Diccionario de Espiritualidad Ignaciana* (Bilbao/Santander: Mensajero/Sal Terrae, 2007), I, 192–95, 194; see also J. Iturrioz, "Años juveniles de S. Ignacio en Arévalo (1506–1517)," *Ignacio de Loyola en Castilla* (Valladolid: Provincia de Castilla de la Compañía de Jesús, 1989), 45–71; Leturia, *El gentilhombre*; and García-Villoslada, *San Ignacio*, 72–78.

[7] Juan Velázquez was married to Doña María de Velasco, who was related to Íñigo's mother. Together they had twelve children, six boys and six girls. Of the boys, three chose careers in military or public administration, the other three clerical careers. Juan Velázquez's sons Miguel, Agustín, Juan, and Arnao, together with one of their servants, Alonso de Montalvo, remained Ignatius's intimate friends. When Ignatius

The Velázquez family had long been in the royal service as counselors and judges, and thus were well connected with the Castilian Crown and other Catholic rulers. Íñigo was to be educated and adapt himself to the cultures of the Castilian royal court, adopting its chivalrous ideals and courtly love "with a great and vain desire to gain honor" [Au 1].[8] However, it was racial differences and their inherent conflicts that disrupted Íñigo's young promising career in the royal court.

In March 1506, after the death of Queen Isabella I, King Ferdinand married Germaine of Foix, a French woman. He appointed his Flemish-born grandson, Carlos I—later the Holy Roman Emperor Charles V—to rule Castile after his death. Instead of taxing the revenue of the Kingdom of Naples to support Queen Germaine, as King Ferdinand had done, the newly crowned Carlos I laid the financial burden on the people of Arévalo and other Castilian towns. Velázquez, whose loyalty lay with Queen Isabella I, led the people of Arévalo to rebel against the king's decision. Lost in a series of political upheavals and royal decisions, Velázquez ended up heavily in debt, retired, and died in Madrid as a "disgraced caballero."[9] At first glance, Velázquez's rebellion could be seen as a token of fidelity to Queen Isabella and the Castilian crown. However, a closer investigation into the downfall of the Velázquez family exposed a "popular movement against the 'foreignization' of the [Castilian] court that was brought about mainly by those who came from the Flanders."[10] In other words, racial tension and its inherent power struggle within the royal court was one of the principal causes of Velázquez's financial collapse and political demise, ending Íñigo's budding career as a courtier.

Having fully invested himself for ten years in Velázquez's circle of influence, Íñigo was suddenly left with an uncertain future. In the

---

was in Rome, he wrote to one of Juan Velázquez's daughters, Doña Catalina, "reconociendo la casa en que había estado" (recognizing the house I was in) (Arranz, "Arévalo," 193; Iturrioz, "Años juveniles," 47).

[8] St. Ignatius of Loyola, "Autobiography," in *Personal Writings: Reminiscences, Spiritual Diary, Select Letters including the Text of the Spiritual Exercises*, ed. J. Munitiz and P. Endean (London: Penguin Books, 2004). Denoted [Au] throughout unless otherwise noted.

[9] García-Villoslada, *San Ignacio*, 101–7; and Iturrioz, "Años juveniles," 54–58.

[10] Iturrioz, "Años juveniles," 56.

end, Velázquez's widow sent him off with five hundred escudos and two horses to search for a new life direction. On her advice, Íñigo left Arévalo and headed to Pamplona in pursuit of a career in the military, where he would serve under Don Antonio Manrique de Lara, the second Duke and Viceroy of Nájera, who had been a loyal subject of Queen Isabella.[11] In a battle in Pamplona, a cannon ball struck Íñigo's knee and set him embarking on a journey of spiritual transformation. As demonstrated, racial difference and its inherent tension played a significant role in those steps of his spiritual conversion.

Íñigo's transformation entailed a long process of conversion *from*, conversion *to*, and conversion *for*.[12] An in-depth analysis on Íñigo's actions from the time after his convalescence in Loyola in 1521 until the time he was asked to leave Jerusalem in 1523 reveals an interior movement from being self-centered to other-centered:

> Going barefoot to Jerusalem on a vegetarian diet in imitation of saintly rigors is not necessarily progress beyond going shod to Pamplona beefed up in imitation of knightly rigors. Loyola has not yet experienced a true conversion of interior disposition. He is merely exchanging one set of appearances and allegiances for another.[13]

In other words, Íñigo's transformation remained external and on his own terms—his determined austerity. Earlier, he himself admitted what inspired him to make the pilgrimage to Jerusalem and to engage in acts of penance was "a similar kind of those things from *Amadis of Gaul* and books of that sort" [Au 17]. As much as he was committed to penances and filled with ardent desires to follow the Lord in every way he knew, he was still "blind" by his racial and religious biases. In one instance, on the way to Montserrat, Íñigo encountered a person of different religious belief and race who insulted the Blessed Virgin Mary. His first inclination was to "search out the Moor and to strike him with his dagger for all that he had said" [Au 16]. As we have often witnessed throughout history, people tend to overcome racial

---

[11] Iturrioz, 57; García-Villoslada, *San Ignacio*, 107–8.

[12] General Congregation 35, decree 2, no. 4.

[13] Marjorie O'Rourke Boyle, *Loyola's Acts: The Rhetoric of the Self* (Oakland, CA: University of California Press, 2021), 38.

tension by either dominating or quashing the existence of those voices which are different from their own. The young Íñigo was not immune from such a destructive self-centered tendency even after the humbling event of Pamplona. It took another blow to his ego for Íñigo to decenter himself and begin to recognize the existence of the other. That fortuitous blow was dealt by the Franciscans in Jerusalem.

More than a year after the incident with the Moor, the gung-ho and self-determined Íñigo, following his dream to walk in the footsteps of Christ and to save souls, reached Jerusalem in 1523. However, because of the tense political and religious climate in the Holy Land, the Franciscans, to whom the Holy See had delegated all the ecclesial power and authority for the region, asked Íñigo to leave. Only after being threatened with excommunication did Íñigo submit himself reluctantly to the Franciscan provincial's order and depart from the Holy Land.

The "great cold" which Íñigo vividly recalled upon arriving in Venice after Jerusalem during the winter of 1524 spoke to his nakedness not only from the lack of proper shelter and clothing, but also from how his ego was being stripped of its self-centeredness. Being kicked out of the Holy Land slowly brought to an end Íñigo's longstanding inner subscription to self-determined behaviors. Ironically, what seemed to be a disappointment and failure to Íñigo at the time functioned as a source of grace that drove Íñigo towards recognizing and reconciling with the existence of the Other. For the first time in his reminiscence, Ignatius mentioned "the will of God" [Au 50]. And in Barcelona, he began to learn how to engage with God and to look for friends. Thus, leaving the Holy Land and returning to Barcelona, all against his will, marked the beginning of a new period in Íñigo's life where he learned to integrate into and adapt himself to a new way of life that no longer centered on himself but on God and others.

Following the advice of others, in 1525, at the age of thirty-four, Íñigo arrived in Barcelona to learn Latin and begin his formal schooling to "help souls." Once again, it was racial and religious discrimination that forced Íñigo to move from Alcalá to Salamanca then finally to the University of Paris. In all of these institutions, he was suspected as either an *alumbrados* or a *nuevo cristiano*, thus victimized by those who considered themselves religiously and racially superior.

During Íñigo's time of studying, the *alumbrados* or the "Illuminists" and the *nuevos cristianos* or the "New Christians" topped the list of those who were most discriminated against and condemned by the Inquisition.[14] The *alumbrados* were accused of rejecting any form of rituals or sacramental elements of the Christian faith and favoring the direct intervention of the Holy Spirit, therefore leading many to judge them to be destructive to the institutional church.[15] The circumstances surrounding the "New Christians" were a bit more complicated. After having united Spain, the Catholic kings signed a decree on March 31, 1492, expelling all Jews from the country unless they converted to Christianity. As a result, about fifty thousand Jews were baptized, and thereafter known as the "New Christians." Even after they joined the church, however, these individuals were often discriminated against, namely, by being denied admission to schools and other social and religious institutions, including religious orders. Consequently, some of the New Christians, who had been baptized by force, continued to observe their Jewish faith in secret.

The Inquisition's "blood cleansing" (*limpieza de sangre*) campaign was aimed at tracking down these New Christians to expel them from the country. In the name of protecting and purifying the Christian faith, such a campaign legitimized the indiscriminate profiling and victimizing of those who appeared differently in their racial make-up and religious practice, as was in the case of Íñigo of Loyola. During the one year and four months of his residence in Alcalá, from March 1526 to June 1527, he was summoned and questioned by the Inquisition three times and once jailed for forty days [Au 62]. Of the three months in Salamanca, he was imprisoned for twenty-two days [Au 68]. Refusing to be harassed and victimized, he left Salamanca for the University of Paris fully aware that "Spaniards might be roasted" there. Thus, Íñigo personally experienced being victimized and discriminated against. Yet through these experiences, the once self-centered and self-determined Íñigo had slowly matured into the individual who valued and advocated for racial and religious diversity and inclusion.

---

[14] M. Sanz de Diego, "Inquisición y San Ignacio," *Diccionario de Espiritualidad Ignaciana* II, 1023–27, 1023.

[15] Alvaro Huerga, *Historia de los alumbrados* (Fundación Universitaria Española, Seminario Cisneros, 1986), 46–47.

During his studies in Paris, two important transformations spoke about how Íñigo had progressed in his indifference: one regarding himself, the other the group of friends he had assembled. Personally, Íñigo became "Ignatius" when he moved from the Collège de Montaigu to the Collège de Sainte-Bárbe of the University of Paris in the fall of 1529. Ignatian scholar William Meissner believed that this name change "may have reflected a humanist trend to Latinize names,"[16] and the late historian John O'Malley suggested that "he mistakenly thought" Ignacio, the Spanish form of Ignatius, to be a variant of Íñigo.[17] However, research by Gabriel María Verd demonstrates that the adoption of the name "Ignatius" was a deliberate and practical choice made by Íñigo in his effort to adapt and accommodate himself to the international environment of the University for the universal good.[18] The name Ignatius, which he adopted from St. Ignatius of Antioch, was certainly more commonly known than Íñigo, as Pedro de Ribadeneira writes:

> In writings, he used different ways to sign: "Poor in goodness, Ignigo" [*De bondad pobre, Ignigo*]; at the end, "Yours in our Lord, Ignigo" [*Vuestro, en el Señor nuestro*]; later he adopted Ignatio for being more universal; and in the end he accommodated himself in courtesy to common usage, because "I have become all things to all people, that I might by all means save some" [*omnia omnibus factus erat, ut omnes lucrifaceret*].[19]

Having wrestled with the racial and religious differences and personally encountered adversity, Ignatius moved towards self-abnegation so to orient his life purpose and self-identity towards the good of the others.

Having displaced himself from the center, Ignatius became ever more sensitive to the needs of the other, and at the same time, was moved to have Christ as the center. Such a movement was seen not

---

[16] William Meissner, *Ignatius of Loyola: The Psychology of a Saint* (New Haven, CT: Yale University Press, 1992), 154.

[17] John O'Malley, *The First Jesuits* (Cambridge, MA: Harvard University Press, 1993), 29.

[18] Verd, "De Íñigo a Ignacio," 113–60, 145–46.

[19] Pedro de Ribadeneira, *De actis Patris nostri Ignatii*, n. 111. *Fontes narrative*, II 393, and *Monumenta Scripta*, I 392.

only in Íñigo's newly adopted name, Ignatius, but also in the name of the group he had congregated. As early as 1524, when Ignatius had begun his study of Latin in Barcelona, three men from different regions of Spain—namely, Calisto de Sa, Lope de Cáceres of Segovia, and Juan Arteaga of Estépa—joined him in a first attempt at forming an apostolic group. The main goals of this group were to imitate Íñigo's way of life and to share in his ministry of spiritual direction. For these reasons, the men in the group were often called *Iñiguistas* or "followers of Íñigo."[20] Evidently, despite his growth in de-centering himself, Íñigo nevertheless remained the center of this group. When Íñigo left Salamanca to study in Paris in 1528, though he had hoped that these men would join him, none showed up. The *Iñiguistas* disbanded.

Ignatius's second attempt at creating a similar group occurred in 1529, a year after his arrival in Paris. Another three men of Spanish origin—namely, Juan de Castro of Burgos, Pedro Peralta of Toledo, and Amador de Elduayén of Pamplona—after having made the Spiritual Exercises,[21] committed themselves to lives of radical poverty and gave away all their possessions, living together in a poorhouse and begging on the streets. However, pressure from their friends and families forced them to split.[22] This group possessed passion, yet lacked a point of balance, an anchor.

In the third and final attempt, though originated by Ignatius, the group extended to include friends of Ignatius's friends who studied at the University of Paris. Unlike the other two initial groups, the make-up of the group of nine members was socially and culturally diverse. Upon their arrival to Paris in 1528, the age ranged from

---

[20] Barton Geger, SJ, "The FIRST First Companions: The Continuing Impact of the Men Who Left Ignatius," *Studies in the Spirituality of Jesuits* 44, no. 2 (Summer 2012): 10.

[21] Ignatius's adapted practices of meditation, prayer, and contemplation in a search for God and how to relate with the Divine in the most personal and direct way. Most importantly, the Spiritual Exercises were Ignatius's "experience before they were written notes, or a manuscript, or formally published" (*El Autógrafo de los Ejercicios espirituales: The Autograph Copy of the Spiritual Exercises*, ed. S. Arzubialde, SJ, and J. García de Castro, SJ [Bilbao: Ediciones Mensajero, 2022], 28).

[22] Geger, "FIRST First Companions," 13–14.

thirteen to thirty-nine.[23] Racially, they were French, Spanish, Savoy-ards, and Portuguese nationals.[24] Spiritually, not everyone made the Spiritual Exercises with Ignatius.[25] In a letter dated July 24, 1537, from Venice Ignatius introduced these men to his old friend Juan de Verdolay in Barcelona with these words:

> They arrived here from Paris, in the middle of January [1537], *nine friends in the Lord*, all masters of arts and well versed in the-ology, four of them are Spanish, two French, two from Savoyard, and one from Portugal.[26]

Fundamentally, something had changed in Ignatius's vision of the group. They were not considered as followers or friends of Ignatius, but "friends in the Lord." The center around which the group re-volved was no longer Ignatius but grounded "in the Lord."

Grounded in the Lord, the reality of racial diversity and its inherent tension within the group was neither ignored nor overlooked. In-stead, it was recognized and dealt with. In the spring of 1539, con-fronting the issue of the members' movement and dispersal due to the high apostolic demands and responsibilities, these "friends in the Lord" gathered in Rome to deliberate the group's future existence and its organizational structure. Most immediately, they recognized the "diverse geographical and cultural backgrounds . . . and perspec-tives" as well as the inherent "conflicting judgments" and tensions among themselves. After a number of sessions, they openly admitted that "we found ourselves divided. . . . [O]ur views and opinions

---

[23] Ignatius was thirty-nine years old, Claude Jay and Paschase Broet, twenty-eight, Pierre Favre and Francis Xavier, twenty-two, Jean Codure, twenty, Simon Rodridguez and Nicolas Bobadilla, nineteen, Diego Lainez, sixteen, and Alfonso Salmeron, thirteen.

[24] J. J. Toner, "The Deliberation That Started the Jesuits: A Commentario on the Deliberatio Primorum Patrum. Newly Translated with a Historical Introduction," *Studies in the Spirituality of Jesuits* 4 (June 1974): 185.

[25] Chronologically, Ignatius directed Favre, Laínez, Salmerón, Rodriguez, Bobadilla, and Xaiver. Favre in turn directed Jay, Codure, and Broet.

[26] *Epp* 1, 119. "De Paris llegaron aquí, mediado enero, nueve amigos en el Señor, todos maestros en artes y asaz versados en teología, los cuatro de ellos españoles, dos franceses, dos de Saboya y uno de Portugal." Emphasis added. The nine companions arrived in Venice from Paris after having completed their studies hoping to travel to the Holy Land together for the sake of saving souls as they had vowed together.

were diversified."[27] However, such a diversity and division did not lead them to separate, but, on the contrary, strengthened and solidified the bond of their affection and union.

Upon confronting the issue that was fundamental to the group's existence—namely, whether they wished to "be joined and united into one body" or not—the response was unanimously in the affirmative. More important than the confirmation itself, the rationality and principle from which they had derived such a response served as a declaration on the group's self-identity as well as the manner of proceeding expected from all the members—past, present, and future. "Since our most merciful and affectionate Lord had seen fit to assemble and bind us to one another," they declared, "we who are frail and from such diverse national and cultural backgrounds, ought not to sever what God has united and bound together." In other words, having recognized their humanity in all its shortcomings and prejudices, Ignatius and his "friends in the Lord" went beyond the experience of meeting Ignatius to encounter the divine as their point of reference, holding all their diversity and adversity in balance. Therefore, not focusing on themselves, each member was to "confirm and strengthen the bond of union, forming ourselves into one single body. Each should have a knowledge of and a concern for the others . . . leading to a richer harvest of souls."[28] Ultimately, each of the members' self-identity as well as the union existing among themselves was meant for the service of others. The long conversion process from a self-centered and self-determined individual such as Íñigo to the God-centered and service-oriented Ignatius slowly reached its completion. Ignatius, who once ardently desired to walk in the footsteps of Christ as did the apostles in the Holy Land, indifferently accepted

---

[27] "The Deliberations of Our First Fathers," 1, Portal to Jesuit Studies, https://jesuitportal.bc.edu/research/documents/1539_deliberationsofourfirstfathers/ (accessed August 14, 2023). Due to the Ottoman–Venetian War (1537–1540), Ignatius and his companions were unable to travel to the Holy Land as they had hoped. Consequently, they decided to travel to Rome and put their services to the pope. After having arrived in Rome, they found themselves dispersed among various apostolic tasks that Pope Paul III entrusted to them. As a result, they decided to assemble before the day of separation and discuss the future of their group. Diverse views and opinions were noted as their first experience at the meeting.

[28] "Deliberations of Our First Fathers," 3.

the mission entrusted by his companions to be the Superior General, administering mostly at a desk in Rome.

Conclusions

Ignatius's conversion can be conceptualized as one from self-centered to other-centered, and preeminently centered in the "other" who creates and loves us, God. But part of that conversion involves a conversion in our relationship with others, one from bias and prejudice to indifference and love. While indifference is not as beautiful as love, it plays a key role in overcoming racial difference and mitigating racial hostility. For indifference is not only a product of conversion, but an animator of conversion. For where racial difference and tensions prevail, and therefore love is all too absent, indifference can recenter us on the path to love. It can remind us of the imperatives of conversion and service in the face of social differences. It helps us examine our interior dispositions as well as our external complicity in structures of sin that stoke racial tensions.

5

The Sins of White Supremacy

Institutionalized Racism and a Composition of Place

Jeannine Hill Fletcher

"In the Spiritual Exercises, sins and their malice are understood more intimately, than in the time when one was not so giving himself to interior things. Gaining now more knowledge of and sorrow for them, he will have greater profit and merit than he had before."

Ignatius of Loyola[1]

What would it look like to employ the Spiritual Exercises to examine our participation in the sin of White supremacy? So named, this exploration begins from the position that the sin of racism in the United States is fundamentally the problem of a racist set of categorizations which hierarchically orders "White" at the top.[2] This sin of American racism involves a "disordered affection" in assessing as more valuable that which is "White." Through the sin of White

[1] Ignatius of Loyola, "General Confession, With Communion," *Spiritual Exercises of Saint Ignatius*, trans. Elder Mullan, SJ (New York: P.J. Kenedy and Sons, 1914), 17.
[2] "White" will be capitalized throughout this essay following the US Census practice of capitalizing the categories of "the races" and APA style guidelines. This is in distinction from lowercase use of terms to designate color.

supremacy benefits accrue directly to those who are identified with the racial categorization of White, and so the disordered affection may be more prevalent among the White persons the disorder serves. Yet because the sin of White supremacy (in valuing White culture, White forms and White persons) *can* be a disordered affection of those who themselves have not been categorized as White, this rendering of the Exercises could be of value wherever one has been located within the dynamics of our US racial project.[3] Here, a distinction among different types of racism might help orient our discussion. Camara Phyllis Jones distinguishes three forms of racism that impact persons of color and White persons in diverse ways. While we most often think about racism as "interpersonal" (visible actions committed between persons), what Jones names as "internalized racism" can take the form of ideas about racial superiority or racial inferiority that come to shape us from the inside. A daily Spiritual Exercise that asks us to undertake an accounting of our thoughts, words, and deeds could fruitfully bring to consciousness these overt and internalized forms.

But in order to draw the fullest benefit from the Exercises, we need also to consider a third form of racism in the structures of White supremacy. Jones presents "institutional racism" in the following way:

> *Institutionalized racism* is defined as differential access to the goods, services, and opportunities of society by race. Institutionalized racism is normative, sometimes legalized, and often manifests as inherited disadvantage. It is structural, having been codified in our institutions of custom, practice, and law, so there need not be an identifiable perpetrator.[4]

When the sins of White supremacy have been codified in our customs, practices and law, we may not even know that we are participating

---

[3] Sociologists Michael Omi and Howard Winant employ the frame of "racial project" to draw attention to the way in which "the races" are constructed categories designed to order humanity and distribute resources through the categories into which persons are sorted. See Omi and Winant, *Racial Formation in the United States*, 3rd ed. (New York: Routledge, 2014).

[4] Camara Phyllis Jones, "Levels of Racism: A Theoretic Framework and a Gardener's Tale," *American Journal of Public Health* (2000): 1212–15, at 1212.

in a racially ordered reality that creates barriers to access of "goods, services, and opportunities." Because "there need not be an identifiable perpetrator" we also may not recognize when racially unjust systems are directed to our benefit. Era by era, US legislation and social formation built a nation that prioritized White well-being. The very structures and institutions that make up our nation (church, school, law, community) have been created unjustly *and* the benefits of past expressions of White supremacy have been "stored" within those institutions. Those of us who are located within predominantly White institutions (both White people and people of color) might be acutely interested in undertaking a new form of the Spiritual Exercises in arriving at a twenty-first-century application for understanding more intimately and gaining more sorrow for the sins embedded in *our* institutions, even our Jesuit institutions.

The invitation to work the muscle of anti-racism with the Spiritual Exercises is a necessary step for Americans of every racial category and identification because the racism of White supremacy has been a national, historical trauma impacting both White persons and persons of color, albeit in different ways. The depth of this sinfulness as the foundational weave of our national history and the very structure of our social reality today invites us to recognize the seriousness of dismantling it and the difficulties in doing so. The advances of emancipation and the civil rights movement are held alongside the continuing assault on Black and Brown bodies through policing and policies in the twenty-first century. The gains of the American Indian Movement placed alongside the ongoing struggle for sovereignty and the protection of native lands. The expansion of the US body-politic to embrace Asian-Americans in immigration legislation of 1965 held in tension with the rise in anti-Asian hate on US soil. And the ongoing expansion of Latinx populations throughout the nation realized even as White protestors keep mounting pressure at our borders. Recognizing the depths of the problems of racial injustice and anticipating the present journey as our era's contribution to the long-haul of undoing American White supremacy, all persons might find benefit in accessing the resources of spiritual capital that Ignatian traditions provide.

We might think of the Exercises as a form of sustenance for the journey of what Dr. Maria Yellow Horse Brave Heart outlines as a process of Truth and Transformation for addressing historical trauma.[5] With Brave Heart, we are asked to recognize that addressing the historical trauma of racism and White supremacy is not an easy fix but a multifaceted, multidimensional process of healing. In a spiraling path, Brave Heart proposes a movement from truth-telling and analysis of the historical trauma, toward releasing the pain and engaging in transformation for the future. As a social worker and mental health expert by training, Brave Heart describes healing from trauma that cannot take place without first naming the trauma that has occurred. This truth-telling includes understanding the history of our nation and the ways in which White supremacy has been intimately woven through each era. The current backlash against facing racial injustice in educational curriculum highlights the necessity of undertaking a naming and truth-telling before healing from trauma can occur. But the second step of Brave Heart's program asks us to deepen our truth-telling in order to come to an understanding of the trauma embedded within our histories. This step of analysis will illuminate root causes of racism and White supremacy and may be able to paint a fuller picture of the ways in which the survivors of racial abuse experience the history differently from those who have benefitted from it. It is only through the pain of truth-telling and analysis, rehearsing past offenses and facing past harms head on, that Brave Heart envisions people might be able to move toward the step of releasing the pain and reconciling with the present. It is only through the painful investigation of our histories that we might collectively understand, heal, and create new and transformed structures for our collective lives together.

Ignatius of Loyola seemed to have understood a similar need for facing a painful reality before moving toward a transformed one, as the Spiritual Exercises invite the seeker into a deep dwelling in the particular and the painful as a process for self-evaluation and self-transformation. How might the deep spirituality of the Exercises be an accompaniment for the movement of truth and transformation that our nation needs? What follows is a reimagining and unpacking of the First Week of the Spiritual Exercises as a way to see the work

---

[5] For an account of Brave Heart's program as adapted by the Jesuit Affiliated Red Cloud Indian School, see https://www.redcloudschool.org/truth-and-healing/about.

of racial justice and dismantling White supremacy as the work Christians are called to do in the world.

Entering into the Spiritual Exercises: Opening Postures toward the First Week

The First Week of St. Ignatius's Spiritual Exercises invites a pain-filled involvement in the sins we have committed as the foundation for deepening spiritual lives. The twenty-first-century reader may wonder whether Ignatius's sixteenth-century audience had as deep an aversion to investigating sin as our contemporaries do. Given the way sin and guilt have burdened Catholic imaginations to the point of paralysis as well as the way "sin" has been wielded dangerously in the tool kit of symbolic capital, it makes perfect sense that many of us resist the deep situating of our feet in the self-loathing that sin-talk can produce.[6] But contemporary readers should take pause in our very resistance to sin-saturation with the insight of James Baldwin, who asked White people to see the ways in which they actively ran from facing their complicity in the sin of racism.[7] In Bryan Massingale's rendering of this sort of sin, the "willful ignorance" of the reality of the depth, breadth, and pervasiveness of White supremacy *and* our cultural, structural and personal participation in it, is a sin that White Christians need to look squarely in the face in order to ground ourselves in the necessary work of addressing, analyzing, and dismantling the racism that has become part of the air we breathe.[8] The first step of the First Week is seeing the sin of White supremacy.

Ignatius, then, boldly asks us to enter into a time when "sin and their malice are understood intimately."[9] Attentive to the poetics of

---

[6] Perhaps this is the aversion White America is experiencing in book banning and curricular refusal to engage Critical Race Theory.

[7] James Baldwin, "A Letter to My Nephew," *The Progressive Magazine*, December 1, 1962, https://progressive.org/magazine/letter-nephew/ (accessed August 5, 2023).

[8] Bryan N. Massingale, "The Ignatian Witness to Truth in a Climate of Injustice," *Conversations on Jesuit Higher Education*, August 12, 2017, https://epublications .marquette.edu/conversations/vol52/iss1/3 (accessed August 5, 2023).

[9] Ignatius of Loyola, *The Spiritual Exercises of Saint Ignatius: A Translation and Commentary*, George E. Ganss, SJ (Chicago: Loyola Press, 1992), 39.

Ignatius's invitation, we might pause to consider the intimacy of this sin. How do we name the sin not simply as "racism" but with the greater precision of "White supremacy" to intimately account for the subtle and submerged ideology that persons, cultures, and practices that have been categorized as "White" are of greater value than any others? Where do we need to look inwardly for the intimacy of this pervasive accounting of humanity and human expression? Internalized racism speaks softly, intimately, cultivated close to hearts and minds, and escaping through lips and limbs sometimes nearly imperceptible, sometimes unknowingly. While internalized racism, and even internalized White supremacy, can impact all persons across the categories of "race," there is a special need for those who have been sorted into the category of "White" to interrogate deeply the systems of supremacy that reside internally, precisely because the disordered affection of White supremacy brings real benefits to those of us who have been categorized and racialized as White. When we name White supremacy as a "disordered affection," we might sense the intimacy of attachments that supremacy stirs.[10] The real, material benefits that Whiteness has brought can create barriers for the kind of deep investigation and contemplation that Ignatius envisions the Exercises to entail.

The regimen of the Spiritual Exercises is a useful measure of the ease with which we might fall into the willful ignorance of our sin of White supremacy. Ignatius describes the formula that the one making the exercises (the exercitant) "should remain for a full hour in each of the five Exercises or contemplations which will be made each day."[11] Over one week, a full thirty-five hours of sustained attention to the disordered affection of White supremacy is recommended. Ignatius's description of the concern raised by "hasty" or "unstable" eagerness to act pairs with this intimate knowledge importantly. The interrogation into the sin of White supremacy is not the guilt-ridden wailing and gnashing of teeth, nor is it the public calling-out of every injustice at every turn; it is turning deeply inward to ground with strength and the suitability to each person "the carrying out of what one wishes to promise."[12] Drawing out the length of

---

[10] Ganss, *Spiritual Exercises*, 143 endnote.
[11] Ganss, 24.
[12] Ganss, 25.

time dedicated to the exploration of disordered affection serves another function for undertaking the Exercises: we are reminded that the transformation of racism is not a quick-fix. Given the depth, breadth, and enduring quality of White supremacy as it has sustained structures, systems, thoughts and practices since the creation of "the races," *undoing* racism must be a similar journey of expansive depth, breadth, and quality if real transformation is to take root.[13]

The First Week: Spiritual Exercises to Overcome Oneself and to Order One's Life without Reaching a Decision through Some Disordered Affection

The opening directives of the Spiritual Exercises orient the penitent in the practice of an Examination of Conscience. In an imagined twenty-first-century schedule, the first day will be directed toward experiencing the rhythm of the retreat focused on the daily disorders. Beginning the day, the retreatants dedicate themselves with a resolve to focus on the sin of White supremacy as "the particular sin or fault he or she wants to correct."[14] Understanding White supremacy as rooted in evaluative thoughts and the categorization of what is "White" as of highest value, those committing to addressing this sin might begin with the process of cataloguing that Ignatius requires seeking the "grace to recall how often one has fallen into the particular sin or fault, in order to correct it in the future."[15] The first day

---

[13] Sociologist Deadric Williams succinctly summarizes the insight of scholars who study racial construction and racism with the idea that "racism created the races." Scholarly consensus identifies that modern construction of "the races" as categories into which people would be sorted was a project that emerged simultaneous to European colonialism precisely as a means by which to sort non-Europeans into categories of "lesser-than." J. Kameron Carter's study of the influential philosopher Immanuel Kant's creation of racial categories helps us to see that the formulation of a set of categories into which persons were to be sorted (by "race") was the product of thought-projects among philosophers, botanists, and emerging anthropologists at a particular time when European nation-states were pursuing a global project of conquest for the accumulation of natural resources and material production. Thus, the very category of "White" was created in the hierarchically ordered categorization as the category of "best," "most human," "closest to the ideal." The drive of White supremacy and European-driven conquest (racism) created the categories of "the races" (with White on top). See Carter's *Race: A Theological Account* (Oxford: Oxford University Press, 2008). See also Omi and Winant, *Racial Formation*.

[14] Ganss, *Spiritual Exercises*, 33.

[15] Ganss, 33.

would be spent calling to mind and chronicling my interpersonal and internalized sins manifest in my thoughts, words and deeds.[16]

Day 1 / Preparations and First Exercise

> 7:00 am Examination of Conscience: resolution to guard against sin of White supremacy
>
> 9:00 am Examination of Conscience: considering sin of White supremacy in *thoughts**
>
> 12:00 noon Examen: Review and record failures[17] in thoughts and *words**
>
> 3:00 pm Examination of Conscience: considering sin of White supremacy in *deeds**
>
> 7:00 pm Examen: List hour by hour a dot for each time he or she fell into the particular sin
>
> *employing memory, understanding, and will

In the imagined schedule for Week One of the Exercises, time is set out to directly chronicle the kinds of sins of White supremacy that can be called to mind employing memory, understanding, and will. The essential thrust of Ignatius's work asks the retreatant to become aware of those things which they have known and experienced and bring them back to the surface for deeper consideration. We can re-trace our steps, so to speak, and illuminate for ourselves our own faults and failures in our thoughts, words, and deeds. This particular day would benefit significantly from the reimagined Exercises artfully constructed by Patrick Saint-Jean in *The Spiritual Work of Racial Justice.*[18] As his text demonstrates, the use of Week One to account for the wide range of expressions in the form of interpersonal and inter-

---

[16] "General Examination of Conscience," Ganss, 35.

[17] Language adopted from Daily Examen Journal, prayer steps as described by Mark E. Thibodeaux, SJ, in *Reimagining the Ignatian Examen: Fresh Ways to Pray from Your Day* (Chicago: Loyola Press, 2015).

[18] Patrick Saint-Jean, SJ, *The Spiritual Work of Racial Justice: A Month of Meditations with Ignatius of Loyola* (Vestal, NY: Anamchara Books, 2021).

nalized racism could last easily a full week, or indeed, a lifetime. In Saint-Jean's text, the investigation of thoughts, words, and deeds is guided by Ibram Kendi's consideration that "racist ideas make people of color think less of themselves, which makes them more vulnerable to racist ideas. Racist ideas make White people think more of themselves, which further attracts them to racist ideas."[19] Saint-Jean leads the reader through the encounters with people of other races shadowed by fear, suspicion, and judgment (33) as well as identifying some of the structures that keep racist realities out of view (47). He asks readers to consider when we have failed to see the image of God in our neighbor (56) and points to specifics of thoughts, words, and deeds that benefit from racism and White supremacy (70), encouraging a vision of intentional cross-racial relationships to remain attentive to the impact of our thoughts, words, and deeds (107). The Jesuit parish of St. Ignatius in San Francisco has similarly developed an online resource to guide practitioners committing themselves to such investigation.[20] Their "Discernment Series" provides a wealth of resources—both in reading and through videos—that might aid in the soul-searching retreat we are considering. To address the sins of White supremacy is to reconceive Christ among those who have been crucified by racism and White supremacy and each day to create an exacting account, "hour by hour . . . from the moment of rising to the present examination,"[21] so that at the end of each day, imagining Christ among the crucified, the penitent can ask: *What have I done for Christ? What am I doing for Christ? What ought I to do for Christ?*[22]

At the end of the first day and the morning of the second, the retreatant might rest deeply in the movement of the spirit Ignatius names as "discernment." Am I drawn toward the benefits and gains

---

[19] Saint-Jean, *Spiritual Work of Racial Justice*, 33.

[20] St. Ignatius Parish, San Francisco, *Discernment Series*, https://www.stignatiussf.org/program/discernment-series-racial-justice. For particularly powerful discussions on the use of imagination see volume 8; and on structural realities of racism see volume 9. The entire series offers an invaluable resource for this work.

[21] Ganss, *Spiritual Exercises*, 33.

[22] Such a consideration of Christ among the crucified people of the world is based on the insights of Ignacio Ellacuría and developed in Jeannine Hill Fletcher, *The Sin of White Supremacy: Christianity, Racism, and Religious Diversity in America* (Maryknoll, NY: Orbis Books, 2017), 142–43.

of Whiteness? Do I experience consolation or desolation in envision-ing a multiracial future as the context in which my life takes place? The beauty of the Ignatian spiritual tradition is precisely the long timeframe of examination and the recognition of the affective ele-ments that inform our understandings. Even if we can name White supremacy as "sin," might some retreatants not experience the lure of this evil in the benefits it presents? In the second day of the First Week, retreatants are invited to name the desired goal of a "growing and intense sorrow and tears for my sins."[23] Some may not experi-ence sorrow for their participation in the sin of White supremacy and Ignatius recommends that one sets the sorrow for one's sins as pre-cisely a goal for this exercise.

Day 2 / Second Exercise:
A court record of my sins in inheritance (the period of my youth)

> 7:00 am Resolution to guard against the sin of White supremacy
>
> 9:00 am *A court record of my sins of inheritance of locality*
>
> 12:00 noon Examen: Review and record failures
>
> 3:00 pm *A court record of my sins of inheritance in relationships and occupation*
>
> 7:00 pm Examen: Review and record failures in locality, relation-ships, and occupation

It becomes increasingly interesting to read the Exercises through the lens of racial justice when we arrive at the second exercise in a week dedicated to enumerating the instances of sin in which we are embedded. For in the first point of focus, the exercitant is asked to create, in Ignatius's words, a "court record of my sins."[24] More pre-cisely, Ignatius asks the one who would take seriously their sins to look back on their personal history and to consider, "year by year, period by period," very particular elements of their lives. Ignatius asks that the one who would take the record of sin seriously would enumerate details about "the locality or house where I lived . . . the

---

[23] "The Second Exercise," *The Second Prelude*, Ganss, *Spiritual Exercises*, 43.
[24] Ganss, 43.

associations I had with others . . . the occupation I was pursuing."[25] This set of directions, focused on geography and habitation is especially important in the United States when so much racialized injustice has filtered through the systems of housing and the location of our homes. But it is precisely here that many may not recognize their condition *as* sin. The most fruitful application of Ignatius's invitation to recount our history and the "locality" of our sins of White supremacy requires supplementation precisely because the forms of "institutional/structural" sin are invisible to us. Here is a most crucial question when we set out our court record and cultivate our understanding with the analytic frame of the racially unjust legislation directly related to habitation: Do we even know the history in which we are embedded? Our retreat proceeds offering three "periods" to consider as Ignatius leads us to deepening our engagement.

Consider your life story, period by period, and the place in which the locality of your house was situated. If you are in the United States, your understanding might be structured by an awareness that every inch of America now under the jurisdiction of the United States was land taken from indigenous nations in the extended project of settler-colonialism. In each period of your residence, do you know who were the original peoples of that land? Do you know the conditions under which that land came to be governed by the United States? Was the land taken violently or purchased (and under what terms); was the transfer of land by treaty or does the land remain unceded? How does the account of my being wrapped up in the sinfulness of the dispossession of indigenous peoples find its way onto the "court record" of my sins? The act of land acknowledgement is a form of spiritual exercise that gives witness to the original peoples who inhabited the land, but the questions still must be probed: Do we feel genuine and deep sorrow for that sin sufficient to seek restitution and renewed relationships with the original peoples?[26]

The second major period our histories and our court record must recall is how the "locality or house where I lived" was involved in the nation's sin of slavery as an economic system of White supremacy.

---

[25] Ganss, 43.

[26] The Native Governance Project offers resources not only for research, but also guidance for establishing relationships of reciprocity and repair. See https://nativegov.org/news/a-guide-to-indigenous-land-acknowledgment/.

While the American education curriculum makes it difficult to claim ignorance of this national reality, it is not clear that all Americans have been asked what relationship *their* locality had in particular to the generations of wealth-building from the stolen lives and stolen labor of peoples of African descent. New histories remind us that it is not only locations where legal enslavement endured into the nineteenth century (that is, "the South") but also Northern cities with earlier histories *and* economies connected to southern slaveholders' money. Whether in the form of early centuries of slavery in the Northeast, investments from slaveholders in cities "on the frontier" of the Midwest, or the struggle for an expansion of slavery into the West in the new US territories at the close of the Mexican-American War, the history of slavery in the United States and its actual impact on our location is often a point that cannot be brought to memory because we have never been taught this history in the first place. And even though we may know that an economy of enslavement built our nation, do we feel sorrow for this sin in the particularity of *our* lives and *our* locations?

One of the reasons many White Americans do not feel sorrow for the sin of slavery is because they see it as someone else's sin, something that happened in the past and for which those of us in the present cannot be held responsible. But Ignatius's Composition of Place attentive to location renders space and place spiritually relevant. If we benefit from ownership of land acquired unjustly, or inhabit "homes" built in an economy of enslavement, are we not the inheritors of the benefits of sin to which we might have a disordered attachment? Contemplating this spiritual geography in a Composition of Place we might need to interrogate our disordered attachment to the wealth of gain from stolen land and stolen labor and to monitor the movement of our spirit as we consider activism of land-return and reparations.

A final invitation from Ignatius in the sixteenth century asks us to consider the home in which we reside in relation to the structures of White supremacy in the twentieth century. For this era is most crucial when it comes to the relationship between "home" and "racism." Yet here again, perhaps many of us were formed in a willful ignorance of the very history that is our inheritance. The locations in which we are now situated across the US were fundamentally impacted by legislation that prioritized home ownership, with the establishment of the Federal Housing Administration (in 1934). Yet the funds that would be dedicated and distributed were informed by a racial hierarchy written into the mortgage-lending manual and used by persons in the real estate industry until well into the 1960s. Practices of the past that distributed government funding for White home ownership but withheld the same funding from families of color became part of the inheritance passed down generationally. If redlining took place in the 1930s and 1940s, and the return on home investment skyrocketed between the 1940s and 1970s, those earlier generations' being structured by the sin of White supremacy would have been passed along to me in the location of my inheritance.[27]

At each step of Ignatius's *Spiritual Exercises*, the penitent is asked to deepen their focus and concern in the court-record of their sin that is building. Week One, Day Three asks us to examine our understanding of the benefits we have accrued as we move into the present, and in Ignatius's second point of this exercise, "to ponder these sins, looking at the foulness and evil."[28] We are invited into the record of our sins and *to see them* as *sins*.

Day 3 / Third Exercise:
A Repetition of the Second Exercise accompanied by Colloquies

> 7:00 am Resolution to guard against the sin of White supremacy in my personal sphere
>
> 9:00 am *A court record of my sins in the present on locality*
>
> 12:00 noon Examen: Review and record failures in locality
>
> 3:00 pm *A court record of my sins of inheritance in relationships and occupation*
>
> 7:00 pm Examen: Review and record failures; engage failures with Colloquies

[27] For a discussion of how White advantage in accessing mortgage lending in the 1940s experienced an exponential increase in White wealth in the housing markets of the 1970s, see Richard Rothstein, *The Color of Law: A Forgotten History of How Our Government Segregated America* (New York: Liveright, 2017).

[28] Ganss, *Spiritual Exercises*, 43.

That this renewed invitation to ponder our sins as foulness and evil comes on Day Three, after the retreatant has already undertaken ten hours of enumerating and considering the court record of their sins, is a particularly potent insight embedded in Ignatius's program. That is, while we may be able to list the sins of our actions and the sins of our inheritance, *do we see them as sinful?* Was the destruction of native cultures and the deceit with which land was taken "foulness and evil"? Is the wealth that accrued through an economy of enslavement saturated in sinfulness? As we ponder the practices of redlining and the dedication of government funds to White wealth building through homeownership, and the withholding of those same funds from people of color, do we name them as "sins"? Our inheritance and our present realities structured by the sin of White supremacy in our locatedness connects directly to the court record of sins that Ignatius asks us to recount also in terms of "relationships" and "occupation." If my locality, my home, was structured in sinful segregations, what forms did my relationships take? What sort of work was being done (in schooling or profession) which year-by-year added to or disrupted the racialized injustice of my personal and family history? The change of heart and mind required to take seriously the sin of White supremacy begins with a willingness to name customs, practices, and law *as* sinful, and to recognize the benefits that have accrued or been withheld through them as sin-filled as well.

To the apparent aversion that many White Americans seem to have when asked to face the sins of White supremacy, Ignatius's program is an intense journey, ever deepening the requirement of truth-telling about our sins. The Third Exercise is relentless in repeating the "court record of my sins" and dwelling on our sinfulness. But the repetition is not mere self-flagellation or amplification of guilt, but a necessary line of questioning for spiritual analysis. If the first expression of this audit of our sinfulness is a form of self-awareness and truth-telling, the approach to the same list of specific sins in this repetition could offer a form of analysis toward understanding. Ignatius's Exercises presuppose that our embrace of our own sinfulness will require an ever-deepening process as the Fourth Exercise is a repetition exactly of the movement of the Third. Ignatius enumerates the deepening and complexifying of our understanding of the sin of racism with a threefold aim:

1. to feel an interior knowledge of my sins, and hatred of them;

2. to feel the disorder of my actions, so that, hating them, I may correct myself and put myself in order;

3. to ask knowledge of the world, in order that, hating it, I may put away from me worldly and vain things.[29]

The flow of these exercises in the First Week invites the contemplation of sinfulness in such a way that the exercitant cannot fail to "see" and is invited to refuse the "willful ignorance" of the structures, systems, and participation in the sins of White supremacy.

Once we have created the court record of our personal sins, we do not need to be paralyzed, for the future weeks of the Exercises will ask us to follow a course of action aligned with Christ toward resurrection, always cognizant of our sins. But before we move on to Weeks Two, Three, and Four in this modified Exercises of Accountability, we have the chance to deepen our understanding of the court record of our sins by not only considering the homes of our family dwellings, but our institutional homes as well.

Day 4 / Fourth Exercise:
A Repetition of the Third, but focused on Institutions

7:00 am Resolution to guard against the sin of White supremacy in my institution

9:00 am *A court record of structural sin in institutional locality*

12:00 noon Examen: Review and record failures in locality of my institution

3:00 pm *A court record of structural sin in institutional relationships and occupation*

For the purpose of this necessary shift, we might consider a definition of "institutions" as those locations that govern the "customs, practices, and laws" of our society, as Jones's definition of institutionalized racism has alerted us. Key institutions include government, religion,

---

[29] Ganss, 45.

and education, so if we are embedded in Jesuit institutions and attempting an authentic interrogation of sins in Week One, the court record of our institutional sins might be especially pertinent. For while the spiritual capital of our Jesuit tradition bequeaths to us the resources of Ignatian spirituality, we must also reckon with the capital residing within Jesuit institutions that is bequeathed to us as the inheritance of racial injustice. Jesuits were among the first Christian missionaries who propelled the projects of settler-colonialism, as evidenced in the *Jesuit Relations* that offers an account of European-Christian encroachment and the logic of Christian supremacy that was its fuel. The deep roots of cultural, linguistic, and religious loss that Native Americans face today were fostered by our Jesuit forebears from the sixteenth-century missions through to twentieth-century boarding schools.[30] In the homes of our Jesuit institutions, our academic forebears produced "knowledge" about the shortcomings of Indigenous peoples in their lifeways and beliefs, while benefitting from legislation that transferred land from them into the hands of White Christians and White Christian institutions.[31] In both the general sense that all land in the United States was stolen from Indigenous peoples, and the more specific sense that legislation provided White settler access to more and more opportunities to claim land, the establishment of twenty-one of the twenty-eight Jesuit institutions of the Association of Jesuit Colleges and Universities within the nineteenth century encourages each institution to ask when and how *their* land came into their possession.[32] Knowledge produced in Jesuit

[30] Allan Greer, ed., *The Jesuit Relations: Natives and Missionaries in Seventeenth Century North America* (Boston: Bedford/St. Martin's, 2000).

[31] While the transfer of land to White settlers is part of the national history for every Jesuit institution, those situated in the West and founded after the 1862 Homestead Act might particularly investigate the ways in which our institutions benefitted directly from proceeds of sales of land taken from tribes. For specific writings from the Jesuits in the nineteenth century see Joseph Mobberly (Georgetown, 1820) and Augustus Thebaud (Fordham, 1877).

[32] The number could be twenty or twenty-two depending on how we count Loyola Marymount (1911)/St. Vincent's (1865): Georgetown (1789), Saint Louis University (1818), Spring Hill (Mobile, 1830), Xavier (Cincinnati, 1831), Holy Cross (Massachusetts, 1843), St. Joseph's (Philadelphia, 1851), Santa Clara (1851), Loyola Maryland (1852), University of San Francisco (1855), Boston College (1863), Loyola Chicago (1870), Canisius College (Buffalo, 1870), St. Peter's University (Jersey City, 1872), University of Detroit Mercy (1877), Creighton (Omaha, 1878), Regis (Denver, 1877),

academic spaces also forged the symbolic capital for both Jesuit-run and other Catholic, Christian, and governmental boarding schools.[33] In the practice of truth-telling that might lead to healing, the Ignatian inspired Exercises of Accountability seem to be a very necessary first step.

The court record of sins of White supremacy, period by period, of our Jesuit network seems like a necessary endeavor to take seriously the Exercises of the First Week. Recalling the insight of historian Shannen Dee Williams, the Catholic Church was the first and largest corporate slaveholder in the Americas, and our Jesuit roots are embedded in this soil.[34] Here, too, we might be overwhelmed with the truth-telling that begins with the buildup of land transferred to the Jesuits in Baltimore through the hands of Catholic bondspeople when James Carroll bequeathed not only his land but also the enslaved workers to the Jesuits. Our truth-telling might include not only those named in Carroll's papers (Dick, Tomboy, Jack, Harry, Daniell, Peter, Dicky, Billy, Maria, Mary, Rachel, Davy, Jenny, Dolly, Toby, Adam, Maria, Pedro, Sampson, Rosa, Glascow, Page, and Judith) as the first enslaved Catholics who built our institutions, but the countless more who labored in service of Church and School in our Catholic, Jesuit network.[35] Might an accounting of the sins of White supremacy include a court record of the specific enslaved Catholics who built *many*

Marquette (Milwaukee, 1881), John Carroll (Ohio, 1886), Gonzaga (Spokane, 1887), University of Scranton (Pennsylvania, 1888), Seattle University (1891), Rockhurst (Kansas City, 1910), Loyola Marymount (Los Angeles, 1911), Loyola New Orleans (1912), Fairfield (Connecticut, 1942), LeMoyne College (Syracuse, 1946), Wheeling Jesuit (est. 1954, no longer within the network). The twenty-eighth college now listed is St. John's Belize (1887); https://www.ajcunet.edu/institutions (accessed January 31, 2022).

[33] Lorenzo Palladino, SJ, *Indian and White in the Northwest: A History of Catholicity in Montana 1831–1891* (Lancaster, PA: Wickersham, 1922), originally published 1894. See also Jesuit contributions to Catholic understanding of indigenous peoples in *The Indian Sentinel* published 1910–1962.

[34] Shannen Dee Williams, "Religious Orders Owning Slaves Isn't New—Black Catholics Have Emphasized This History for Years," *America*, August 6, 2019, https://www.americamagazine.org/faith/2019/08/06/religious-orders-owning-slaves-isnt-new-black-catholics-have-emphasized-history.

[35] Maryland Province Archives, "James Carroll, 'An Account of My Negroes,'" September 27, 1715," *Georgetown Slavery Archive*, https://slaveryarchive.georgetown.edu/items/show/135 (accessed June 2, 2022).

Jesuit institutions, but remain unnamed and uncredited?[36] To account for our sins, our institutional homes would need to be audited for the benefits they received in the period of slavery through the structures of sin that built our dwellings and the ways in which money from an economy of enslavement saved our schools, endowed our pursuits, and paid our tuition.

Tracing the same periodization as we did in our personal accounting, we might turn to our institutional histories in the mid-twentieth century, to ask to what extent did Catholic and Jesuit institutions as *White-serving and predominantly White* contribute to the assessor's review? As Jesuit institutions of Church and School continue to be stakeholders in our local communities, what are the sins of White supremacy we continue to perpetrate in our localities, our relationships, and our occupations? And which of our Jesuit institutions were creating "knowledge" about "the races" that might have fed into the assessor's hand? The ideologies and practices, customs and laws of White supremacy did not drop from the sky. They were cultivated in the institutions of our nation: Church and School, Family and Government. In this, the leading knowledge production of Jesuit education surely had (and has) a role to play. In undertaking twenty-first-century knowledge-production and applying our spiritual heritage of Ignatian Exercises, might Jesuit institutions become models for all Catholic institutions and Christian institutions, preparing the ground for the work of reparations that might come to fruition as national legislation following House Resolution 40?

The deepening spiral of return to the court record of my sins moves the seeker into ever deepening saturation in the reality of our sinfulness, as if a spiral staircase, drawing ever deeper and finally into the Fifth Exercise that is a Meditation on Hell. Here Ignatius stirs the imagination through the senses to see the huge fires, hear the wailing and blasphemies, smell the smoke and rotting things, taste the bitter

---

[36] Jesuit institutions are aided in this work by the *Georgetown Slavery Archive* and the Midwest Province *Slavery, Memory and Reconciliation* project. See, for example, Kelly Schmidt, "A National Legacy of Enslavement: An Overview of the Work of the Slavery, History, Memory and Reconciliation Project," *Journal of Jesuit Studies* 8 (2021): 81–107; and Adam Rothman, "The Jesuits and Slavery," *Journal of Jesuit Studies* 8 (2021): 1–10. Each Jesuit institution, however, would need to examine their own histories for a fuller picture of Jesuit institutional complicity.

flavors of tears, sadness, and the worm of conscience, and touch the burning flames. In the closing of this Exercise the exercitant realizes that they are in hell with the many textures it entails but they are not finally in hell and instead raise their gratitude to Christ for his pity and salvation.[37]

Day 5 / The Fifth Exercise:
A Meditation on Hell using the Imagination

  7:00 am Resolution to guard against the sin of White supremacy

  9:00 am A Meditation on Hell using the *Eyes* of the imagination, *Hearing*, and *Stench*

  12:00 noon Examen: review and record

  3:00 pm A Meditation on Hell using *Taste* and *Touch*

  7:00 pm Examen: review and record

The challenge in this Meditation on Hell is that too often those who are the beneficiaries of the sins of White supremacy in institutional form do not experience the results of this sin as "hell." But the eyes of the imagination might see predominantly White institutions out of touch with the suffering they are causing, and see exclusively White spaces as evidence of deep structures of racism. The ears of the imagination might hear the words of White supremacy woven into White Christian preaching and White Christian curriculum. The sense of smell lifted up in the imagination might experience the clean air of suburban life and not know that environmental devastation is being breathed into the lungs of children and elders in poor neighborhoods. In our White-benefitting institutions we might taste organic foods and dabble in cultural cuisines of the world, but are we cognizant of any environmentally racist tolls these practices might reflect? We might touch the forms of wealth that surround us and not know that instead of the wealth of salvation in intercommunion with God and others, we are surrounded by a hell of our own making within the walls of White supremacy.

---

[37] Ganss, *Spiritual Exercises*, 47.

There will be time in the Third Week to employ the senses in an imaginative effort to feel the suffering of those who suffer, after the Second Week has invited retreatants to walk in the way of Christ, and long before we experience the joy of the resurrection anticipated in the Fourth Week. Those who have moved on through the First Week of the Exercises to the subsequent weeks will know that this journey into the depths of hell and the salvation of Christ is not the end but only the beginning of the journey that continues through discipleship, death, and resurrection. Experiencing the reality of our sinfulness and the depths of hell is, in Ignatius's ambulation, only the beginning of the Christian's journey: "For what fills and satisfies the soul consists, not in knowing much, but in our understanding the realities profoundly and in savoring them interiorly."[38] When we savor intimately the understandings of our sins, perhaps the Ignatian spirituality of the Exercises of Accountability might serve the project of truth and transformation our nation requires.

[38] Ganss, 22.

$$=== 6 ===$$

The Gift of Tears

White *Metanoia* at the Foot of the Black Cross[1]

Christopher Pramuk

In August of 2017, I flew from Denver to Charleston, South Carolina, to participate in a retreat at Mepkin Abbey, a Trappist monastery on the outskirts of the city. While there, I also spent time with local organizations, including the monks, who, in the wake of the massacre of nine members of the historic Mother Emanuel AME Church, have been doing a great deal of work in the area of racial justice and reconciliation. The opening evening of the retreat was held in downtown Old Charleston, just blocks from Mother Emanuel. As we drove past the church, my host slowed the car to a stop, and together we sat for a while in silence. It felt to me like hallowed ground, perhaps in the way that Gettysburg, or Golgotha, is sacred ground.

Mepkin Abbey is situated on land that was a former slave plantation. At the edge of the property near the woods, I noticed signs indicating a path to an "African American Cemetery" on the property. On the second day of the retreat, just before sunrise, I set out for a walk, traversing several miles through corn and cotton fields—I had never seen a cotton field, despite being raised in the South—finding

---

[1] Portions of this chapter were originally developed in Christopher Pramuk, "At the Foot of the Black Cross in America," *Jesuit Higher Education* 12, no. 1 (June 2023): 9–15. Used with permission.

my way in the half-light along a rough path through the woods until I came upon an iron arch opening into the small cemetery. I arrived just as the treetops were starting to glow with the dawn light. The whole landscape seemed to breathe with what German theologian Johann Baptist Metz calls "dangerous memory."[2] Even the trees, draped with what locals call "resurrection moss," form a kind of mystic canopy over everything, seeming to hold the presence of the dead. And I could almost hear the slaves singing in the field.

I wanna die easy when I die

I wanna die easy when I die

I wanna die easy when I die

shout salvation as I rise

I wanna die easy when I die. . . .

Wade in the water

Wade in the water children

Wade in the water

God's gonna' trouble the water. . . .

In his *Narrative of the Life of Fredrick Douglass, An American Slave*, Douglass describes hearing his fellow slaves singing as they made their way between the fields and the farmhouse after nightfall, making "the dense old woods, for miles around, reverberate with their wild songs, revealing at once the highest joy and the deepest sadness." "Every tone," he writes, "was a testimony against slavery, and a prayer to God for deliverance from chains. The hearing of those wild notes always depressed my spirit, and filled me with ineffable sadness. I have frequently found myself in tears while hearing them."[3] When I teach Douglass's narrative in class, we begin by reading aloud together just the first few pages of the text, slowly, taking turns around the circle. There is a music in Douglass's writing that breaks open the heart, and if we allow it, our sense of the sacred. I can say

---

[2] Johann Baptist Metz, *Faith in History and Society: Toward a Fundamental Theology*, trans. J. Matthew Ashley (New York: Crossroad, 2007), 182–85.

[3] "Narrative of the Life of Frederick Douglass," in *The Classic Slave Narratives*, ed. Henry Louis Gates (New York: Signet, 2012), 315–403, at 324–25.

that "I have frequently found myself in tears" when hearing these pages read aloud in the voices of my students, white, Black, and Brown, the next generation.

Catholic theologian David Tracy, in his influential study, *The Analogical Imagination*, describes the "classic" as follows: "When a work of art so captures a paradigmatic experience of [an] event of truth, it becomes in that moment normative. Its memory enters as a catalyst into all our other memories, and, now subtly, now compellingly, transforms our perceptions of the real."[4] For anyone who has felt the power in Frederick Douglass's storytelling; the emotional impact of the spirituals and sorrow songs, or of Billie Holiday's recording of "Strange Fruit," allowing her performance to truly get under the skin, it becomes impossible to behold any "pastoral scene of the gallant South"[5] in the same way. Our "perceptions of the real," as Tracy has it, are forever changed. Whether the cotton fields and forests surrounding Mepkin Abbey or the magnificently restored plantation houses, a big tourist draw in the rural South today, such landscapes can no longer be enjoyed without at once "seeing" the bodies of Black men hanging from their fragrant trees, or enslaved women whipped raw, chained to the hitching post just this side of the mansion's grand entrance. The classic, says Tracy, "confronts and provokes us in our present horizon with the feeling that 'something else might be the case.' "[6]

During the First Week of *The Spiritual Exercises* of St. Ignatius, following a series of meditations in which we—that is, the retreatant under the guidance of a director—are asked to gaze long and hard at our sins, Ignatius invites us to "imagine Christ our Lord suspended on the cross before you," and prayerfully to meditate on three questions: "What have I done for Christ? What am I doing for Christ?

---

[4] David Tracy, *The Analogical Imagination: Christianity and the Culture of Pluralism* (New York: Crossroad, 1998), 115.

[5] Billie Holiday, "Strange Fruit" (Commodore, 1940), composed by Lewis Allan, a.k.a. Abel Meeropol, 1939; see Christopher Pramuk, *Hope Sings, So Beautiful: Graced Encounters across the Color Line* (Collegeville, MN: Liturgical Press, 2013), 53–66; also Christopher Pramuk, " 'Strange Fruit': Black Suffering/White Revelation," *Theological Studies* 67 (June 2006): 345–77.

[6] Tracy, *Analogical Imagination*, 102.

What ought I to do for Christ?"[7] He then directs us, as we gaze on Christ "in so pitiful a state as he hangs on the cross," to engage in a conversation, or "colloquy," with Jesus, "speaking in the way one friend speaks to another."[8] It is a remarkable contemplation, intimate and vulnerable, linking the honest reckoning with one's sins during the First Week—for Ignatius, a grace that ought to fill us with "shame and confusion about myself"—with the terrible suffering of a beloved friend. What would I say to Jesus in such a moment of reckoning? What would Jesus say in response to me?

In truth, he might struggle to say anything. Death by crucifixion, as medical experts have long suggested, is death by suffocation. The weight of the body, suspended by the arms, eventually renders the exhausted victim unable to breathe. The breaking of the legs of the two men crucified with Jesus by the Roman soldiers (John 19:32) would have ensured a quick, gasping death, and thus might be called, with terrible irony, an act of mercy. To witness such a manner of death must have been "pitiful" indeed, like watching a protracted drowning, powerless to render aid. The dying words of Jesus bear frightful impact when grasped against the physiological horror of crucifixion. Short bursts of speech are all that a body thus tortured could manage. *"I thirst."* "Father, why have you abandoned me?" *"Forgive them."* "Mother, behold your son." *"It is finished."* Like the sorrow songs that rise up from the bloodied soil of American history, the Spiritual Exercises have endured for 500 years because they continue to "confront and provoke us in our present horizon" with the transformative power of the Gospel narrative.[9]

---

[7] *Ignatius of Loyola: Spiritual Exercises and Selected Writings*, ed. George E. Ganss, SJ (Mahwah, NJ: Paulist Press, 1991), no. 53, p. 138.

[8] *Ignatius of Loyola*, no. 54, p. 138.

[9] Rather than the "classic," in his more recent work Tracy emphasizes the revelatory power of "fragments," appealing to the writings of Frederick Douglass and the Black theology of James Cone. While the fragment shares qualities of a classic in being intensely particular while having universal appeal, the former is distinguished by its capacity to trouble and undermine Western, Eurocentric metanarratives and totality systems. See David Tracy, *Filaments: Theological Profiles*, Selected Essays, vol. 2 (Chicago: University of Chicago, 2020), 351–64. For an excellent discussion of Tracy's development from one to the other of these two frameworks, see Stephen Okey, *A Theology of Conversation: An Introduction to David Tracy* (Collegeville, MN: Liturgical Press, 2018), 76–97.

If African Americans have long intuited a link between the passion of Jesus and lynching— the unjust brutalization and murder of people of color, like Jesus, at the hands of state-sanctioned violence—it is fair to conclude that white Christians today are only just beginning to grasp the resonances between this central narrative of their faith and the ongoing scourge of personal, structural, and racialized violence. The human drama of the passion narratives are not so far from the horrors of Charleston and Charlottesville, Ferguson and Minneapolis, Staten Island and Waller County, Texas. Consider the dying words of Eric Garner, face-down on the pavement, an officer's elbow around his neck, "*I can't breathe, I can't breathe,*" no less than eleven times. Or George Floyd, the same three desperate words, more than twenty times, and this, "Mama, mama, mama, mama. . . . Mom, I love you. I love you." And finally, "Please, sir. Please. Please."[10] Or Elijah McClain, of Aurora, Colorado, just before he was given a powerful dose of ketamine, and passed into unconsciousness, forever.

I can't breathe   I have my ID right here

     My name is Elijah McClain   That's my house

I was just going home   *I'm an introvert*

         I'm just different

That's all   I'm so sorry

   I have no gun   *I don't do that stuff*

I don't do any fighting

         Why are you attacking me?

   You are all phenomenal

         You are beautiful

   And I love you[11]

---

[10] Richard A. Oppel Jr. and Kim Barker, "New Transcripts Detail Last Moments for George Floyd," *The New York Times* (July 8, 2020), https://www.nytimes.com/2020/07/08/us/george-floyd-body-camera-transcripts.html.

[11] Dan Evon, "Are These Elijah McClain's Last Words on Police Video?," *Snopes.com* (June 26, 2020), https://www.snopes.com/fact-check/elijah-mcclains-last-words.

I used to dismiss the colloquy with Christ during the First Week of the Exercises as a somewhat idealized picture of the crucifixion. At least I had a hard time imagining myself in the scene, much less conversing with Jesus as he hangs from the cross. But I've looked again, through eyes now shaped by a litany of deaths that seem to have forced many white Americans to the foot of a cross that has overshadowed the lives of African Americans for 400 years. With "shame and confusion," I've concluded that my prior dismissals of the colloquy were unjust. Gently, Ignatius invites me to try again. Dare to place yourself in the scene. What would you say to a person in the throes of such anguish? "I'm sorry." *"I can't help you."* "I'm here." *"God loves you."* "Try not to be afraid." *"It'll be over soon."* I pause, and shudder to imagine what they might say to me.

This raw human discomfort, I've come to see, is the point of the colloquy. Ignatius has us pray for nothing less than the grace of shame and confusion during the First Week, a felt sense of powerlessness—our own, certainly, and crucially, the victim's—"for what we have done and what we have failed to do." The colloquy holds us in this dreadful liminal space, ugly and vulnerable, violent and paralyzing; in a word, damning. Ignatius would not have us spiritualize, sanitize, or whitewash our encounter with Christ crucified, nor downplay its implied link to our personal sin, our agency, our freedom. But why? After all, whether the subject of our contemplation is Jesus of Nazareth or Elijah McClain, Trayvon Marton, or Freddie Gray, what possible grace can emerge from placing ourselves inside such scenes, played out in the imagination, felt through all the senses, absorbed through the eyes of the heart? Could it be, as the title of this volume suggests, the grace of freedom: freedom from the prison of violence, shame, guilt, and paralysis, and freedom for a more generative life of truth and reconciliation, solidarity and love?[12]

---

[12] The merging across time and space of images of Jesus with Elijah McClain and others throughout this essay might be described, with Metz, as an exercise in *anamnestic reason*, a reason that remembers. The Catholic notion of *anamnesis* presumes a communion with the dead that moves in two directions, from giver to receiver and back again, crossing bounds of time and eternity. See Johann Baptist Metz, *A Passion for God: The Mystical-Political Dimension of Christianity*, trans. J. Matthew Ashley (Mahwah, NJ: Paulist Press, 1998), 142–43.

When police officers and EMTs bore down on Elijah McClain, he was wearing a face mask and waving his arms around, probably singing, his friends say, as he walked home from a convenience store. "It doesn't make sense," said one of his massage therapy clients, calling the police response "brutal." "He was the sweetest, purest person I have ever met. He was definitely a light in a whole lot of darkness."[13] Photographs of Elijah playing his violin to the animals in a local shelter during his lunch break circulated the internet in the months following his death. "He had a child-like spirit," another long-time client says. "Elijah McClain was not conditioned to the norms of America. . . . He was never into, like, fitting in. He just was who he was."[14] Here we come to the heart of the matter, occasioned by an honest reckoning with Christ crucified at the boundaries between personal and social freedom, individual and corporate sin. Elijah McClain, thanks be to God, "was not conditioned to the norms of America." Neither was Sandra Bland, who refused to accommodate herself—her body, her dignity, her agency—to a bullying police officer, lights flashing, taser drawn, bearing down on her with all the power and arrogance of the state. Three days later she was found hanging dead in her jail cell.[15] *To what extent have I become conditioned to the norms of America*, resting comfortably in the assurance that neither I, nor my children, nor anyone I love, could ever be subjected to the same fate?[16]

The cross of Jesus, Jesuit theologian Jon Sobrino reminds us, "before being *the* cross, is *a* cross and . . . there have been many more before and after it." Sobrino is right to add a fourth question to our

---

[13] Marna Arnett, quoted in Grant Stringer, "Those Who Knew Elijah Balk at Aurora Police Account of His Death," *Aurora Sentinel* (October 27, 2019), https://sentinel colorado.com/news/metro/unlikely-suspect-those-who-knew-elijah-balk-at-aurora -police-account-of-his-death/ (accessed December 30, 2021).

[14] April Young, quoted in Stringer, "Those Who Knew Elijah."

[15] See Christopher Pramuk, "On Not Following the Script: The Defiant Dignity of Sandra Bland," HopeSingsSoBeautiful.org (July 26, 2015), https://www.hopesings sobeautiful.org/2015/07/26/on-not-following-the-script-the-defiant-dignity-of -sandra-bland/.

[16] To be conditioned to the norms of white supremacy—and the corresponding benefits of white privilege—would in Ignatian terms be a "disordered attachment," a terrible lack of "indifference," a betrayal of God's gratuitous love and mercy with grave consequences for ourselves and certainly for the victims of injustice.

reckoning with sin during the First Week of the Exercises: "What am I doing to take the crucified peoples down from the cross?"[17] Like so many of Jesus's parables and teachings—think of the Good Samaritan story, or the judgment scene of Matthew 25, "Whatsoever you do to the least of my brothers and sisters"—the colloquy with Christ as he is dying on the cross draws the scope of our freedom into a wider field of vision that, once seen, cannot be unseen. I can no longer behold the suffering of my neighbor without at once beholding the face of Christ, Emmanuel, the humanity of God with us. Elijah McClain has become for me an almost unbearably tender icon of Christ crucified; he is Wisdom-Sophia, God unveiled in the rejected cornerstone, the divine Child who plays "hide and seek" within all the people, daring us not to conform to the dictates of a rapacious and violent society. Like a lamb led to the slaughter, She says, "I love you," and "I'm just different," and "Why are you attacking me?" in the face of the world's power.[18]

The "gift of tears," or *penthos*, an idea richly explored in ancient Christian monasticism, expresses a spiritual wisdom embraced by many religious traditions that the capacity for grief is crucial in our path to growth and transformation. As Doug Christie writes of the desert mothers and fathers, tears of grief and "compunction" signaled "a willingness to open oneself to [the reality of sin], to mourn for what had been lost or was in danger of being lost, and to open oneself to the possibility of renewal, regeneration."[19] To put it negatively, an individual's or a society's incapacity or refusal to grieve what is lost to us when an Elijah McClain or Tamir Rice or Breonna Taylor no

---

[17] See Jon Sobrino, *The Principle of Mercy: Taking the Crucified People from the Cross* (Maryknoll, NY: Orbis Books, 1994).

[18] The controversy surrounding an icon displayed at Catholic University of America depicting George Floyd's dead body being held by his mother, in the style of traditional pieta imagery of Christ and Mary, suggests that not everyone is comfortable with the identification of Christ with Black victims like Floyd or Elijah McClain. See Nate Tinner-Williams, "'Needless Controversy and Confusion': CUA President Cancels George Floyd Icon Following Second Theft," *Black Catholic Messenger* (December 22, 2021), https://www.blackcatholicmessenger.com/cua-garvey-george-floyd-icon-canceled/.

[19] Doug Christie, *The Blue Sapphire of the Mind: Notes for a Contemplative Ecology* (New York: Oxford University Press, 2013), 76. Cf. the Spiritual Exercises, nos. 203, 206, and 316, which gesture to tears of grief as a means of consolation, the flowering of deepening love for and solidarity with the suffering Christ.

longer walk the earth has little hope for authentic peace, renewal, regeneration. It was Nietzsche, suggests Metz, who inverted Jesus's beatitude, "Blessed are those who mourn," to its cynical corollary under the blind will to power, "Blessed are the forgetful."[20]

The norms of white supremacy dictate such amnesia. They counter that I am innocent of Elijah McClain's death; that Sandra Bland should never have resisted the officer; that Eric Garner, Ahmaud Arbery, and George Floyd were all petty criminals who brought their deaths upon themselves. My defense, as a white person, may take the form of the shocked bystander, "Lord, when did I see you unjustly imprisoned, denied your dignity, presumed guilty because of your name, your zip code, the color of your skin?" Or that of Cain, whose claims of innocence and ignorance about his brother's death—"Am I my brother's keeper?"—seem prerequisite in the cynical climate of American power politics today. Both strategies, as Pope Francis laments, trap the imagination in a bubble of solipsism, untruth, and indifference. "We have become used to the suffering of others; it doesn't affect me; it doesn't concern me; it's none of my business!"[21] "Any man who is capable of being satisfied with himself as he is," wrote Friedrich Schleiermacher, "will always manage to find a way out of the argument."[22]

---

[20] See Johann Baptist Metz et al., in *The End of Time? The Provocation of Talking about God* (Mahwah, NJ: Paulist Press, 2005), 37–38. Metz describes mourning not as weakness but in biblical terms as a mark of Israel's intensely covenantal relationship (and often intense wrestling) with God. "Mourning is hope in resistance . . . [resisting] the forgetfulness of the forgotten that goes by the name of progress and development among us. . . . Have we left ourselves, and others, in the dark about the biblical meaning of consolation?" (Metz, *Passion for God*, 160).

[21] Pope Francis, Homily During the Visit to Lampedusa, July 8, 2013, https://www.vatican.va/content/francesco/en/homilies/2013/documents/papa-francesco_20130708_omelia-lampedusa.html.

[22] Friedrich Schleiermacher, *The Christian Faith* (Edinburgh: T&T Clark, 1989), 69. As I write these lines, the newly sworn-in governor of Virginia has just issued an executive order "to restore excellence in education by ending the use of divisive concepts, including Critical Race Theory (CRT), in public education." Several other states have also banned the teaching of CRT, described as "political indoctrination" by the governor. Exhibit B is the controversy surrounding *The New York Times*'s 1619 Project and its lead creator, Nikole Hannah-Jones. Never has Walter Benjamin's famous dictum—"History is written by the victors"—seemed so dangerously prescient in the US.

The genius of the Spiritual Exercises is precisely their refusal of all argument. In their reordering of freedom's attachments, the Exercises appeal not foremost to the head, to humane ideals, ethical principles, or even cherished dogma; they draw us into the heart, the realm of desire and love—and yes, shame and confusion—by way of the imagination.[23] John Henry Newman had it right: "The heart is commonly reached, not through the reason, but through the imagination, by means of direct impressions, by the testimony of facts and events, by history, by description. Persons influence us, voices melt us, looks subdue us, deeds inflame us. . . . Christianity is a history supernatural, and almost scenic: it tells us what its Author is, by telling us what He has done."[24] Indeed, Newman celebrates the Spiritual Exercises for their wholesale immersion, "from below," as it were, in the actual life of Christ. Not incidentally, the Negro spirituals mediate the same kind of intimacy with Jesus, his suffering, his kindness, his mercy. An elderly Black man, speaking of the power of the spirituals and the "ring shout" that still echo from the prayer houses of rural Charleston, puts it this way: "I think singing is the key that opens the heavenly door."[25]

In short, much like the spirituals, the "logic" of the Spiritual Exercises is not logical at all. It says that God and humanity are united to a degree we could never have thought possible, and that love, mercy, and compassion are the deepest laws of our being. It says that God meets our sin, truthfully acknowledged and sincerely turned away from, with gratuitous forgiveness, setting our freedom free, as it were, from the prison of shame, self-loathing, and paralysis. If in each of the First Week's meditations we are to pray for the grace of shame over what our sin has done to the world, they end with "an exclamation of wonder and surging emotion" with the realization that we

---

[23] "For, what fills and satisfies the soul consists, not in knowing much, but in our understanding the realities profoundly and in savoring them interiorly." See *Ignatius of Loyola*, no. 2, p. 121. "I do not theologize about the redemptive significance of Calvary," writes Jesuit Walter Burghardt. "I link a pierced hand to mine." See Burghardt's classic essay, "Contemplation: A Long Loving Look at the Real," in *An Ignatian Spirituality Reader*, ed. George W. Traub, SJ (Chicago: Loyola Press, 2008), 89–98.

[24] John Henry Newman, *An Essay in Aid of a Grammar of Assent* (Notre Dame, IN: University of Notre Dame, 1979), 89, 91–92.

[25] See "The Ring Shout and the Birth of African American Religion," from *Eyes on the Prize: America's Civil Rights Years* (PBS/Blackside, 1987).

are still held and loved into existence; that indeed, the angels and saints "have interceded and prayed for me," and even "the heavens, the sun, the moon, the stars, and the elements; the fruits, birds, fishes and animals," and more, the earth itself, have conspired with God not to "swallow me up" in eternal suffering.[26] In the life of Christ, says Newman, with no small wonder, "we are allowed to discern the attributes of the Invisible God, drawn out into action in accommodation to our weakness."[27] We are saved not in spite of our brokenness but because of it.

Moreover, by engaging the imagination with a history "almost scenic," the Exercises comprise a powerful school for empathy, nurturing our capacity and willingness (i.e., our freedom), in the pattern of Christ, to place ourselves inside the life-worlds of others.

> *What would it feel like to die by suffocation, bystanders crying out, an officer's knee pressed into my neck? (Surely, I, too, would cry out for my mother.) If Elijah McClain were my own son, how would I go on living? How would my life be different had I been born and raised in the projects of the South Bronx; the Lakota reservation of Pine Ridge, South Dakota; the streets of South Central LA? How would my kids' lives be different?*

Expanding to the social relationships and political discernments that bind us:

> *Who can help me to understand the memory of this place? What would they say is required for life to flourish in this environment? What gifts remain hidden under a bushel basket, beneath histories of neglect, economic and political inequity, misuse of the soil and trees, air and rivers? Dare we begin to imagine together what is yet possible?*

To imagine together and thus to expand our vision of the possible: these are the marks of freedom's growth into the *magis* of divine-human partnership, the invitation to order our desires and gifts to the "greater glory of God" in this, our moment in history. The Exercises presume our capacity to discover ourselves in the ever-moving dance of multiple freedoms, co-creators with God in what the Hebrew

---

[26] See *Ignatius of Loyola*, nos. 59–60, pp. 139–40.
[27] John Henry Newman, *Fifteen Sermons Preached Before the University of Oxford* (Notre Dame, IN: University of Notre Dame Press, 1997), 26.

Bible calls "covenant," Dr. King calls "Beloved Community," Jesuit Fr. Greg Boyle calls "kinship," and Jesus of Nazareth calls the "Reign of God."[28]

It is important to note that Sobrino's addendum to the contemplation of Christ on the cross during the First Week—"What are we doing to take the crucified peoples down from the cross?"—has not yet taken on flesh, the dynamic of Weeks Two, Three, and Four of the Exercises. In other words, the "crucified peoples" can easily remain for us an abstraction, faceless objects of a moral command, rather than subjects of a burgeoning desire to join with others in building beloved community. I haven't yet come to know my sisters and brothers by their real names, their joys and hopes, enfleshed in their life stories, their music, poetry, food, dance, and worship. Nor have I yet discovered the deepest gospel paradox of all: that my happiness, my joy, my flourishing, is bound up with theirs, just as my sin, my selfishness, my social myopia, is bound up with theirs.[29]

"Hope not only imagines; it *imagines with* others," writes the Jesuit William Lynch.[30] Despite the dictates of American individualism, the myth of the self-made man, the Hollywood superhero (or machine) who needs no one, there is no shame in acknowledging our dependence on others, our mutual need for help. Again, Lynch: "The truth is that hope is related to help in such a way that you cannot talk about one without talking of the other. Hope is truly on the inside of us, but hope is an interior sense that there is help on the outside of us."[31]

[28] The "diseased social imagination," by contrast, renders people hopeless, incapable of imagining "a way out of no way," much less building a path forward with others. See Willie James Jennings, *The Christian Imagination: Theology and the Origins of Race* (New Haven, CT: Yale University Press, 2010), 6–9, 58–59, 208, 250.

[29] Encounter "is the key to truth," insists Pope Francis. "Because truth is not only the definition of situations and things from a certain distance, by abstract and logical reasoning. It is more than that. Truth is also fidelity. It makes you name people with their real name, as the Lord names them, before categorizing them or defining 'their situation.'" Pope Francis, "Homily for Holy Thursday Chrism Mass," March 29, 2018. https://www.vatican.va/content/francesco/en/homilies/2018/documents/papa-francesco_20180329_omelia-crisma.html# (accessed August 5, 2023).

[30] William Lynch, *Images of Hope: Imagination as Healer of the Hopeless* (Baltimore: Helicon Press, 1965), 23.

[31] Lynch, *Images of Hope*, 40. The Second Week of the Exercises facilitates the healing of imagination in the realization that there is indeed "help on the outside of us." With meditations like the Two Standards and the Three Degrees of Loving Humility, we are invited into a deep, imaginative reordering of desire in solidarity with Jesus.

As Ignatius himself would learn, from his convalescence at Loyola to his studies at the University of Paris, our vision of the possible is enlarged by discerning with others and acting in mutual encouragement and collaboration. Once the headstrong *hidalgo*, Ignatius laid down his sword at the foot of the Black Madonna of Montserrat, recognizing with painstaking humility—a dying to self-absorption that would consume him for many months at Manresa—that he would need her grace to overcome his disordered affections, including the impulse to religious arrogance and violence.[32]

For white Christians, to lose oneself under the Black cross in America (or the Black Madonna!) is to begin to find oneself in the joy of an enlarged sense of kinship; it is to be known, loved, and forgiven, by our real name.[33] Whether in the classroom, churches, or streets—as in the protests that swept the country following the murder of George Floyd—it is to make of our lives a work of art, a poem of solidarity and sacrificial love. "The revolutionaries, whether on the right or the left, will attack and destroy," writes Lynch. "Persons of imagination will imagine; they will build and compose. . . . They will not fall back on simple thrusts of the will but on acts of imagination."[34] The women who tended to his physical and spiritual healing at Loyola; Our Lady of Montserrat; his companions in the newly established Society of Jesus; all of these were pivotal in Ignatius's journey from "I" to "we." For white Christians, the first step may be to pray for the courage to "crossover" into unfamiliar communities, from whom the Spirit is calling us to learn what it means to imagine, build, and compose another possible world.[35]

---

[32] See the incident with the "Moor" on the road to Montserrat, for example, which nearly incited Ignatius to murder.

[33] This is largely the argument of my book *Hope Sings, So Beautiful*. On the Black Madonna and the feminine divine, see *Hope Sings*, 115–18; also Christopher Pramuk, *At Play in Creation: Merton's Awakening to the Feminine Divine* (Collegeville, MN: Liturgical Press, 2015), especially 51–58, 81–85.

[34] William Lynch, "Death as Nothingness," *Continuum* 5 (1967): 459–69, at 459–60. Lynch continues, "This in fact should be a great goal of the universities (and seminaries), to turn out men who know what is the matter and who are intent on acts of imagination which will try to do something about it" (460).

[35] See Pramuk, *Hope Sings*, 45–51, 147–53. In his encyclical letter *Fratelli Tutti: On Fraternity and Social Friendship*, Pope Francis uses the term "social poets" to describe persons or social movements who act as "sowers of change, promoters of a process involving millions of actions, great and small, creatively intertwined like words in a poem" (no. 169). He applies this same language movingly—"our poetic capacity, our

In sum, the sin that Ignatius would have us confront during the First Week may well be our own or others' acts of overt racial aggression or insensitivity ("what I/we have done"), or, it may be more habitual, unconscious failures of imagination, courage, and creativity ("what I/we have failed to do") in the face of white supremacy—another term, by the way, that risks paralysis by abstraction. Not to put too fine a point on it, but I haven't the faintest idea how to respond concretely in freedom and love to the "crucified peoples," to "white supremacy," or even to "white privilege." I do know how to relate to other human beings with names and families, hopes and dreams, like mine, for a better world. Again, much as in the Good Samaritan parable (Luke 10:25-37), Jesus's advice to the rich young man (Mark 10:17-31), or any number of gospel stories, this means finding creative and sometimes costly ways to cross the barriers that divide us, including the categorical ones, the labels that keep us at a distance.[36] In the end, as Thomas Merton wrote to a young peace activist in 1966, when the sickness of society runs bone-deep, when citizens "are fed on myths" by mass media, bombarded by slogans and can no longer think straight, "it is the reality of personal relationships that saves everything."[37] Because the disease of white supremacy is both personal and structural, so must be the conversion that leads to its cure.

This brings us back to those three damning words, "I can't breathe," spoken into the void of death at the hands of white power. If I am not wrong in my interpretation of the First Week to suggest that white Christians should embrace and not flee from the grace of "shame and confusion" at the foot of the Black cross, one may still reasonably ask how shame can be for us a vehicle of grace? Indeed, how can it be anything but paralyzing in our movement toward active, empathic,

---

capacity to dream together"—to the George Floyd protests in his address to the World Meeting of Popular Movements, October 16, 2021. For a montage of images accompanying this address, see Catholic News Service, "Pope Likens George Floyd Protests to Good Samaritan Parable," October 18, 2021, https://www.youtube.com/watch?v=hyWFr0Qmqs8.

[36] See Pope Francis on the "culture of the adjective," "Homily for Holy Thursday Chrism Mass," n. 29 above.

[37] Letter to Jim Forest, in Thomas Merton, *The Hidden Ground of Love: Letters on Religious Experience and Social Concerns*, ed. William H. Shannon (New York: Farrar, Straus and Giroux, 1985), 294–97.

solidaristic love? Under the dynamic of the First Week, would Christ desire that I bear responsibility for the deaths of the nine church members gunned down by a twenty-one-year-old white supremacist during Bible study at Mother Emanuel AME Church? Would he further hold me accountable for the "white collar violence" that disproportionately traps communities of color in multigenerational poverty, despair, mass incarceration, and violence?[38] And in the end, to what extent are such interior exercises in (white) self-examination—if not self-flagellation—actually *helpful* for the (Black) living, much less for the dead? In short, is shame the best vehicle for the personal and cultural *metanoia* we desire to see? If Ignatius would be our guide, the answer to this last question, I believe, is yes, though a carefully qualified yes. A sense of shame, grief, or guilt can indeed be a transformative grace, a necessary and liberating first moment in the path to reconciliation and solidarity in the work of justice, so long as it is not the last moment.

"Shame," of course, can mean very different things. There is the kind of shame that comes over us in the honest appraisal of our sins, when I face the full truth of how my actions, or failure to act, has harmed others. And there is the kind of shame that descends over us when we have been shamed by others, whether by our actions or inactions, or worse, because of *who we are*, irrespective of our actions. The former can be healthy, healing, reconciling, a first step to living in the truth. The latter is never healthy, and almost always about power. Its energy is debilitating, effectively saying to the one shamed, "Grovel all you want. You can never say you're sorry enough because I'll never let you off the hook." Or worse, "Because of who you are,

---

[38] "Few of us would admit to wanting to murder another human being. And yet we allow a societal system to exist that literally kills people of color, through lack of good medical care, unequal legal rights, and the effects of poverty." Patrick Saint-Jean, SJ, *The Spiritual Work of Racial Justice: A Month of Meditations with Ignatius of Loyola* (Vestal, NY: Anamchara Books, 2021), 54. I borrow the term "white collar violence" from Thomas Merton's remarkable essay, "Toward a Theology of Resistance." "[It] must be remembered that the crime that breaks out of the ghetto is only the fruit of a greater and more pervasive violence: the injustice which forces people to live in the ghetto in the first place. The problem of violence, then, is not the problem of a few rioters and rebels, but the problem of a whole social structure which is outwardly ordered and respectable, and inwardly ridden by psychopathic obsessions and delusions." See Thomas Merton, *Faith and Violence: Christian Teaching and Christian Practice* (Notre Dame, IN: University of Notre Dame, 1968), 3–13, at 3–4.

you are *already guilty*, disordered, dangerous, irredeemable, the enemy." To internalize such a message from other people—to say nothing of religion or the church—is death to the human spirit. There is a merciless, puritan streak in American culture that seems to me, in Ignatian terms, frankly demonic. From the right or left, it takes pleasure in categorizing, attacking, punishing, and shaming, with no concern for persons, and certainly little thought of mutuality, growth in understanding, or forgiveness on the way to reconciliation and common purpose.[39]

"When God tells you of a sickness," writes Thomas Merton, "it is because He means, at the same time, to provide a remedy. It is the Devil who tells us that we are ill and taunts us for it, reminds us of our helplessness by making us even more helpless."[40] Commenting on Jesus's response to the woman caught in the act of adultery (John 8:1-11), Howard Thurman notes that Jesus did not shame or condemn her. He "met the woman where she was, and he treated her as if she were already where she willed to be. In dealing with her he 'believed' her into the fulfillment of her possibilities. He stirred her confidence into activity. He placed a crown over her head which for the rest of her life she would keep trying to grow tall enough to wear. *'Free at last, free at last. Thank God Almighty, I'm free at last.'*"[41] As to the persons ready to stone her, Jesus disarmed their righteous anger with a deep breath, writing in the dirt, and a pointed invitation to self-examination.

---

[39] See Michael Eric Dyson, "Where Is the Forgiveness and Grace in Cancel Culture?," written on the occasion of Desmond Tutu's death, *The New York Times* (December 28, 2021), https://www.nytimes.com/2021/12/28/opinion/desmond-tutu-america-justice.html. Few thinkers have diagnosed the destructive "absolutizing instinct" in American culture more effectively, in my view, than William Lynch. See the excellent study by John F. Kane, *Building the Human City: William F. Lynch's Ignatian Spirituality for Public Life* (Eugene, OR: Pickwick, 2016).

[40] Thomas Merton, journal of March 3, 1953, cited in *The Intimate Merton: His Life from His Journals*, ed. Patrick Hart and Jonathan Montaldo (New York: HarperCollins, 1999), 113. Cf. *Ignatius of Loyola*, Spiritual Exercises, no. 315: "[It] is characteristic of the evil spirit to cause gnawing anxiety, to sadden, and to set up obstacles" for those who are progressing "from good to better in the service of God our Lord" (201). Ignatius came to realize that his struggle with scruples at Manresa—an inability to accept God's (or his own) forgiveness for past sins, which nearly drove him to suicide—was not from God but from the evil spirit, "the enemy of our human nature."

[41] Howard Thurman, *Jesus and the Disinherited* (Nashville: Abingdon Press, 1949), 106.

Perhaps more than any other thinker, the late Canadian Catholic theologian Gregory Baum has helped me sort out my own complex feelings as a white Christian around the question of guilt. Baum dedicated much of his career to examining the relationship between Christianity and politics, faith and culture, the public dimensions of a believer's life. Born in Germany in 1923, the son of Jewish mother, his family fled to Canada in 1940 as war refugees. Writing about that war and the church's complicity in the Shoah, Baum proposes a distinction between "guilt by personal implication," which means to knowingly participate in sinful structures or refuse to resist them, and "guilt by common heritage," which applies to persons or communities who, even if not personally implicated, may still "willingly share in the burden of guilt" because they share "a common heritage and are spiritually identified" with those who are (or were) personally responsible for history's atrocities. As an example of the latter, Baum points to young Germans who were not alive during World War II and yet strongly believe that they must assume the heavy burden of past evils. Why? "Without grieving over the past, they argue, people cannot come to a truthful understanding of the present nor adopt a responsible orientation to the future."[42]

I could hardly say it better as to why I believe white Americans are called to grieve and bear responsibility for the legacy and ongoing scourge of racial injustice in American society. To assume a share of culpability, as Baum suggests, is not always about guilt or shame in the proper sense, though it may be that. Often, "it is more aptly described as grieving or sorrowing," the readiness to mourn, and a keener sense of personal responsibility."[43] Young people in Germany are taught the hard truths of their history—made to stand squarely on the German "ground beneath the cross"—and as such, are educated from their youth with an acute awareness of the dangers that fascist groupthink and racist "othering" pose to a humane society. Jesuit theologian Karl Rahner, himself exiled from Germany during the war, put it this way: "There are no islands [where we do not already]

[42] Gregory Baum, *Essays in Critical Theology* (Kansas City, MO: Sheed & Ward, 1994), 199–200.

[43] Baum, *Essays in Critical Theology*, 200. Cf. Saint-Jean, *Spiritual Work of Racial Justice*, 232–34, on the importance of emotions for Ignatius, including anger, as "the passion that moves the will to justice" (Aquinas).

bear the stamp of the guilt of others, directly or indirectly, from close or from afar."[44] Rabbi Abraham Joshua Heschel, who barely escaped Europe in 1940 and would lose his mother and several sisters to the Nazis, put it succinctly: "Some are guilty, all are responsible."[45]

The fact that the Spiritual Exercises do not rely on rational arguments to link our freedom with the sufferings of the world does not mean that there are not convincing arguments to be made. Indeed, as Baum's example of young people in Germany suggests, one would think that an honest look at the bare facts of American history—the literal and cultural erasure of Native Americans, the internment of Japanese Americans and the rise of anti-Asian hate crimes today, the gutting of the Voting Rights Act and the systematic suppression of the vote targeting communities of color—would be enough to convict any thinking person, religious or not, with their eyes half-open. Alas, the very notion of a "common heritage" that binds us across diverse identities seems ever more tenuous in our dangerously balkanized political landscape. While we need more than ever to find ways to cultivate rational and unifying public discourse, I would like to conclude by reiterating the pivotal role of imagination, affect, and desire in Ignatius's vision of *metanoia*, and by extension, the importance of Black literature and theology, music and the arts, as a vehicle for the conversion of white Christians. Such multivalent expressions of Black experience, which speak powerfully to both head and heart, have been for me an enduring source of renewed vision of what is possible for God and human beings. To recall David Tracy, the classics of Black literature and music especially, "now subtly, now compellingly," have transformed my "perception of the real" in profoundly immersive ways, akin to the dynamic of the Spiritual Exercises.[46]

---

[44] Karl Rahner, *Foundations of Christian Faith* (New York: Crossroads, 1978), 109.

[45] Abraham Joshua Heschel, *Moral Grandeur and Spiritual Audacity: Essays*, ed. Susannah Heschel (New York: Farrar, Straus and Giroux, 1996), 231. For a thoroughly Ignatian treatment of guilt, forgiveness, and what he calls a "humanizing shame and confusion" in the face of unjust suffering of the poor and in light of middle-class privilege, see Dean Brackley, *The Call to Discernment in Troubled Times* (New York: Crossroad, 2004), 29–38. "The outcast calls forth from within us parts of ourselves that we have banished into unconscious exile, and heals us" (36).

[46] On using these resources in the undergraduate classroom, see Christopher Pramuk, "The Question of God in the Struggle for Racial Justice," *Horizons* 48, no. 1 (June 2021): 172–94; Pramuk, *The Artist Alive: Explorations in Music, Art and Theology* (Winona, MN: Anselm Academic, 2019), chaps. 5 and 6; and Pramuk, "Proximity,

Let me offer a last glimpse of a work of art that has helped to situate me, my students, and many others, at the foot of the Black cross in America. In 1998, Denver sculptor Jan Van Ek was commissioned by a local church to create a crucifix with a corpus depicting Christ as an African American man. Using a life-cast of a Denver native, she created an arresting, larger-than-life bronze sculpture of the crucified Christ, whose features are clearly African.[47] The church that requested the work was unable to complete its part in the commission, and the sculpture languished for years in the workroom of the foundry where it was cast. Some ten years later, foundry owner Ray Fedde donated the sculpture to Regis University, a Jesuit university in the heart of northwest Denver, where I teach. Fedde also fabricated a massive steel cross for its installation. In August 2010, the crucifix was installed in a meditation garden just west of the St. John Francis Regis Chapel, against a panoramic view of the mountains and surrounded by native plantings. Known as the "Black Jesus" in the Regis community, the work has become a pilgrimage site for many, from students and staff seeking a quiet place for prayer, to faculty bringing their class for discussion around the flagstone table at the foot of the cross. Why?

Let me suggest one possibility in the words of New Testament scholar N. T. Wright. "When art comes to terms with both the wounds of the world and the promise of resurrection, and learns how to express and respond to both at once, we will be on the way to a fresh vision, a fresh mission."[48] For white Americans and for white followers of Jesus, the Black crucifix holds us before the wounds of a people,

---

Disruption, and Grace: Notes for a Pedagogy of Racial Justice and Reconciliation," in *You Say You Want a Revolution? 1968–2018 in Theological Perspective*, ed. Susie Paulik Babka, Elena Procario-Foley, and Sandra Yocum (Maryknoll, NY: Orbis Books, 2019), 135–57. On Ignatian spirituality in the life and art of iconographer Fr. William Hart McNichols, including the identification of Christ crucified with LGBTQ persons, see *Artist Alive*, chap. 8; and Michael O'Laughlin, *Hidden Mercy: AIDS, Catholics, and the Untold Stories of Compassion in the Face of Fear* (Minneapolis: Broadleaf, 2021), especially chap. 18, "AIDS Crucifixion."

[47] An image of the sculpture can be seen on the second page of "Regis University Visual Art": https://static1.squarespace.com/static/55d1dd88e4b0dee65a6594f0/t/5604369ee4b01128f1904c21/1443116702380/Regis-Art+at+Regis.pdf.

[48] See N. T. Wright, *Surprised by Hope* (New York: HarperCollins, 1989), 222–24. The insight speaks just as pointedly, I think, to the distinctive mission of Jesuit universities and educational apostolates like Regis.

our African American brothers and sisters—the Christ of the First Week. That it does so in a setting of abundant life, and in winter, the promise of new life breaking forth from seeming barrenness, is not incidental. Like the broken gravestones at Mepkin Abbey, we encounter Christ crucified in an earthen landscape that says, as wind stirs in the aspens surrounding Jesus, "Behold, death is not the last word"—the Christ, and the grace, of the Fourth Week. "Hope," writes biblical scholar Walter Brueggemann, "must be told, in image, in figure, in poem, in vision. It must be told sideways, told as one who dwells with the others in the abyss."[49] His way of love, though rent with pain, is beautiful.

Some months ago, a faculty colleague shared the following story. "I was speaking with a new pharmacy student who was visiting Regis with his African American stepfather. During the campus tour, when he encountered the crucified Black Jesus near the chapel, he filled up with tears, and said, 'This place must be committed to racial justice to have art like this on the campus.' " There it is again: the unsettling, and at once consoling, gift of tears. As a white faculty member and committed Catholic, I can only hope that Regis embodies the truth of those words in our collective work as a university and in the daily lives of our students. From an Ignatian view, it should be said, there is no single blueprint or uniform way for people of faith, nor for a university community, to respond rightly to the unsettling reality of racial injustice. Each of us, just as every Jesuit apostolate, will be called according to the distinct gifts we have to offer in response to the challenges, opportunities, and limitations that concretely face us and the society we serve. Still, I hope the discussion above is enough to suggest the following Ignatian insights that can guide the way of *metanoia* and discernment across diverse situations.

First, if you are white, don't run from the crosses carried by communities of color. Read and listen intently to the stories of people of color. Look intently at your own privilege. Ask God for the grace of understanding, empathy, and courageous imagination.

Second, don't run from your own racial biases and limitations, fears and failures. See them, name them, and ask God—and those you

---

[49] Walter Brueggemann, *Disruptive Grace: Reflections on God, Scripture and the Church,* ed. Carolyn J. Sharp (Minneapolis: Fortress, 2011), 153.

may have offended—for the grace to make peace with them. In the words of Rumi, the great Sufi poet, "The dark thought, the shame, the malice, / meet them at the door laughing, / and invite them in." Be grateful to learn from them, and then release them. Resolve that each day, through the struggle itself, you can become a new creation.[50]

Third, resist the temptation to judge others from a privileged distance. Proximity is God's doorway to grace. Find ways to draw near, to initiate encounters with the most vulnerable and marginalized communities. And then, repeat steps one through three. What once was novel and frightening can become a life-changing spiritual exercise, a source of fulfillment and joy, a habit of being. "Religion, the end of isolation, begins with a consciousness that something is asked of us,"[51] says Rabbi Abraham Joshua Heschel. Ignatian spirituality at its most exciting and most authentic, I believe, is a response to that covenantal call.

Lastly, look for beauty in others and beauty will overwhelm you. Radiate kindness and it will come back to you, seventy times seven. Pray for mercy and mercy will be given you. In sum, contemplate what is and dare to imagine what is yet possible. Together, in freedom and grace, we can become a new creation, pilgrims in the way of justice, reconciliation, and love.[52]

---

[50] The term *metanoia* in the New Testament, notes the Catholic ethicist Fr. Bryan Massingale, means "more than a mere change." It denotes a "profound *about face*," an "evolution" into a new creation in Christ Jesus (2 Cor 5:17), who dwells with us in the abyss. Akin to the transformation of a caterpillar into butterfly, "God wants us to be more than we think we can be," says Massingale, but such transformation will not be easy. It involves "the death of an old way of being," and thus anticipates the resurrection, not a mere "resuscitation." Bryan Massingale, keynote address to the Ignatian Family Teach-In, November 6, 2021, at https://www.youtube.com/watch?v=327QS9xXIj8&t=5s.

[51] Abraham Joshua Heschel, *Man Is Not Alone: A Philosophy of Religion* (New York: Farrar, Straus and Giroux, 1951), 68–69.

[52] For the development of a number of key ideas in this chapter I am especially indebted to William Hart (Fr. Bill) McNichols, Notre Dame scholar J. Matthew Ashley, and my Regis University friend and colleague, Jason Taylor.

7

Resting Under the Standard of Christ

The Spiritual Exercises and Discerning White Supremacy

Maureen H. O'Connell

In the spring semester of 2021, the academic leadership team at my university decided to forgo spring break week in order to avoid a spike in Covid infections on campus. This left us with more "contact hours" of instruction than needed, so leadership built three "academic enrichment days" into the academic calendar. Rather than convene formal classes, on these days students would engage in extracurricular learning activities designed by groups of faculty. As a member of the university's Anti-Racist Working Group (ARWG), I was invited to pull together a team to create an enrichment day about Lasallian commitments to anti-racism.

The prospect excited me. After years of collaborating with colleagues to design and offer programming for students and faculty this seemed like a great opportunity revisit our repository of resources. I thought we could dust off a template we had used for a day-long "Teach in for Racial Justice" in the Spring of 2017. I started imagining how we could build out that program to include all kinds of things: conversations with neighbors, social justice walking tours of campus, a lunch-time workshop for colleagues, a guided sitting meditation, an art exhibit in our university museum. My mind was off to the races.

My colleagues' responses pulled me up short. They had little interest in creating additional academic programming for a semester that was already too long, too full with managing the impact of Covid on our students, too taxing with meeting the needs of their families. They were too busy doing the work of reckoning with the legacy of racism on our campus via a Joint Commission the President and our Faculty Senate had organized to assess our situation and offer ways forward.[1] Some were frustrated by the obtuseness to these realities that the ask signaled. But when one colleague suggested the very request was an expression of the racism we were trying to resist with our work on the ARWG, I was taken aback. How could an institutional commitment to holding space for academic engagement around racism and anti-racism be racist, particularly in light of demands from people of color in our institution that we demonstrate commitments to our mission, that we *do* something? How could an invitation to bring the gifts we had to that kind of collective effort be racist, especially in light of course evaluations of teaching that suggest our students rather regularly encounter racism with our faculty? How could I be participating in a culture of white body supremacy with my willingness to facilitate my colleagues' engagement if I was more than willing to do the heavy lifting such an endeavor would require? I was flummoxed and flatfooted, once again, by my whiteness.

Ignatius clearly knew the swirl of temptation in situations like this. Throughout his Spiritual Exercises, he creates space for retreatants to meditate on the "Two Standards." Ignatius invites us to imagine a battlefield with two armies amassing: one under the banner or standard of Christ, one under the banner of Satan. Which standard, Ignatius prompts, will you choose? At first, the answer seems fairly straightforward. Of course, if presented such a clear choice on the moral battlefields of our lives, we're going to choose Christ's side of the equation. But if Ignatius invites meditation on this scene four different times in his Spiritual Exercises, perhaps the decision is not as easy as we think, especially when the temptation luring us away from Christ and toward Satan is a sense of self, others, and the good warped by white body supremacy.

---

[1] See La Salle University's Joint Commission on Diversity, Equity, and Inclusion: https://www.lasalle.edu/mission-and-heritage/joint-commission/.

The Two Standards meditation can help me recognize the insidious ways that white body supremacy permeates so many of the choices I make, especially when I believe that those choices are anchored in ideas about racial justice and in desires to advance it. This meditation also helps me to appreciate just how challenging discerning between good and evil really is in our culture of white body supremacy. Finally, it helps me recognize how those of us most committed to the work of anti-racism can unexpectedly find ourselves under the standard of Satan in that work.

In what follows, I will highlight some graces that Two Standard meditation can offer those of us either raced as white or attempting to stand with Christ in the context of institutional cultures of white body supremacy, especially Catholic ones. These became evident to me as I continue to reflect on my colleagues' alternative to that program-rich anti-racism enrichment day. "How about a day of rest," they proposed. "Rest is anti-racist." I'll suggest that rest is truly a spiritual discipline for many white people, especially white Catholics, and as such can be a tremendous resource for racial justice.

Discerning White Supremacy Via the Two Standards

The Two Standards meditation is in many ways autobiographical, as it reflects Ignatius's own story as a solider who once enjoyed and defended the vainglory ways of the world but who converted to equally militant service of the way of Christ. Roger Haight, SJ, notes how the very imaginative scene itself reflects the dualistic worldview of the time, as well as the primacy of the battle between good and evil with which Ignatius was familiar on personal and intellectual levels. "These alternate worldviews, cultures, programs or lifestyles," those of Christ and Satan, "become internalized in every person, define the divided self, and create the struggle between egoism and a self-transcending attraction to higher ideals."[2] Ultimately, according to Roger Dawson, SJ, the central probing question of the Two Standards meditation is this: "From where do I get my identity?"[3] Since

[2] Roger Haight, SJ, *Christian Spirituality for Seekers: Reflections on the Spiritual Exercises of Ignatius Loyola* (Maryknoll, NY: Orbis Books, 2012), 55–56.

[3] Roger Dawson, SJ, " 'Give Them Exactly What They Want': The Meditation on the Two Standards," September 2, 2011, https://www.thinkingfaith.org/articles/20110902_1.htm (accessed August 5, 2023).

racism is so wrapped up in identities—inherited and constructed, felt and performed, individual and collective—this seems a basic and yet fundamental question to ponder in the work of dismantling and reconstructing our approach to racial identities.

Dawson's interpretation of three aspects of this meditation can assist with discerning where the temptation of whiteness or white body supremacy—both personal and institutional—warps our self-understandings, distorts our sense of the good we are to pursue, including the good of racial justice, and hijacks the means by which we think we ought to pursue these goods.

Dawson's first element for discernment in the Two Standards meditation has to do with *poverty and our ability to respond to God.* The standard of Christ invites us to poverty—spiritual or actual—through an ongoing and critical attention to our relationship with our possessions. How free are we to discern and respond to Christ's ongoing call to discipleship? On the personal level, moving toward Christ entails asking ourselves whether we possess things or are possessed by them. The standard of Satan, on the other hand, "tempts people, often under the appearance of good, to covet riches," which end up displacing God from the center of attention or the ground of being.[4]

So how does this help us pay attention to the temptation of white supremacy? First, it can help us recognize white supremacy as idolatry and as such a primary violation of our covenantal relationship with God and others. Eddie Glaude defines white supremacy in terms of a value gap and habits, "which come to us in worlds not of our own making" that sustain it. In other words, white supremacy is the belief, socially constructed and passed down from generation to generation, "that white people are valued more than others" and "the things we do, without thinking" that perpetuate that belief.[5] The belief that white people are the most valuable of creation leads us to value white notions of God above all others, fashioning God into a particular image, and to associate godliness with those who share that image and dehumanizing those who do not. The belief in the value of white people above all else then compels us to sacrifice, often violently, facets of what it means to be human, as well as how to

---

[4] Dawson, "Meditation on Two Standards."

[5] Eddie Glaude Jr., *Democracy in Black: How Race Still Enslaves the American Soul* (New York: Penguin Random House, 2016), 6 and 183.

express that humanity, which don't fit the dominant mold of whiteness. The Two Standards meditation, then, asks us to discern our ultimate values vis a vis our own relationship to whiteness and how we live those values.

Moreover, the meditation can help us to discern better ways of relating to the goods afforded us by virtue of our racial identities. Certainly, this might entail making an inventory of the unearned social benefits we may receive simply because of our racial identity. But more importantly, we might think of these things as instruments for entering into nonviolent conflict with our cultures and systems of white supremacy. Choosing the standard of Christ invites us not only to be aware of benefits we accrue by virtue of our racial identity, but also how we use those benefits and privileges. Peggy McIntosh's famous image of the knapsack of white privilege comes to mind. The point of racial justice is not to deny the resources we receive by virtue of our racial identities but to ensure that all others share them as well.[6] This can apply to institutions: institutions fall under the standard of Satan when they "[foster] hierarchical and competitive social systems in which the lives of most are dominated by the few who reap an abundance of society's benefits while many go without adequate opportunities to achieve their self-fulfillment and fair share of the goods of God's creation." Those aligned with the standard of Christ "[foster] social systems of mutual understanding, personal subjectivity, freedom, and a true sense of humanity."[7]

A second aspect of Dawson's interpretation of the Two Standards pertains *to our understanding of the purpose of our lives*. In other words, the meditation asks us to reflect on how we are using our resources and power. Is it all about us or all about our relationships with others? Satan lures us into thinking that the point of our lives is to be highly regarded, which is particularly hard to avoid in our contemporary culture of social influencers in social media echo chambers. If our primary goal is to increase esteem through affirmation of and renumeration for our public allegiances to products, people, and ideologies—to be perceived as "woke" or "not racist" or "one of the good

---

[6] Peggy McIntosh, "White Privilege: Unpacking the Invisible Knapsack," in *Understanding Prejudice and Discrimination*, ed. Scott Plous (New York: McGraw-Hill, 2003), 191–96.

[7] Dawson, "Meditation on Two Standards."

white people"—then our imaginations will be held captive by the parameters of what already is. In these spaces, going viral, even with messages around anti-racism, is more prized than embodied candor and/or getting grounded in lived truths about belonging to each other. All of this undermines our awareness of our distinct gifts, as well as the means and ends to which we use them.

This temptation toward a life's purpose oriented around the ego only gets amplified in a culture of white supremacy, which for those of us who are raced as white manifests in internalized notions of our specialness, our superior intellect, and our moral goodness. Jeannine Hill Fletcher notes Ignatius's awareness to the central role such a temptation played for Christ himself: "like Jesus's critique of religious supremacies of his day, we might be reminded of the ever-present temptation to give in to another set of desires: the desires of symbolic capital that promise us (as they did Jesus in the desert) the rewards of glory, honor, credit, praise, and fame," which are a "constant pull" in the lives of humans and Christian communities too.[8] This under-tow warps our sense of agency and purpose in the world.

To stand under the banner of Christ, therefore, is to spend the ener-gies of one's life in service of an evolving process of becoming more human ourselves, as well as making sure that our systems and insti-tutions open that evolutionary process to others. The Two Standards meditation can help us tune in to the why and how of our commit-ments to anti-racism. Are our motivations for engaging in anti-racism work purely egocentric or self-interested or are we tuned into others' laments and dreams? Do we function in such a way that centers racial justice efforts on white experiences, particularly our own, or are we capable of collaboration that centers on others? Do we understand our impact on others in terms of public performances that signal a desire for attention and affirmation, or do we seek to make an impact through continually learning how to model justice for others through our actions?

Dawson's third interpretation of the Two Standards meditation asks to *look as honestly as possible at the impact of our choices on ourselves.* Do our choices cultivate pride or false senses of self-importance that

---

[8] Jeannine Hill Fletcher, *The Sin of White Supremacy: Christianity, Racism, and Reli-gious Diversity in America* (Maryknoll, NY: Orbis Books, 2017), 163.

buffer us from an ongoing accounting to people in pain, or do our choices humble us, fostering a humility that keeps us vulnerable and always ready to serve others? In other words, do we move toward the banner of Christ by being candid with ourselves, naming our failings and our mistakes, and committing to grow from them? Or do we armor up, to use the imagery of Pope Francis's "armor-plated selves," and remain stuck in rigid ideological postures under the banner of Satan?[9] Pope Francis posits this as the choice between awareness and ideology, in which he defines the former as "being conscious of what's at stake in the fate of humanity" and the latter in terms of "a prism through which we judge everything," or being "incapable of moving outside of [our] own little worlds."[10]

Racial justice activists rooted in the spiritual dimensions of both white supremacy and anti-racism concur and implicitly call our attention to the embodied dimension of the choice Ignatius presents to retreatants in the Two Standards meditation. "Supremacy systems want us to be ill-equipped to feel liberation, courage, hope and love," explains Jardena Peacock. "When we avoid the oppression, the pain and trauma, then we remain ill-equipped to step into that place of liberation. We show up as less of who we are. . . ."[11]

We need to take a break—a rest—from these ways of living, these ways of understanding ourselves, these ways of doing the work of justice.

Resting Under the Standard of Christ

Dan Berrigan, SJ, once told a group of Fordham first-year students, only a few hours into their orientation to the institution, the key lesson gained from his experiences with resisting the Vietnam War portrayed in *The Trial of the Catonsville Nine*: "Know what you stand for, and *stand* there." I'm struck by the ironic combination of extreme action and inaction in that koan. Surely, it takes ongoing effort to discern what our deepest commitments are and assess whether or

---

[9] Pope Francis, *Let Us Dream: The Path to a Better Future* (New York: Simon & Schuster, 2020), 27.

[10] Pope Francis, *Let Us Dream*, 27.

[11] Jardana Peacock, *Practice Showing Up: A Guidebook for White People Working for Racial Justice* (Mountain View, CA: Creative Commons, 2018), 20.

not we live in a way that aligns with those commitments. At the same time, discipleship simply requires standing, being, presence, a decision to remain inert so as not to be pulled in the wrong direction or to lend your energies to the initiatives of false prophets.

"We shall not be, we shall not be moved," goes the African American spiritual pulling from Psalm 1:3. It is not a coincidence that some who link rest to anti-racism are cultural descendants of the Black Christianity that prophesied in song the power of intentional inactivity, of inertia by choice, of resisting the task master's tempo. "This is about more than naps," explains Tricia Hersey, founder of the Nap Ministry and author of *Rest as Resistance: A Manifesto*. Hersey "unbounds" a variety of disciplines—theology, the arts, community organizing, public health. She makes it clear that her encouragement for actual rest is not a part of the wellness industry that exploits the labor of others, but rather, a fundamental human right.[12] "It is not about fluffy pillows, expensive sheets, silk sleep masks or any other external, frivolous, consumerist gimmick. It is about a deep unraveling from white supremacy and capitalism."[13]

Scripture scholar Walter Brueggemann recognizes as much in his examination of the moral imperative to rest articulated in the covenant between Yahweh and the people of Israel. The Sabbath is protection against the "restless anxiety of Pharaoh."[14] In fact, Brueggemann explains that to rest is to remember that we are made in the image of a God who rested and to tap into God's power to resist "coercive and competitive production" through "covenantal enterprises of compassionate solidarity";[15] to resist exclusive membership by insisting that "work stoppage, an ordinance that everyone can honor" is the only requirement to belong to the People of God;[16] to resist multitasking that "yields a divided self" with a single-minded focus on shalom;[17]

---

[12] See http://www.triciahersey.com/about.html and Tricia Hersey, *Rest as Resistance: A Manifesto* (New York: Little, Brown, 2022).

[13] Tricia Hersey, "Rest Is Anything That Connects Your Mind and Body," The Nap Ministry, February 21, 2022, https://thenapministry.wordpress.com/2022/02/21/rest-is-anything-that-connects-your-mind-and-body/.

[14] Walter Brueggemann, *Sabbath as Resistance: Saying No to the Culture of Now* (Louisville, KY: Westminster John Knox Press, 2014), xiii.

[15] Brueggemann, *Sabbath as Resistance*, 44–45 and 39.

[16] Brueggemann, 56.

[17] Brueggemann, 67.

to resist coveting that is rooted in idolatry and greed with "time for a self-embrace of our true identity" as that of humans made for communion with God and others.[18]

I suspect that this is what my colleagues, all of whom were women but particularly those of color, were suggesting in terms of insisting on an intentional day of intentional resting. We were nearly a year into the Covid pandemic in which the burdens of avoiding or dealing with infection were not evenly distributed, where the impacts of already strained social infrastructure were not equally felt, in which so much labor to keep our institutions open and the people within them functioning at basic levels was rendered invisible. Their expressed preference for our enrichment day was not simply about refraining from adding to already full plates but rather intentionally choosing to rest instead and explaining the rationale for doing so. To their minds, and in keeping with Hersey's approach, this accomplished the goal of a day dedicated to anti-racism. "We are deeply committed to dismantling white supremacy and capitalism by using rest as the foundation for this disruption," Hersey says of the liberatory practice of napping, which she says is a spiritual practice.[19]

In light of that dimension, let's consider what adding the notion of actual "rest" to each of Dawson's three interpretations of the difference between the Two Standards might mean in terms of actual resting as a way of moving toward the banner (Standard) of Christ.

First, *in terms of relationship to our possessions*, resting under the banner of Christ calls us to look for and name the interplay between white supremacy and capitalism, or to put it more plainly "racial capital," which has "devastated nonwhite citizens in the United States" through its ability to separate, differentiate, and manipulate people in the context of transactional relationships.[20] To refrain from consumption is to rest from the transactional relationships that re-inscribe racialized hierarchies and reduce people to commodities. It might also mean taking a break from the more familiar way we tend

[18] Brueggemann, 86–88.

[19] Hersey, "Rest That Connects."

[20] See Olga Segura, *Birth of a Movement: Black Lives Matter and the Catholic Church* (Maryknoll, NY: Orbis Books, 2021), who relies on Cedric Robinson, *Black Marxism: The Making of the Black Radical Tradition* (Chapel Hill, NC: University of North Carolina Press, 2000).

to respond to the needs that our white supremacist capitalism creates: charitable giving. Ignatius implicitly calls us to recognize the ways in which white people, particularly white women and white Catholic women, have been formed with a kind of charitable industriousness that keeps us focused on and exhausted by meeting the immediate need right in front of us while root causes go unexamined and the status quo remains intact. Willie James Jennings highlights the interplay between racism and capitalism in the earliest days of colonialism in America via three roles Europeans stepped into upon arrival—merchant, soldier, and missionary—in order to exercise power and control over people and the environment. These roles persist. To my mind, the missionary is the trickiest part to play because they keep peace, but one without justice; they educate but with an intention to force cultural assimilation; and they sanctify but with an eye for aligning faith with political power—and all in the name of God.[21] That missionary posture of doing good in the name of meeting need is harmful. We need to take a rest from it.

Likewise, we might pay attention to ways in which the busy work we do to sustain our Catholic institutions makes it easy for us to lose track of whether they are actually serving all, particularly the least, or of the impact our approaches to that service is having on particular groups of people. In other words, we might be attentive to how we make a preferential option for the good of the institution in the name of all of the good it might do but lose sight of the human cost. We might reflect on the constant busyness of developing new programs in order to keep our institutions open but which often don't actually serve our students, especially in those programs still tethered to that missionary impulse of forced assimilation to cultures that don't reflect their stories, their sense of self. "Too often, our vision has turned into creating institutions rather than developing people," says John Perkins. I contend that the Two Standards meditation can help us, in Perkins's words, "keep our focus on the people of God—reconciling them to God and to each other."[22]

---

[21] Willie James Jennings, "Disfigurations of Christian Identity: Performing Identity as Theological Method," in *Lived Theology: New Perspectives on Method, Style, and Pedagogy*, ed. Charles Marsh, Peter Slade, and Sarah Azaransky (New York: Oxford University Press, 2017), 67–85.

[22] Shane Claiborne and John M. Perkins, *Follow Me to Freedom: Leading and Following as an Ordinary Radical* (Norwood, MA: Regal Press, 2009), 60.

Second, in terms of *discerning what we do with our impact*, the Two Standards meditation invites us to interrupt all of our exhausting "not racist" performances. By this I mean the reactive, theatrical, dopamine-inducing ways we signal to others that we are not racist. Performance is focused on being right in the eyes of influencers or popular opinion, on being perceived as being one of "the good" people, on curating a public persona or brand. It seeks moments for spectacle, not movements for change. For all of these reasons, performative non-racism is exhausting and depleting. We cannot build trust this way; in fact, performance often erodes trust. Since it is so egocentric, we cannot build collective power this way. We can easily get burned and burned out with performance.[23] What's worse, our burnout negatively impacts others engaged in anti-racism work.[24]

Interestingly, modeling anti-racism, while much more intentionally active, can offer rest and recovery from performance. When we model anti-racism, we are purposeful with how we expend our energies, looking for places where we can collaborate with and learn from others in spending our impact. We are not obsessed with being right but deeply committed to being curious about how to get it right with the help of others.[25] Rather than expend energies defending positions or explaining intentions or justifying actions, we can "turn to wonder," a far more malleable state that can be a grounding experience offering respite from exhausting and obstructionist posturing.[26] We can be energized by visions of what we're working toward, building power with others along the way. We're less batted around by public opinion or the need to be seen as good individuals because we're buoyed by the relational good of kinship instead.

---

[23] Abraham Lateiner, "The Gift of White Burnout," EmbraceRace, https://www.embracerace.org/resources/the-gift-of-white-burnout.

[24] Paul C. Gorski and Noura Erakat, "Racism, Whiteness, and Burnout in Antiracism Movements: How White Racial Justice Activists Elevate Burnout in Racial Justice Activists of Color in the United States," *Ethnicities* 19, no. 5 (October 2019): 784–808.

[25] Brené Brown, "The Courage to Not Know," BreneBrown.com, February 13, 2020, https://brenebrown.com/articles/2020/02/13/the-courage-to-not-know/.

[26] See Erestus Tucker's "Touchstones" via the Center for Courage and Renewal, which I encountered through the Association of American Colleges and Universities' Racial Healing and Transformation training program in July 2021: https://www.wm.edu/as/center-liberal-arts/_documents/350-resources/touchstones.pdf.

Third and finally, Ignatius's meditation provides an opportunity for us to discern the impact white supremacy has on white people, including those working toward racial justice. Robin DiAngelo explains the impact of generations of white supremacy on white people in terms of "white fragility" or "the reduced psychological stamina racial insulation inculcates."[27] We get triggered when we become or are made aware of the anti-blackness at the heart of our frames for understanding ourselves, others, and our worldview. Common responses, all of which create "racial stress" for us and others, include "anger, withdrawal, emotional incapacitation, guilt, argumentation, and cognitive dissonance." This kind of stress undermines our abilities to use our gifts effectively, especially in communal settings. It also works to restore the racial equilibrium that existed before the triggering event, keeping everyone going in exhausting and traumatic circles. DiAngelo's recommended remedy is to be "be less white" or "less racially oppressive" through a variety of practices that we might recognize as emanating from ways of being rather than tasks to be done or actions to be taken: listen, breathe, reflect, take time to process.[28]

Resmaa Menakem is helpful here in linking rest with the intentional work of regulating our individual and collective nervous systems or what he calls "settling" into a path to healing pain. He notes that his settled self helps regulate other nervous systems as well. "This does not happen through a process of mirroring, or cognitive training, or verbal communication. What takes place is energetic, chemical, biological—a syncing of vibrations and energies. My nervous system does not model the way; over time, it helps other nervous systems access the same infinite source that mine does."[29] Resting, in other words, begets more rest. It is a generative practice of tapping into a reservoir of settledness that is always available to us, or what he calls the "Infinite Source." I can't help but think in terms of resting under the standard of Christ, of settling into the infinite source of healing

[27] Robin DiAngelo, *White Fragility: Why It's So Hard for White People to Talk about Racism* (Boston: Beacon Press, 2018), 181.

[28] DiAngelo, *White Fragility*, 147–50.

[29] Resmaa Menakem, *My Grandmother's Hands: Racialized Trauma and the Pathway to Mending Our Hearts and Bodies* (Las Vegas: Central Recovery Press, 2017), 152.

love that lies below the surface of our noisy minds and industrious bodies. Menakem points to the anti-racist potentials of settling: "If you're white, you may discover that when you can settle and manage your body, you won't feel a need to manage Black ones—or a need to ask Black ones to manage yours. You'll also be better able to manage, challenge, and disrupt white-body supremacy."[30]

Rest as Resistance and Justice

So my colleagues suggested that the university community—students and faculty at least—intentionally rest for that academic enrichment day in February 2021, and recommended that I curate a few resources we might share with our university community, which ended up being quietly remarkable.[31] Maybe these can help us understand that resting under the standard of Christ is a tool for forming us as anti-racist disciples.

Slowing Down. Speeding things up—time, productivity, efficiency, rates of return—is a manifestation of our corporatized culture.[32] If we recognize the colonizing tendencies of humans' first corporations—violently racializing peoples, exploiting labor and natural resources, hijacking natural rhythms of life, devasting webs of interdependence between humans and the natural world—then we have an ethical imperative to interrupt the dehumanizing pace of the corporatized cultures in which we live, move, and have our being. Moreover, if we consider the historical interplay between *Christianity* and those early corporatizing impulses—normalizing violence, falsely aligning the desires of the merchant classes of Christian empires with God's desires to save heathen souls, forcing the assimilation of indigenous cultures into Western Christianity[33]—then disrupting the pace of contemporary corporate cultures is practice of anti-racist discipleship.

---

[30] Menakem, *My Grandmother's Hands*, 152.

[31] "Using Rest as a Tool to Fight Racism," La Salle News, February 1, 2021, https://www.lasalle.edu/blog/2021/02/01/using-rest-as-a-tool-to-fight-racism/.

[32] For a description of this in the context of higher education, see Maggie Berg and Barbara K. Seeber, *The Slow Professor: Challenging the Culture of Speed in the Academy* (Toronto: University of Toronto Press, 2016), 1–15.

[33] Jennings, "Disfigurations of Christian Identity."

Slowing down "can fuel us" with "contemplation, connectedness, fruition, and complexity," all of which are important tools to protect against the colonization of our minds and homogeneity in our thinking and acting.[34] In their examination of the impact of corporate culture on higher education—faculty, students, curriculum—Berg and Seeber cite the distinction environmentalist David Orr makes between "fast" and "slow" knowledge. Fast knowledge is linear, standardized, franchizeable, and likely to constrict intellectual diversity. Slow knowledge, on the other hand is complex, focused on particular contexts, and seeks to preserve patterns that help us make connections to other ways of thinking.[35] Slowing down is a form of self-care in that it allows for an intentional and authentic process of self-becoming in which we grant ourselves the freedom for self-exploration, self-discovery, the chance to be mastered by something as opposed to hurriedly working to master something in order to move on to the next task.[36] Becoming anti-racist, a lifelong process, requires this kind of intentional, slowed down, deep reflection.

In his 2020 reflection during the Covid pandemic, Pope Francis lifts up the importance of a "stoppage" in the life of those attempting to be faithful to God. "A stoppage can always be a good time for sifting, for reviewing the past, for remembering with gratitude who we are, what we have been given, and where we have gone astray."[37] Stoppages reveal to us what we need to change and help us stay tethered to social change as primarily an awareness of self and of reality through the perspective of others, and not an ideology that "armor-plates" our hearts.[38]

Dreaming. Hersey insists that her nap ministry is against capitalism that exploits labor, that depletes resources. But she also suggests napping is *for* something: for dreaming, making space for what might be possible beyond the busy boundaries of what is. "We cling to the power of collective care and collective rest opening the DREAM-SPACE that will allow us to invent and imagine a New World rooted

---

[34] Berg and Seeber, *Slow Professor*, 57.

[35] Berg and Seeber, 58, citing David W. Orr, *The Nature of Design: Ecology, Culture, and Human Intention* (New York: Oxford University Press, 2002).

[36] Berg and Seeber, 59.

[37] Pope Francis, *Let Us Dream*, 35.

[38] Pope Francis, 27.

in rest."[39] Scientists and health care professionals are increasingly agreeing on the benefits of daydreaming or "thinking for pleasure," which is different from ruminating or undisciplined mind-wandering. Daydreaming involves purposeful thinking about "meaningful and pleasant things," which has the power to "reshape our emotions and make us happier" and can be a skill we can draw on when under stress.[40] Disciplined daydreamers are more likely to be innovative thinkers since it allows us to "imagine new realities." In some ways, Pope Francis alludes to this human capability in his distinction between fundamentalism and discernment, particularly in times of chaos like the one we find ourselves in. Where "fundamentalist mindsets offer to shelter people from destabilizing situations in exchange from a kind of existential quietism," discernment encourages seeking refuge through a different relationship to truth, one marked by a humility that slows down and "creates room for [us] to encounter the truth."[41]

Presence. Rest also makes presence possible: presence to and of God, ourselves, and others. "Those who remember and keep Sabbath find they are less driven, less coerced, less frantic to meet deadlines," says Brueggemann, "free to be rather than to do."[42] David Fleming notes that this is the central point of the Two Standards meditation. "Christ our king calls us to be *with* him. The essence of the call is not to do some specific work, but, above all, to be with the One who calls, imaged in the everyday details of living like our king lives. We are to share Christ's life, to think like him, to do what he does."[43]

Meditative practices of many faith traditions cultivate a heightened awareness of the present moment in order to find vast, still space between ruminating on the past or worrying about the future. Currently, the Synod on Synodality process underway in the Catholic

[39] Tricia Hersey, "Slowly Emerging after a 3 Week Sabbath," The Nap Ministry, July 14, 2020, https://thenapministry.wordpress.com/2020/07/14/slowly-emerging -after-a-3-week-sabbath/.

[40] Alison Escalante, "New Research Finds Daydreaming Is Good for Our Health," *Forbes*, March 23, 2021, https://www.forbes.com/sites/alisonescalante/2021/03/23 /daydreaming-is-under-attack-now-researchers-say-its-good-for-our-health /?sh=6ccccae67ee1.

[41] Pope Francis, *Let Us Dream*, 55.

[42] Brueggemann, *Sabbath as Resistance*, 42.

[43] Estrus Tucker, "Touchstones," The Center for Courage and Renewal, https:// www.wm.edu/as/center-liberal-arts/_documents/350-resources/touchstones.pdf.

Church tethers itself to that still space in order to create the possibility for communal discernment about hurts of the past and the possibilities for the future. While Pope Francis may have convened the three-year process with the intention of continuing the renewal of the church begun at Vatican II—a heavy lift, no doubt—its critical first phase is one of listening to the Spirit at work in our lives and in the lives of others in our communities. In short, the process hinges on tuning into the indwelling of the Spirit, the permanent presence of the Spirit, with the hope that that posture of attunement will become a central—if not *the* central—disposition of the church.

All of this intentionality, stepping into circles of open-hearted sharing and dreaming, stilling ourselves in order to perceive what God, through the Spirit, is up to, provides restful space where new springs can be tapped. "The spirituality for synodality gives form to the amazing discovery of the hidden energies of love, self-commitment, generosity and sharing that lie within us, sometimes unattended and forgotten: a sort of 'dowry' received in baptism but often neglected." As such, it is the hope that through a synodal way of being church, the People of God can be transformed by and through the Spirit, into "a place of refuge for all who live with the realities of a vulnerable and precarious life."[44]

Conclusion: I Will Give You Rest

A good friend and anti-racist teacher, Dr. Tia Noelle Pratt, intentionally capitalizes her term for ongoing efforts toward racial justice. She calls it "THE WORK." "I've specifically used capital letters in this description because it's essential that we think of it and visualize it with the importance of capital letters," Pratt explains.[45] Anti-racist ways of being and doing is indeed work, perhaps the most pressing work for those of us who have been raced as white and must contend with what Pratt calls "the erroneous assumption that none of this,"

---

[44] Vatican Office of the Synod, "Towards a Spirituality for Synodality," 7, 12, https://www.synod.va/en/highlights/towards-a-spirituality-for-synodality.html.

[45] Tia Noelle Pratt, contribution to a roundtable on my book *Undoing the Knots: Five Generations of American Catholic Anti-Blackness* (Boston: Beacon Press, 2021), in *American Catholic Studies* 133, no. 2 (2022): 61–64.

by which she means cultures of white body supremacy—"have anything to do with [us]."[46] Given that our brothers and sisters of color, and the natural environments around the globe in which many of them live, cry out in lamentation and demand interrupts us with the urgency of THE WORK. Undoing cultures, systems, institutions, and internalized senses of self warped by white supremacy is hard. It is exhausting. And, for white Christians, it can be the battlefield to which Ignatius points in his meditation on the Two Standards. For Christians, especially those raced and spiritually formed as white, white supremacy can hijack our desire to contribute to THE WORK with the temptation to use the tools white supremacy has handed down to us in our efforts to dismantle it: industriousness, take-chargeness, corporatized efficiency and focus on outcomes, and linear progress. Ignatius's invites us to awaken to a different approach to THE WORK, one that originates from a place of actual rest under the standard of Christ as we have come to understand that idea in this essay—both as resistance to white supremacy and as creative alternatives to it.

---

[46] Tia Noelle Pratt, "The Call Is Coming from Inside the House," foreword to Segura's *Birth of a Movement*, xi.

8

Recuerda Que Jesús También Fue Niño

An Undocumented Reflection
on the Spiritual Exercises

Armando Guerrero Estrada
and Paulina Delgadillo

After three days they found him in the temple, sitting among
the teachers, listening to them and asking them questions.
And all who heard him were amazed at his understanding
and his answers.

Luke 2:46-47

Armando Guerrero Estrada (AGE): Referencing Jon Sobrino, Mark W.
Potter states that "solidarity can best be understood as the praxis of
discipleship that flows out of a particular encounter with Jesus Christ
mediated through the suffering ones of history."[1] If, for Sobrino,
solidarity flows from the encounter or *el encuentro con Jesús*, what
could solidarity look like if one were to encounter *el niño Jesus*? In
what ways must solidarity differ when one comes face to face with
the adolescent Jesus who, in the temple at Jerusalem, begins to come

---

[1] Mark W. Potter, "Solidarity as Spiritual Exercise: Accompanying Migrants at the
US/Mexico Border," *Political Theology* 12, no. 6 (2011): 832.

to conscientization about his vocation and public ministry?[2] What are the ramifications of such a reflection on solidarity for those of us working with and alongside "today's suffering ones of history": undocumented migrant youth and young adults?

In the second and third days of Week Two of the Spiritual Exercises, Ignatius of Loyola encourages contemplation on the "Presentation in the Temple" and the "Obedience of the Child Jesus to His Parents." In what follows, Armando Guerrero Estrada and Paulina Delgadillo offer a brief reflection on Luke 2:41-52 inspired from their social location as two Jesuit-educated and undocumented/DACAmented, Mexican-born theologians.[3] This reflection stems from Guerrero Estrada's article "The Holy Disobedience of an UndocuJesus: Re-Reading Luke 2:41-52 Alongside Immigrant Youth," where he lays the foundation for an undocu-biblical criticism from an undocumented, Catholic perspective.[4] In the 2021 article, Guerrero Estrada affirmed that "[t]hough the scholarship on undocumented immigrant youth and unaccompanied minors has increased, there remains a need for a biblical ethics of migration focused on children, adolescents, and young adults. Better yet, a biblical interpretation *from the perspective of an undocumented young immigrant.*"[5] This collaboration is an attempt to take Jean-Pierre Ruiz's call to "read in *voz alta*" seriously, a call that moves readers away from a private practice of biblical interpretation and instead encourages a practice of reading out loud and *en conjunto.*[6] Doing so, he argues, "brings to the surface a

    [2] Elisabeth Schüssler Fiorenza, "Luke 2:41-52," *Union Seminary Review* 36, no. 4 (October 1982): 399, https://doi.org/10.1177/002096438203600409.

    [3] Armando Guerrero Estrada is a doctoral candidate in theology and education at the School of Theology and Ministry, Boston College. He serves as the inaugural director of the PASOS Network at Dominican University, a network committed to the expansion of culturally sustaining university practices. He also teaches in the theology department and co-advises the Undocumented and Immigrant Allyance student organization. Paulina Delgadillo is currently pursuing a master of pastoral studies at Catholic Theological Union and is a graduate of Dominican University, where she majored in theology and natural sciences.

    [4] See Armando Guerrero, "The Holy Disobedience of an UndocuJesus: Re-Reading Luke 2:41-52 Alongside Immigrant Youth," *Journal of Hispanic/Latino Theology* 3, no. 2 (2021): 205–30.

    [5] Guerrero, "Holy Disobedience," 3.

    [6] Jean-Pierre Ruiz, *Readings from the Edges: The Bible and People on the Move* (Maryknoll, NY: Orbis Books, 2011), 52.

number of insights that . . . helps us to appreciate the complexity of the immigration debate" and strengthens solidarity in the struggle for justice.[7] How can a biblical interpretation of the Child Jesus read in *voz alta* alongside undocumented youth move us towards solidarity and justice?

AGE: Paulina, at the end of this pericope we read that the Child Jesus went to Nazareth with his parents and was obedient to them. This emphasis on obedience is in juxtaposition to his holy disobedience, i.e., staying behind to be in his Father's house without Mary and Joseph's permission. In what ways does the holy disobedience of the Child Jesus in Luke 2:41-52 speak to your identity as a young, undocumented Latina Catholic, who has been informed by Jesuit spirituality?

Paulina Delgadillo (PD): One of the ways I interpret this stems from my lived experience and social location. My parents and I came to the United States twenty years ago, not knowing the language, area, people, or what was going to become of us. I am an undocumented young Latina woman. Who would ever take me seriously? I knew deep down [that] I felt like a child who was underestimated and misunderstood because of my age. Growing up, my undocumented status was not as present as it felt when I got to high school. In grammar school many of my classmates had family members or parents who might reflect my and my family's situation; my status was not something that limited me in any way. My parents did not want me to go to the public schools near the area because the dropout rate was high and there was a lack of resources. They wanted me to achieve my dreams—their dreams—of getting an education and doing something not because of the money but because I was passionate about it.

I had applied to a prestigious Jesuit high school; all my friends knew I would get in, as if they knew I was meant to do great things. What ran through my head was not if I could get in, but if I was worthy. I remember the moments in high school where I would pray to God to please allow me not to be undocumented. This happened

---

[7] Ruiz, *Readings from the Edges*, 49.

often when other students would talk about their vacations, and going to all these different places that I knew I would never be able to travel to—at least not anytime soon. When all my friends started taking driving lessons and got their licenses, I always told them I liked taking public transportation so there was no need for me to get mine. Or when my best friend asked me to go to Spain on a school trip with her, it broke my heart that I couldn't tell her the real reason because I didn't want to burden her. I said it was a money issue and that I was afraid of planes. All my friends were going on college visits and traveling and here I was navigating feelings of insecurity: Was this future even a possibility for me? Was pursuing higher education even worth it? Did my education matter in the midst of a world where I was constantly being told "no" and telling people "no" to educational experiences because of my status. I was being obedient to those around me, to norms and expectations of those around me, but there was a part of me that hoped she could one day be obedient to my heart. It was hard enough being a young woman navigating education and the world; throw into the mix being undocumented and Latina. What do I bring to the table? Do I have a voice or a place at the table where others sit? In Luke 2:41-52, the teenage Jesus sits amongst those considered the smartest and the wisest people in that time. The passage speaks to how everyone around him was amazed at his input.

AGE: You've attended a Jesuit high school, a Dominican university, and are about to begin your studies at Catholic Theological Union. In "The Holy Disobedience of an UndocuJesus," I argue that Jesus is welcomed by the temple teachers and sits among them, listening and asking questions. "Had the teachers not provided a welcoming environment, would Jesus have had the courage to stay with them, let alone sit among them, ask questions, and engage them in conversation?"[8] Like the temple teachers, have the professors and institutions you've attended provided a brave space for you to share your wisdom and bring your full, undocumented self to the table?

---

[8] Guerrero, "Holy Disobedience," 12.

PD: My life has been full of moments where I have felt unheard, unseen, unsafe, and unloved; I have gone my whole life to Catholic schools and been in spaces where that should not happen. I would hear classmates, teachers, and faculty talk about justice with passion. I would begin to feel safe and hopeful. Yet at the same time, outside of the classroom or certain spaces, I would hear others speak about how immigrants should go back to their country, say phrases that were hurtful to minoritized communities, or complain to their parents that the school was a bad influence for teaching about justice (or a certain topic in social justice). I would see people with "We Stand with Immigrants" stickers yet I never once heard them say it out loud, owning it. One would think [that] seeing that sticker and learning about social justice would make me, an undocumented young Latina, feel safe, but that sticker gave me a false hope—did they actually care or was it just for show? I was learning about social justice and learning how to see God in everyone and in all things, but were others doing that with me?

Going to a Jesuit school, I learned about St. Ignatius and about Ignatian spirituality: "being a man and woman for and with others." It seemed to me that this could be a place where I can finally be my whole self and be accepted. I was able to connect to what Ignatius taught, while at the same time think about the ways where I didn't feel that his teaching applied to me. For example, dealing with two expectations and feeling "ni de aquí, ni de allá" is a common feeling shared among the immigrant population.[9] What would Ignatius think of me—an undocumented young Latina woman? Like Jesus, my immigration status, age, gender, and social location influenced the way I saw the world and how the world saw me. Back then, if someone asked me about my experience, I would keep it to myself. I would have felt as though nobody would be "amazed" or "astounded" with what I had to say. Thankfully, I have learned that people *are* willing to listen to me.

At Dominican, a Hispanic Serving Institution, one of the first things that I noticed was that I was not the outlier. I was not the only one who shared this experience. On one of my first days, I met four people who were undocumented and who were open about their status,

---

[9] "From neither here nor there." For more on this, see Guerrero, 12–19.

without any fear of what others might think. For the first time, I felt a warmth, unity, and hope of being undocumented with people I had known for mere hours. Having students and professors who understood and saw me as worthy and with lots to offer—whether it be in class, in student clubs, or events—was something I didn't know I craved so much until I tasted it. As I investigated graduate school programs, I had to do something scary and ask the question to institutions: Are you willing to work with a student who is undocumented? It was scary. I had been so blessed at Dominican and by the opportunities I had here despite my status. I wondered if a graduate school had anything similar. Now I am so proud to say that I have a full scholarship to attend graduate school at Catholic Theological Union. To feel like you belong and that you bring so much to the table is a feeling that makes me hopeful. I am beyond blessed to have that space and opportunity as I pursue higher education.

AGE: For many undocumented students, like Paulina, the education system can serve as a place of deep belonging and radical hospitality; it can become a safe haven as they transition into illegality. Roberto Gonzales defines illegality as the process of coming to understand one's status as an undocumented individual, a process that begins in the education system for many youth and young adults.[10] While the education system can be a positive experience, the same system can also be exclusionary. Gonzales rightly states, "Historically, public schools have wielded the power to either replicate societal inequalities or equalize the playing field."[11] Teachers, administrators, and mentors are critical partners in equalizing the playing field for undocumented students. In the case of the temple teachers, they expressed an authentic form of radical solidarity with the Child Jesus, where he felt like he belonged. Is there anyone who has shown you that same form of solidarity?

PD: A mentor and wonderful human being said to me the following: "Oh, my girl, until you are free, safe, empowered, and protected, my *liberation* is farce. This is the Gospel. I am with you always." In my

---

[10] Roberto G. Gonzales, *Lives in Limbo: Undocumented and Coming of Age in America* (Oakland CA: University of California Press, 2016), xix.

[11] Gonzales, *Lives in Limbo*, 13.

opinion, being men and women for and with others is not about speaking the right words and reading a book, we need to live it, while reflecting on where and how we can be better. My mentor's words finally allowed me to be my true self, my *cura personalis*. When the elections of 2020 were happening, I remember doing lots of outreach to get votes especially from underrepresented communities, and I was advocating to those around me to vote because it was a privilege I did not have. My two best friends, who had supported me through the good and bad days, the storms and the sunlight, did not even know at this point about my undocumented status, and I remember I sent them a text to vote because I wasn't able to. They asked why not and I told them why. Their responses were the following: "I love you and you better believe I am going to get myself to VOTE" along with "I care for you! And I'll still care regardless of whatever factors!" For the first time I saw how my friends realized and understood that their actions affected me and that they would do anything in their power to make it known that they loved me. They embraced my *cura personalis* with love and reminded me that I was worthy.

AGE: Are there any final remarks about how this pericope, perhaps how this passage, plays out in your everyday life, *en lo cotidiano*?

PD: Growing up, my mom would always tell me, "Recuerda que Jesús también fue niño."[12] She would say this especially in times where things might seem stressful and out of control or even when I was being rebellious. It was her way of telling me that things would be okay, take it as a learning experience. There is something so empowering about that. Despite what the world might think or say about me because of my age, gender, or legal status, I think I understand what my mom was trying to tell me. If Jesus, despite his age, was able to be listened to and heard, so can I. Who would have thought that the little girl who learned English from watching PBS kids would be here, getting her degree?

AGE: For many undocumented and DACAmented students, Luke 2:41-52 can provide an avenue for the conscientization or realization

---

[12] "Remember, Jesus was also a child." Paulina's translation.

of their agency and self-worth. Through the image of the Child Jesus, they can feel empowered to share the cultural, epistemological, and social wealth of their communities and their lived realities as immigrant youth and young adults. As Paulina demonstrates, despite certain limitations or challenges, undocumented and DACAmented immigrant students challenge the performative nature of solidarity. Wearing stickers and waving flags are great initial steps; however, these actions must be accompanied by a radical sense of solidarity that provides a brave space for immigrant students to be their true selves and to bring their full selves to the classroom and beyond.

Inspired by the temple teachers, an anti-racist reading of Luke 2:41-52 coupled with a contemplation of the Spiritual Exercises can inspire allies and accomplices to engage in radical solidarity with migrant youth and young adults that flows from an encounter with the Child Jesus. Such an encounter, however, must be accompanied by culturally responsive and culturally sustaining practices that view undocumented and DACAmented students as ecclesial agents in the church and society. In the United States, more than half of all Catholics under the age of eighteen are Hispanic, many of whom are immigrants or children of immigrants. The Catholic Church and Catholic education must embrace the signs of the times and engage in radical solidarity with today's migrant youth and young adults—not the future of the church, but the "now of the church."

$$=9=$$

Mephibosheth and Me

An Interpretive Ignatian Prayer of Memory and Imagination

María Teresa Morgan

There is a primal bond between us and the land of our birth;[1] a force that becomes all the more encompassing when we have been torn away from it by violence, when that land becomes a mythical place that no longer exists and where we cannot return; it charts the memory of our longing. As an immigrant and/or exile,[2] I am keenly aware of this category of absence; a dislocation that has framed my story within the biblical metanarrative of exile and journeying.

---

[1] For an insightful study on geography, identity, and spirituality see Belden C. Lane, *Landscapes of the Sacred: Geography and Narrative in American Spirituality* (Mahwah, NJ: Paulist Press, 1988).

[2] Both terms are highly debated and become a source of contention and classism. The nomenclature of "immigrants," "exiles," and "refugees" is also politically charged as evidenced in the recent controversy regarding Susan Eckstein's presentation at Florida International University in Miami of her book *Cuban Privilege: The Making of Immigrant Inequality in America*, and the response by Orlando Gutiérrez-Boronat, "Cubans' Lives Definitely Were at Risk under Castro. That's Why We Became Refugees," *The Miami Herald*, "Guest Opinion," https://www.miamiherald.com/opinion/op-ed/article270358782.html.

For disclosure, I, along with all the other Pedro Pan children, came with a visa waiver and was admitted to the US as a refugee. I identify as "and/both exile and immigrant" because I believe all exiles are also immigrants and vice versa.

Throughout this path the Ignatian practice of imaging,[3] consisting in placing ourselves within the narrative of Scripture, has been instinctive, for being displaced early in life has led me to seek for a sense of belonging somewhere in the history of the People of God. This brief reflection presents an illustration of Ignatian contemplation through the engagement of the imagination and memory based on the narrative of Mephibosheth and that of the Pedro Pan children. Allow me then to tell you both stories.

Mephibosheth, who appears throughout 2 Samuel 4–21, was the son of Jonathan, with whom David made a covenant of love and friendship. When Jonathan and his father Saul perished at Mount Gilboa, a revolt ensued in Saul's palace. Amidst the chaos and upheaval Mephibosheth's nurse fled with the child in her arms and in her panic stumbled and dropped him, resulting in crippling injuries that rendered Mephibosheth disabled for life. After becoming king, David inquired as to the whereabouts of the child and welcomed him into his home. David granted Mephibosheth a place at his table for the rest of his life. The scriptural passages above are brief but contain a wealth of applications that are relevant to the situation of children who have been uprooted by the calamities of history. For this purpose, I will now transition to the story of the Pedro Pan children and proceed to establish similarities that connect both narratives, applying the Composition of Place found in Ignatian spirituality.

Operation Pedro Pan refers to the 14,000 unaccompanied children who came from Cuba from 1960 to 1962: the largest documented exodus of unaccompanied children in the Western Hemisphere. I am one of those children. The reader may ask, what would prompt parents to send their children, alone, into another country? There have been books and doctoral dissertations presenting differing versions as to the reasons for Operation Pedro Pan. The various arguments lie outside the scope of my reflection, for to get involved with them would be a desecration of lost lives and those who loved them, of

---

[3] Robert J. Egan, "Jesus in the Heart's Imagination: Reflections on Ignatian Contemplation," *The Way*, 62–72, chrome-extension://efaidnbmnnnibpcajpcglclefindmkaj/https://www.theway.org.uk/back/s082Egan.pdf. My education in Ignatian contemplation is based primarily on this article.

stories that need to be honored and not debated.[4] Because of this, I choose to speak of my own experience and of what I witnessed in my family and city when, after the Bay of Pigs fiasco in 1961, there were roundups and imprisonment of opponents to the Castro regime, executions by firing squads, increased repression, closure of Catholic schools and churches, expulsions of religious and priests, and confiscation of the property of whoever was suspected of not agreeing with the ideology of the "revolution." Stripped of most everything and rightly fearing for my father's life after he was arrested and sent to the infamous Boniato prison, my parents had no choice but to send us away to safety. It was through these events that my world (and that of countless others) was breached and my story plundered.

I don't remember how Mephibosheth and me got acquainted some four decades ago, whether through my reading of the Scriptures or whether I heard about him somewhere, but his saga resonated with me as it mirrored my own. Sometime later I wrote a poem about him and all exiled children. It was published in "Laity in Action" but the lack of feedback resounded like a thud. I suppose readers had never heard of him and Mephibosheth and poetry made for an odd mixture! I am glad to have been given this second chance and hope to rehabilitate my previous, clumsy attempt to make ourselves known.

What did I see in Mephibosheth? How did I pray through his story? How was God's providence manifested in this prayer? How has this one-act drama of my by now lengthy sojourn informed my discipleship? The above are all questions posed by the exercise of Ignatian contemplation that have a profound impact in our attempt to understand the presence of God in our lives. To these I now turn my attention by intertwining diverse elements posed by these questions.

Narrative, by nature, is disclosive. Praying with the passage of 2 Samuel 4:4 evoked the consequences of the upheaval(s) in my homeland. My country, the land that nursed me, fled in panic and in the chaos dropped me. Since that time long ago, shards of memories, of landscapes, of my beloved grandfather to whom I never got a chance to say goodbye, come to greet me, peering over the edges of my

[4] Refer to Johann Metz regarding "the suffering of the stranger" and "solidarity denied" in *Love's Strategy: The Political Theology of Johann Baptist Metz*, ed. John K. Downey (Harrisburg, PA: Trinity Press International, 1999), 171.

consciousness, as they also must have come looking for Mephibosheth. I am not from where I am and liminal spaces continue to claim me.

We know that human experience is fraught with ambivalence; light and darkness, loss and gain, grief and joy often come together in the perspective of reflective prayer. Though I left "in darkness and concealment" it has been nonetheless a "happy venture"[5] For the country that welcomed me, the United States, offered me a place at the table: one of relative security and peace, of freedom, opportunities, and abundance of blessings. I affirm my immense gratitude to this country, to my parents for the risk they took in order to protect us, grateful to the Archdiocese of Miami, to Archbishop Carroll and Monsignor Bryan Walsh who made possible the Pedro Pan Operation, grateful to Pepe and Lourdes González-Maribona, the parents that welcomed us as their own until we were reunited with our parents.

The Ignatian prayer of imagination and memory has enabled me to experience God's love amidst the conflicts that are an inevitable part of life and become all the more destructive when they involve families and entire countries. The practice of imagination and memory is also one of hope born out of those same broken memories;[6] it has rescued my narrative from the grip of the flotsam of history and reframed it within the story of the passion, death, and resurrection of Jesus, as all our stories are ultimately bound to find their meaning.[7] This prayer has given me the gift of compassion towards immigrants, such an unpopular, ignored, and very often despised

---

[5] John of the Cross, *The Dark Night of the Soul*, my translation.

[6] For the past two decades the work of Elizabeth Johnson has shaped my understanding of the connection between solidarity, memory, and hope. See Elizabeth Johnson, *Friends of God and Prophets: A Feminist Theological Reading of the Communion of Saints* (New York: Continuum, 1999). I have also been influenced by the single image of the "Rose of Memory" in T. S. Eliot's "Ash Wednesday." Though the poet most likely alludes to the vision of Mary in Dante's *Paradiso* the open-ended nature of poetry allows for my interpretation of memory transformed and graced through God's mercy. T. S. Eliot, "Ash Wednesday," https://thepoetryplace.wordpress.com /2010/02/17/ash-wednesday-by-t-s-eliot/.

[7] Egan, "Heart's Imagination," 63. No reflection on memory, on our broken world, on suffering, narrative, hope, and compassion can fail to refer these themes back to Johannes Metz's nor to exclude his concept of *dangerous memory*: "I put forth the notion of a *memoria passionis* which is at the same time both universalizable and particular: the memory of others' suffering. I develop this basic theological-political category in resistance to the cultural amnesia of our time." Metz, *Love's Strategy*, 174.

group clamoring at the borders and margins of our society: for I know well the heart of an alien, because I am one (Exod 23:9).[8] This practice of imagination and memory has also led me in so far as I am able, to lend a hand across the crossing of their waters (Exod 14:19-31).

Conclusion

I doubt that other Pedro Pans have prayed with the passage of Mephibosheth. He is not an easy person to find as only a few lines about him appear in the Scriptures. But Ignatian spirituality discerns God's presence in every aspect of creation, in every worthy human endeavor[9] and includes the manifold manifestations of imagination and memory: "finding God in all things, and all things in God." Last year I toured the Pedro Pan Exhibit at the Cuban Museum of the Diaspora. The exhibit memorialized our experience in a collective gathering of memories. I got to sign the suitcase that stands starkly as the centerpiece of the display, a suitcase that every Pedro Pan that toured the memorial was invited to sign. Rituals of solidarity, imagination, and memory, crafted by a gathering of our testimonies, by small items that we brought with us so as to hold on to the continuity of our identities, pictures of happier times, a blown-up mural of a historical and remembered event I feared would bring back such pain that I turned away my eyes. The exhibit is now permanently housed at Barry University in Miami Shores so that our story may not be forgotten.

I am only one of "a great multitude . . . from every nation, from all tribes and peoples and languages" (Rev 7:9-11). Like Mephibosheth and me, countless children have been and are being sent away in haste and desperation. I am connected to them, to my other Pedro Pans, for our stories are bound in the skeins of our trauma. I hope

---

[8] The scriptural command against oppressing the alien together with the summons to welcome the stranger is an often repeated theme appearing in Exodus 22:21; 23:9; Leviticus 19:33-34; 25:23; Numbers 15:15; Deuteronomy 10:19; 23:7; 24:14; 24:17-22; 27:19; Ezekiel 22:7; 22:29; 47:22; Zechariah 7:10; and, finally, in Matthew 25:35. The chosen passage from Exodus 23:9 is particularly relevant in Ignatian spirituality for it bids us to examine our hearts so as to discover in our encounter with the immigrant stranger that we once were aliens.

[9] Egan, "Heart's Imagination," 64, 65.

that through the diverse manifestations of the Ignatian practice of imagination and memory the vision will come to all, the vision of how "the new years walk, restoring / Through a bright cloud of tears, the years, restoring / With a new verse the ancient rhyme, Redeem / The time . . ."[10]

---

[10] Eliot, "Ash Wednesday."

=== 10 ===

Ignatian Discernment in a Diverse Ecosystem

Marilyn L. Nash

As a young adult in the 1990s, I volunteered with a local nonprofit uprooting invasive scotch broom along the Duwamish River. Scotch broom is a nonnative plant in the Pacific Northwest, crowding out native species and harming local habitat. It's a tall, upright shrub with bright yellow flowers that bloom along the highways and rivers in the late spring. I find it quite beautiful with its shocks of color in the lush, green landscape. Yet, scotch broom isn't meant to be in this place. Its purpose is out of alignment with local ecosystems, so despite its beauty, it causes harm.

After an exhausting but satisfying morning ripping out the stubborn plants by their roots, our guide treated the group to a brief hike around the site. The river holds great cultural significance for the Duwamish dxʷdəwʔabš tribe, whose homelands include the territory also known as Seattle and much of Greater King County in Washington State. Although federally unrecognized, the Duwamish people have been land and water protectors since time immemorial.

Hidden among ships, cranes, and stacked containers is the mouth of the Duwamish—a once-meandering healthy river that was deliberately straightened into a waterway to accommodate industry. Centuries of colonization and industrialization have resulted in heavy pollution, negatively impacting people and lands and native species in the region. Endangered salmon and diminishing salmon runs have cultural and practical significance to tribes who continue to lead the way to restore the river and revive the runs.

Our guide explained these efforts and shared his enthusiasm that after many years and much labor, the salmon were beginning to spawn. The slow process of restoration was having a good day and it was consoling for our group to see the fruits of our peripheral effort.

There was a woman in the group, agitated as she listened to him speak about the river and the struggle to restore the fish. I can still hear the ignorant and well-intended urgency in her question. "I don't understand why it took so long. Why wouldn't you just get some salmon and salmon eggs and repopulate the river when you noticed they were gone?"

I wish I could remember the guide's name, to honor the deep wisdom of his generous, thoughtful response. In my memory, he paused, allowed the question to hang in the air, and then spoke into that silence.

"I hear the desire and intention in your question. But it does not work that way. Look around you. The salmon live in this river, but they are part of this entire ecosystem. If one does not understand the relationship of the salmon to the river, and of the river to the quality of the water, and the water to the silt along the bottom; if one does not understand the relationship of the salmon to the insects attracted to the river, and the insects to the small vegetation along the banks; if one does not understand the relationship of the vegetation to the trees, and the impacts of invasive plants and the benefits of indigenous flora; if one doesn't understand the relationship of the salmon to all of these things, then one could act out of the most well-intentioned place—simply replacing the fish where they belong—but it would fail, because there is a greater habitat, a greater context to consider."

I pay that story forward when speaking about discernment. Sometimes, I try to recreate his expectant silence, an attempt to highlight the vital significance of mindful, contextual decision-making. His words illustrate the potential for harmful impact despite good intent and *the importance of considering context when making choices*. Whatever our intent might be, our impact relies more on understanding the ecology or culture within which we make our decisions.

The single most important context for faith filled, values-based decision-making in this land we now call the United States is the culture of racism and Whiteness—albeit, possibly the most neglected as well.

In conversations about faith and spirituality—especially in regard to racism— it is important to begin with as much truth as possible, creating an atmosphere that allows for the vulnerability necessary for challenging conversations and genuine learning.

As I write this essay I am on unceded, ancestral homelands of the Coast Salish People, specifically the territory of Puyallup and Duwamish tribes, who have lived and continue to live on these lands and waters since time immemorial. I am a white, cis, LGBQ-identifying woman, the oldest of six children from a rural Pennsylvanian, Catholic family. I am aware that who I am, my stories and generational legacies, influence my perspectives on faith, justice, and discernment. I offer myself to this essay, and to you, reader and colleague, as no more and no less than who I am.

When I was invited to contribute to a collection addressing *colorblindness* and the Spiritual Exercises of St. Ignatius, I knew immediately that I wanted to write an accessible, story-based essay about discernment and the culture of Whiteness. It feels important to resist the urge to attempt a dense, overly intellectualized piece about something I believe should be more about meandering and paying attention.

My experience with the Spiritual Exercises is not academic. I am not a theologian by the academy's definition nor a Jesuit priest, unless desire and call matter more than rules of admission. I have, however, spent many years making, offering, guiding, and living the Spiritual Exercises in my ordinary life, and almost as many years teaching and facilitating conversations about Ignatian spirituality and discernment professionally. My wisdom comes from students and stories, young adults and elders, retreats and classrooms, conversations and prayers. It is deeply rooted in my relationships with other womxn[1] in this mission, with Jesuits who understand lay

---

[1] The use of the word *womxn* in the context of this essay is meant to disrupt a limited or transphobic understanding of gender or a presumption of whiteness, and is intended to signal the inclusion of those who are often traditionally excluded— specifically Black women, Indigenous women, women of color, queer and transgender women. Language is constantly changing and encouraging us forward, and this is not a term used by everyone. The author would like to emphasize that transwomen are women, and that gender is a fluid, nonbinary social construct.

collaboration, and most importantly with directees, students, and colleagues of color who share perspectives and stories of discernment in our current social context.

For many years, I led teams of directors facilitating Ignatian silent retreats for university students. I encouraged directors to diversify prayers, songs, poems, and stories from the expected canon of predominantly white, Jesuit priests. Diversifying the ministerial resources we use to animate the Exercises is a barely baseline effort to be more inclusive, yet somehow this still seems radical in many Ignatian spaces. I have encountered Jesuit centers, schools, and non-profits proclaiming a desire for "more diverse" participants without ever considering the default Eurocentric lens through which retreats, programs, and formation will be offered once "they" arrive. We cling to traditions as if they were absolute law, rather than seeds and roots that beg for continued growth and transformation. I was formed through the words of Chardin, Hopkins, Fleming, Lonsdale, Rahner, Arrupe, Kolvenbach, and other valuable, orthodox resources. We do not have to abandon this rich lineage in order to contemplate colorful, expansive wisdom from other lived experiences.

The particular university retreat program I helped to lead didn't shy away from stories of faith and justice, but as is true of most white-dominant institutions, racial justice—especially at that time—was peripheral if mentioned at all. There was an unspoken sense that the Spiritual Exercises themselves would naturally land in each person according to their specific context or identity—that they should be offered in a neutral, pure, or in other words, *color-blind* approach.

I remember a conversation with a Jesuit after one of the retreats where many of the directors had more deliberately attempted to interrogate the way we spoke of suffering in the Third Week. He cautioned me, instructed me to be more careful, not to allow the political or social views of directors to interfere with the way the Exercises are offered. He was concerned that our retreat talks contained stories beyond their scope and purpose, that we had used nontraditional music, poetry, and images to cater to the myriad of student identities in the room. He encouraged me to simplify the retreat. *Essentially? Let the exercises do what the exercises do.*

At the time I felt chagrin—branded brazen in unordained attempts to expand and contextualize something that did not belong to me as a lay director . . . much less a woman.

Later, I would recognize the depth of fear present in his concerns. Fear of change . . . fear of the Spirit's unruly revelations . . . fear of progression. I would remember that the gospels and life of Jesus are certainly not neutral. I would remember that the Exercises are intended to be in relationship to a director and a community. I would remember that the Exercises are in fact meant to be brazen, rooted in the experiences and writings of a man long before he would become a priest and saint. I would remember standing in Loyola castle's conversion chapel in Azpeitia, Spain, placing my hands flat on the altar that now stands in the center of the room where Ignatius first began to listen to his body, emotions, and the voice of the Spirit. I would remember leaning my weight on my hands and closing my eyes as a strong physical sensation traveled up my arms to my heart, feeling a direct connection to the Ignatian charism I now helped to animate. I remember smiling, presuming that Ignatius had likely not imagined me as part of his legacy. I doubt he could have foreseen the groups of womxn who claim and lead the mission at Jesuit works across the country; the IgnatianQ retreat for LGBTQ+ Jesuit college students; the Jesuit and lay collaborations and offerings that would reach beyond Catholic and in some places, even Christian boundaries; or the tables vibrating with conversations about spirituality and race. I felt an awe of Ignatius not because he was perfect or irreproachable. Rather, my admiration was for his very human journey to seek God and grow in understanding over the course of his entire life; his willingness to confess fault and doubt; and most of all the genius of creating the structure of the Exercises. Ignatius co-created something out of his own time and context that would find its way to us now, exercises that by their very nature demand continued transformation. Generations after that cannonball, we continue to discern and reveal the will of God over the course of our lives—calling us deeper, forward, and beyond what he—what we—once understood to be true.

I acknowledge that brazenness and intent alone are not enough— especially as white directors and leaders. We must be clear about our positionality, perspective, and motivations. Most importantly, we must be willing to fail and learn. We must remain active discerners ourselves.

I recall one of my first attempts to center the topic of racial justice on the silent retreats. It felt bold to address race directly, and as I looked out into the diverse faces of students, I remember wanting to be a *good* white director, I wanted them to be proud of me. I wanted to shake up and disturb the white students and directors, but maybe more so at that time, I wanted to *help* the black and brown students in that room. I wanted them to see themselves in the retreat. I wanted them to see that we were trying. But you can't bring the salmon back to a river simply because you want to.

My memory of the details of the talk I gave that weekend is blurred by many subsequent ones. What I remember clearly is the conversation I had with a young woman of color following it. In the silence, student after student touched my shoulder, sent affirming glances, or nodded gratitude for my offering as they left the room where we'd gathered for the evening's presentation. I was flooded with what surely felt like consolation and the kind of pride one feels after effort and bravery. The student who stayed behind allowed everyone to leave so she could break the silence and speak to me. Like the others, she began by thanking me. She acknowledged that she'd never heard a white person speak about race in a religious setting. She said what I did was important. She was glad her classmates heard the talk. Then she looked at me so generously—like so many other women of color before and since her, despite the burden I'd laid upon her—and explained to me what had actually happened in that room. While I felt like I offered an inclusive talk into a diverse room, I had really only directed it to the white students. This is often how it happens, whiteness centering whiteness, even—especially—in conversations about racial justice. I saw what she meant immediately, the obviousness of it hidden by my unexamined saviorism and lens of Whiteness. Her parting sentence evoked an embodied experience of the First Week—a blend of desire and longing combined with the generous, stinging sorrow of an inadequate offering. *"I long for a talk that speaks to me, not about me."*

Her ungrudging and forthright feedback, delivered into my haze of unexamined consolation, had the effect of stretching me—uncomfortably—into a more vulnerable, humbling, true consolation.

Even the deepest, most sincere consolation if plagued by ignorance needs to be assessed and understood in the fullness of its context. As most conversion moments will do, mine would shift and transform my understanding of discernment. I would wonder, how do I continue to trust my own consolation as a sign of alignment with the

Spirit of God? I don't believe my consolation was entirely false that evening. I began to understand that even true consolation can be misinterpreted through the *distorted lens of limited perspective and imagination*. I would come to understand that my consolation that night had been a cocktail of true consolation, false consolation, and ignorant consolation.

When I reflect on this moment, the true consolation I experienced affirmed the Spirit's desire for me to be bolder, to address race and Whiteness, to risk enough that I was willing to fail. I knew it was real because it was inviting me to grow and become more, as opposed to the falseness of my initial attraction to a more superficial self-satisfaction and unexamined saviorism.

My imagination has grown since then. Rather than meaning I make fewer mistakes, it means I expect them more often now—especially when I'm trying to grow. I understand the importance of claiming the perspective of my own identity and being clear whom I am addressing and when I might be overreaching. I welcome and seek feedback to remain accountable, and I know that the Exercises can never be fully liberated for retreatants of color by even the most well-intentioned of white directors alone. In the words of Maya Angelou, "Do the best you can until you know better. Then when you know better, do better." We are called to *more*.

If we reduce all experiences of consolation to *irrefutable* signs of alignment with the will of God, we will have no reason to examine them further. We must understand that we are not perfect receivers or translators of the movements of the Spirit. It is neither God, nor God's self-communication in question. Rather, if genuine self and contextual *awareness* are indeed presuppositions to practicing discernment, then contextual *ignorance*—deliberate or implicit—of the cultural impacts of racism and Whiteness is a *distortion* of discernment.

The closer one is to power and privilege in identity, role, or sphere of influence, the more one's experience of consolation—and discernment overall—should be examined.

Discernment is central to the way of proceeding as offered by St. Ignatius. The radical concept that we can attend to our own emotions, felt sensations, and encounters in order to sense the will of God in our lives converted the heart of Ignatius more than once. As he recovered at Loyola, the forced stillness drew his awareness to the intimate movements of the Spirit. Like anyone growing in awareness, it would take a while until he had the wisdom and words to move beyond sentiments of happiness and sadness to describe what he was experiencing. He would continue to nuance and organize his experiences over the course of his life. Ignatius understood that we are not meant to discern alone. The Exercises and accompanying Rules of Discernment, while they have their origin in one man's life, would be experienced, tested, and honed among his companions and first retreatants. We are the legacy and caretakers of that transformative work.

The First Principle and Foundation clarifies what and for whom and to what purpose we are discerning. It prepares us to understand that *discernment is an unfolding story*, a collective story of God spilling Godself into the world in search of relationship and a desire to manifest Love.

Ignatius's early discernment led him to a long night in confession witnessed by the Black Madonna at Montserrat. The liberation he experienced was deeply consoling. I imagine that later, when visited by doubt, he grasped for attachment to this first liberative confession without fully understanding that his love of God *inspired* the confession, rather than his confession *making him worthy* of God's love. He would fall into an arduous period of despair, shame, and confession without forgiveness. This would be disrupted by profound revelations and the *eyes of his understanding would be opened*. Ignatius never fully articulated this mystical experience, but we can understand its fruits. We know Ignatius embraced a spirituality grounded in mutuality, freedom, and a profound gratitude for all of creation. I imagine him bathed in the consoling love of God, gifted with glimpses of an intricately connected story of a transforming creation, and an abundant God's intimate desire for our response in return.

We do it a disservice to think of our response to this love as individual assignments we are trying to guess or get right. Rather, we are called to co-labor with God and one another in a continual unfolding of Creation. We are "from, of and for Love."[2] Every manifes-

---

[2] Jacqueline Syrup and Marie Schwan, CSJ, *Forgiveness a Guide for Prayer* (Winona, MN: St. Mary's Press, 1985), 11.

tation, every thread, every part of creation unfolding to tell one story, an ecosystem of God's love in the world.

The First Principle and Foundation—inspired by the message of Jesus—is insistent that each of us—each story—matters. The veil of racism and a culture of Whiteness distort this narrative and instead of abundance, we learn to move out of scarcity and fear. In that version, some lives end up mattering more than others.

Bryan Massingale, priest, author, and educator, has a helpful first chapter in his book *Racial Justice and the Catholic Church*, for understanding racism as culture.[3] It can be challenging to explain a culture in which we are immersed every day. Its power rests in the fact that it is pervasive and hidden in norms and standards that at first seem to have little to do with race. Massingale doesn't use the terms Whiteness or white supremacy culture, two other ways of describing the default expectations and practices that uphold the culture of racism. Whiteness is more than a conversation about white people. It shows up in the "attitudes and behaviors" that are considered normal and appropriate.[4] Intentional or implicit, the culture of Whiteness is dangerous because it can have dire consequences for those who cannot or choose not to adapt.

If we are not *intentionally* accounting for racism as culture when teaching or practicing discernment, then we are *implicitly* listening and choosing through that lens. Listening is the crux of discernment. Listening to our bodies, our emotions and felt senses, for the Spirit's movement in our relationships and encounters, for the voice of God inviting us to co-participate in the unfolding of the world. Imagine, however, a translucent veil filtering our senses. The veil is always there—seen or unseen—and has been for generations. Occasionally there are events—elections, protests, prophets, pandemics, deaths—that reveal or attempt to reveal it. Yet, it remains.

The true work of discernment should be about the business of dismantling this pervasive, harmful barrier to our collective freedom—identifying unfreedoms in the systems, structures, policies, and practices in which we live, move, and have our being. Until that

---

[3] Bryan N. Massingale, "What Is Racism?," *Racial Justice and the Catholic Church* (Maryknoll, NY: Orbis Books, 2010), 1–42.

[4] Massingale, *Racial Justice*, 22.

time, we need to deliberately account for its distortion and the bitter fruits of its impact on our personal and collective decision-making.

Recalling our opening story, even the best or most righteous of intent can still result in harmful impact. This is in part because we are practicing discernment in the midst of our human realities. One of the most harmful lies of Whiteness is that we are individuals, discerning on our own. The more consciously we grow in awareness of ourselves and our shared context, the more we understand how much that awareness matters. There is no faith worth believing in if it does not lead us all to freedom.

Burdening Ignatius with understanding racism in the US in the twenty-first century is unreasonable. Yet, we are called to observe the signs of *our* time. We can begin by understanding how Whiteness shows up in cultural norms and assumptions, so that we can recognize it. Tema Okun's work on the characteristics of White Supremacy Culture (WSC) goes into more detail about the default of expectations of dominant culture.[5] They cloud our ability to unfold into our call and purpose by distorting what we think is possible or appropriate.

Okun describes multiple characteristics prevalent in our institutions, media, and the undergirding systems of this country. Closer to home, these same characteristics can show up in our theologies, liturgies, and Jesuit works. Most of the characteristics—for example perfectionism or individualism[6]—are also impediments to authentic spiritual life, meaning that ironically, while these characteristics benefit some more than others and result in real harm to marginalized identities, they aren't conducive to a healthy spiritual life for any of us.

---

[5] Tema Okun, *White Supremacy Culture—Still Here*, www.whitesupremacyculture. info, 2021. This piece on white supremacy culture builds on the work of many people, including (but not limited to) Andrea Ayvazian, Bree Carlson, Beverly Daniel Tatum, M. E. Dueker, Nancy Emond, Kenneth Jones, Jonn Lunsford, Sharon Martinas, Joan Olsson, David Rogers, James Williams, Sally Yee, as well as the work of Grassroots Leadership, Equity Institute Inc., the People's Institute for Survival and Beyond, the Challenging White Supremacy workshop, the Lillie Allen Institute, the Western States Center, and the contributions of hundreds of participants in the DR process. Some sections are based on the work of Daniel Buford, a lead trainer with the People's Institute for Survival and Beyond who has done extensive research on white supremacy culture.

[6] Okun, *White Supremacy Culture*.

Whiteness can impede good discernment by distorting our experience of consolation. All too often, we mistake comfort for consolation, or fail to recognize that true consolation can *feel* uncomfortable.

Consolation isn't simply a glad feeling acting as a clue to God's will. Consolation *is* God self-communicating, a sacramental sign of God's grace and desire, an affirmation that we are in alignment with a just and loving God's story.

In the beginning, love spilled out into creation, becoming particularized into the threads of each person, creature, and moment—expressing and becoming a diverse, ongoing, laboring story of love to which each of us are personally called to participate. When we are in alignment with the story, when we manifest the love God intended to manifest through us—we experience true consolation.

We need more nuanced conversations about felt senses and emotions. Ignatius himself grew more complex as his experiences became more complex. He understood that sometimes feelings of discomfort or disease could be the good spirit trying to shift a retreatant from a place of sin. He dealt with this by first suggesting there are two ways of experiencing spirits, those on the committed spiritual path, desiring to listen to the will of God, and those moving from sin to sin. In the first case, consoling feelings would encourage and affirm, while feelings of despair would indicate that we should wait to make a choice and certainly not one rooted in that despair. In the second case, for someone not on the spiritual path, consoling feelings could be deceptive—and one should listen more closely to feelings that agitate and "trouble" one's current trajectory.

The second way Ignatius accounted for various experiences of consolation was to indicate the three times of decision-making for those desiring to be guided by the Spirit. The first of these times is the experience of inner clarity and certainty, inferring the need for a less explicit discernment and election in those cases.

I respect Ignatius for understanding that God might deal with us differently depending on who we are and in what state we are in. Yet there is an inherent danger in the way we translate this—a danger in believing that "being on the spiritual path," aka having good intent, means the spirit of consolation won't show up in agitating or troubling ways; or presuming that an experience of certain consolation does not need to be as further examined. I'm not even sure this was Ignatius's intention, yet it is often how I hear it taught or described.

Following the will of God for both Jesus and Ignatius was often disruptive and countercultural, especially to those who believed themselves to be committed to the spiritual path and above recrimination. Liberation can *feel* disruptive, transformation can *feel* uncomfortable—and still, true consolation can be present.

I imagine that there truly is a different experience for those on the absolute extreme of deliberately courting evil and violence. What I mostly encounter, however, are human beings who try and sometimes fail, who want to want to find their true selves, folks struggling to believe they are beloved and worthy, people who aren't sure how to listen for the Spirit, folks who are trapped in the burden of individual, decontextualized discernment, and many who are caught up in or complicit in systems and traps of Whiteness and power. Our commitment and clarity varies throughout the course of our lives; our need for comfort or affliction doesn't always align with good intentions.

The trap inherent to this unexamined way of thinking is that those who are on a committed spiritual path might not be open to the experience of *God* communicating through disturbance or discomfort.

Power, privilege, and wealth have a tendency to narrow our experiences, limit imagination, and convince us that comfort *is* consolation. The God Ignatius describes and Jesus embodies desires growth and abundance and boundlessness of love. Those of us who are closest to power by role, identity, or sphere of influence could very well experience consolation (God's will) much more like a troubling of the waters, a stretching of the heart, invitations to discomfort and sacrifice. It is harder for a rich man to enter heaven than a camel through the eye of a needle.[7] Power and privilege impacts the way we interpret and discern the Spirit.

As Massingale says so directly, in his article in America magazine, "It is white comfort that sets the limits of conversations regarding racial justice."[8] We know that discomfort is a necessary sign and ex-

---

[7] Matthew 19:23-24.

[8] Bryan N. Massingale, "Racism Is a Sickness of the Soul: Can Jesuit Spirituality Help Us Heal?," *America* (November 20, 2017).

perience of growth. We also know Whiteness feigns feeling unsafe or desolate when invited into discomfort.

Discernment requires both honesty and vulnerability—this is how we grow—stretching our hearts for the *magis*. Consolation expands. With self-awareness, this can feel wonderful—like taking a breath more fully than usual, ribs expanding, muscles moving, more oxygen. Sometimes though, stretching is painful, tearing apart layers of restrictive fascia in order to provide our heart with more range of motion. This kind of consolation, while *uncomfortable*, is *still* expansive, liberating, and true.

When we become too attached to a singular perspective, it can take some strong encouragement to move. Ironically, staying still in this restricted state can feel *comfortable*; if we don't move, if we don't look beyond ourselves, we will not notice the restriction. This kind of contentment can be confused with consolation, even though it prevents us from more fully embracing Spirit and community. We *can* discern the difference in God's true comfort because it is yielding, healthy, generous, and inviting. False comfort is discerned by its unyielding, exacting, prescriptive demand or inability to move beyond ourselves toward real encounters and transformation.

In light of the cultural context of race and Whiteness, and these questions about consolation, I return to the belief that power and privilege need to be deliberate lenses for discernment. More specifically, the closer one is to power and privilege in identity, role, or sphere of influence, the more one must intentionally include Whiteness and racism in the election process. As directors and Ignatian leaders, not only must we more eagerly lean into this kind of examination ourselves, we must create circumstances that make it possible for directees as well.

If indeed a consolation is true and genuine then it will withstand being held up to the light of examination. While it might shift under the inspection of this sharp lens—discernment is never wasted. In fact, once examined we will understand that it is the *consolation* that we are called to follow into freedom—even when, especially when, it moves beyond what we expected.

I was fortunate to be part of a small community that supported an acquaintance—a white, cis woman—through a significant decision-making process about whether or not she should run for local office.

Plagued by indecision, she entered into a discernment. Patiently, she sifted out the negative self-talk that questioned her worth and value as a woman. She prayed and did imaginative exercises. Over the course of weeks, she spoke to friends and colleagues, drew colorful mind maps to sort out financial and family obligations, gathered information and contemplated her gifts and resources. The deeper she traversed into this discernment, the more consoled she grew and she found herself growing more and more certain as she imagined serving her community in this way. I have very little doubt that her consolation was real, though not fully examined.

Then she invited one more layer of election. Later, she explained that the initial consolation was so powerful, she almost hesitated to question it further. Instead, she made a deliberate decision to consider the context of identity, power, and Whiteness.

If she ran and won she would be representing a primarily immigrant community of color. She found herself and her consolation troubled by a deeper value she was trying to cultivate. Running for office would bring more power into her life and influence the lives of neighbors with whom she did not share the same context.

She decided not to run for office. That could be a fine place to end—with a realization that something isn't for us because of the time and context we are in.

She moved through her disappointment and confusion and continued to consider the entire ecosystem around her. She realized she could follow her consolation into a new outcome, one that truthfully, had been veiled by Whiteness as an initial option.

In lieu of running, she found another neighbor who was also considering running for office and would be much more representative of the community and decided to actively support her. In their own ways, these two women each broke through barriers of Whiteness to arrive at deeper, truer consoling responses for each of them.

Whiteness is a default lens. If we are not acknowledging it, we are complicit with it. The culture of racism and Whiteness does not mean the Exercises need to be changed to *help* people of color experience them. It means the Exercises are being offered through a veil that has the potential to distort and even pervert our understanding and interpretation of the voice of God in our lives and our world. Liberating the Exercises—exercises, by the way, whose purpose is to liberate—will mean *more God* for all of us.

As a white Catholic, committed to living at the intersection of faith and racial justice, I know how discomfort can hold me back. I witness it all around me, often in those of us with the best of intentions. When we over-emphasize that white Christians are well-intentioned or mean well, we prioritize comfort over true discernment. We are in dire need of a troubling, expanding discernment willing to lift its gaze to account for the stories around us.

One of the lies of Whiteness is that we can know ourselves outside the context of community. We don't exist as separate, self-sustaining creatures—like the salmon, we can only exist in our healthy, flourishing fullness in relationship to the rest of a diverse creation. Like industry and pollution alter the life cycle of the river and the salmon—so too does Whiteness (which is enmeshed in misogyny, hierarchy, sexism, forced binaries, homophobia, ableism, etc.) distort the ways we choose to manifest our faith.

I was asked to reflect on the question, should the Spiritual Exercises be offered in a color-blind fashion? Let me insist, we are not offering the Exercises in a neutral fashion now. We are *already* offering and making the Exercises through a lens of Whiteness and dominant culture. We can't *not* offer it through some lens, whether intentionally or ignorantly. If we are willing to bring our awareness to this we can account for it, seeking more and more freedom.

As we consider the way forward, I implore us to imagine that there is *more* than we can see, or choose, or manifest on our own. Dismantling racism isn't even the end point. There is a horizon after racial justice—a powerful, creative joy when we become truly available to God's desires to fully manifest in this world.

I cannot definitively answer the question of whether or not the Spiritual Exercises of St. Ignatius have the potential to be a source of liberation for retreatants and communities of color. I will trust and listen to the colleagues and friends who are interrogating and exploring that question.

I can, however, say with conviction that it is vital to name and disturb the default veil or lens of Whiteness that pervades the way we talk about and practice spiritual discernment. I can say with confidence that we cannot speak about *listening* for God, without acknowledging the ways the culture of racism distorts *how* we listen. I can say with confidence that the Spirit and wisdom to do so are already available and among our Ignatian communities. I can say with confidence that this desire and longing are not new, or singular, or fleeting.

> Take a deep breath.
> What do you feel? Daunted? Excited? Ready? Reluctant?
> Whatever whisper or wellspring of Hope lies within us, let it be a lamp unto our feet.
> Let us grow in awareness of ourselves, our contexts, and the ecosystems around us.
> Let us free our hearts, root ourselves in community and right relationships.
> Then let us listen—and allow ourselves and the Exercises to grow— to expand—
> to be boundlessly at the mercy of God's imagination, not ours alone.
> Let us allow the eyes of our understanding to be opened.

11

Seeing Bodies

Using the Separate Lenses Frantz Fanon and Ignatius of Loyola for Healing

Patrick Saint-Jean, SJ

The body is vital to our understanding of race. Ignatius of Loyola insisted that the body is also essential to our relationship with God; he believed in the Incarnation—the literal "enfleshment" of divinity in the body of Jesus Christ. A psychoanalytic theorist, Frantz Fanon, lacks the Ignatian focus on Jesus, and yet he too uses the body as a source of human meaning. Fanon believed it was the center of self-reference. Ignatius and Fanon refer to the human body as a central component in our understanding of reality. At the same time, both speak of the body in terms of something greater than mere physical existence; for Ignatius and Fanon, physical flesh *embodies* meaning. For good or ill, our bodies carry meaning out into the physical, tangible world. They are visible signifiers of identity, capable of being *seen*.

While Fanon centralized the body, his predecessor, Sigmund Freud, the father of psychoanalysis, had a less embodied philosophy. Despite his emphasis on the phallus, Freud saw physical reality as having a subordinate, secondary status to mental activity. Today, Freud himself may be considered academically passé, but his belief in the objective reality of mental activity still influences the way most of us think about the world. As W. H. Auden commented about Freud, "If often he was wrong and, at times absurd, to us he is no more a person now but a whole climate of opinion under whom we conduct our different lives."[1] Because of Freud's influence (at least in part), we speak of maladaptive mental activity as though it were as specific and identifiable as a virus, we use mental abstractions to describe both ourselves and others, and we often overlook the real-life physical causalities that exist around us. This form of disembodied thinking has facilitated the concept of mental "color-blindedness" that has become so prevalent among whites.

"I don't see color." That statement has recently been spoken again and again by white people, and they say it with utter conviction. After all, if they can live in an intellectual realm where race is unreal, then they are excused from any accusation of racism. They can speak as though they are disembodied minds perceiving other minds in a mental dimension where the physical agonies of racism do not exist. From this rarified perspective, whites hover above racism; it no longer troubles their field of vision because they claim to function from a purely intellectual, even spiritual level. Meanwhile, of course, those of us who inhabit Black bodies know full well that racism is a physical fact, one that threatens our flesh at so many levels that it is nearly omnipresent in our lives. Race may have no real scientific foundation, but it is nevertheless engrained in us, both as individuals and as a society. Its effects are undeniable in the "real world," the physical world inhabited by visible bodies.

Invisibility

The claim to "not see color" is a lie that strives to render race invisible. Many white progressives and liberals, as well as some conservatives, have embraced this comforting falsehood. While Sigmund Freud's ideology may have facilitated the belief in an abstract, intangible reality, this way of looking at the world also has deep roots in Christianity.

The gospel message is based on incarnation—the literal expression of divinity in (visible) human flesh. Somewhere along the way, how-

---

[1] W. H. Auden, "In Memory of Sigmund Freud," in *In Solitude, for Company*, ed. Katherine Bucknell and Nicholas Jenkins (Oxford: Clarendon Press, 1995), 143.

ever, the church lost sight of this. The church replaced Jesus's message of union among many with its firm belief in duality: spirit and body, good and evil, white and black. Now, instead of the body being the site of God's tangible presence and revelation, it became a source of sin and temptation. The ethereal "spirit" became the emphasis, while the body appeared to go missing from Christian theology.

The body was still there, Colleen Griffith writes, "buried in the deep recesses of Christian tradition. The mythic story of Creation affirmed its goodness. Incarnation gave it theological significance. Resurrection deemed it integral to human fullness of life."[2] And yet the importance and sanctity of the body all but disappeared from Christianity. Charles Taylor refers to this as a kind of "excarnation" within Christianity that is the very antithesis of Christ's original message. Divine love, Taylor writes, can only be created and expressed in "enfleshment"; it "moves outward from the guts."[3]

The denial of divine incarnation is not a modern invention. In the second century after Christ, Docetism[4] was already rejecting the reality of Christ's physical body. The Docetists believed that Christ did not, in fact, become flesh; he just *appeared* to have a body, an illusion he put on for the convenience of his followers. According to Docetist theology, Christ is completely divine; his body—his humanity—was merely a disguise with no foundation in physical reality. His historicity was thus denied, for he was never born, never actually walked the earth, never died, and hence was never resurrected.[5]

A couple of centuries later, the Nestorians[6] again voiced doubts that God and humanity could be physically joined. To get around this mystery, they insisted that Christ must have had two distinct

---

[2] Colleen M. Griffith, "Spirituality and the Body," in *Ethics and Spirituality*, Readings in Moral Theology No. 17, ed. Charles E. Curran and Lisa A. Fullam (Mahwah, NJ: Paulist Press, 2014), 235.

[3] Charles Taylor, *A Secular Age* (Harvard, MA: Belknap, 2018), 741, 771.

[4] The word *Docetism* has its roots in the Greek language, meaning "to seem" or "to show."

[5] In response to the Docetists, St. Irenaeus affirmed that the flesh is the "hinge" or "axis" of human salvation through Christ, and in 325 CE, the Council of Nicaea affirmed, with Irenaeus, that "Jesus is true God and true Human."

[6] This heresy is named after Nestorius, a fifth-century Patriarch of Constantinople. (Historians are not clear, however, if he actually held all the views attributed to him concerning the humanity and divinity of Christ.)

natures—one human, the other divine—which functioned separately from one another. This meant that when Jesus died on the cross, his human flesh experienced agony, but his divine nature was untouched, immune to physical suffering.[7]

The church officially labeled these ideas as "heresy," and yet they continue to persist in our world today. The concept of a fusion of the divine with our tangible, visible flesh is so incomprehensible that for all practical purposes, Christianity quietly sets it aside. The physical senses, including sight, are thus discredited, while Christians insist they live in a "spiritual" realm, a symbolic space that allows us to project invisibility onto bodies our physical eyes can clearly see.

Cardinal Ratzinger noted this problem within Christianity, saying:

> At the very moment that we discover the corporality of the human being with all the fibres of our existence, in such a way that we can only understand His spirit as incarnate, in such a way that Christ *is* body, not *has* body, people try to save the Christian faith by completely disembodying it, by taking refuge in a region of "mere" mind, of pure self-satisfying interpretation, which seems to be immune from criticism only through its lack of contact with reality.[8]

The "Mystical Body of Christ" is a concept that facilitates the imaginary construct of invisibility. It refers to the belief that all Christians are united within Christ's "spiritual" body. Faced with the challenges of World War II, Jesuit author Emile Mersch wrote in 1939 that within this spiritual body, "there is no longer any separation." The Mystical Body, he claimed, makes it impossible for Christians to hide "under their egoisms of class, of race, or of persons, under theories of massacre and of hostilities, of reprisals and of parties."[9] A few years later, in 1943, Pope Pius XII issued a papal encyclical on the

---

[7] The Council of Ephesus in 431 CE rejected Nestorianism and affirmed the unity of Christ's two natures.

[8] Joseph Ratzinger, *Introduction to Christianity*, 2nd ed. (San Francisco: Ignatius Press, 2004), 278–79. The Cardinal went on to say, "But Christian faith really means precisely the acknowledgement that God is not the prisoner of his own eternity, not limited to the solely spiritual; that he is capable of operating here and now, in the midst of my world, and that he did operate in it through Jesus."

[9] Emile Mersch, *Morality and the Mystical Body* (New York: P. J. Kenedy & Sons, 1939), 172, 176.

doctrine, saying that the Mystical Body offers humanity a "divinely-given unity—by which all men of every race are united to Christ in the bond of brotherhood."[10] The encyclical sought to give spiritual comfort to a war-torn Europe, but even as it pointed to Christ's mystical body as a form of interracial communion, it also prioritized spiritual union through and with Christ over the pursuit of earthly justice or peace. It exhorted people suffering from the loss of homes and loved ones to look to the mystical body for encouragement, to look beyond earth at heaven.

The Mystical Body of Christ is an idea that still claims to offer an answer to the problem of racism. White Christians still use it as a way to support their assertion that they "don't see color." S. Kyle Johnson gives a good analysis of why the concept of the Mystical Body tends to move us away from the visible body and into the realm of invisible spirit:

> First, the doctrine often lends itself to language of reconciliation as opposed to liberation or racial justice. Second, a "color-blind discourse" is employed: Wherever emphasis is placed on the Church as a continued incarnation, Christ's mystical flesh is described in an unresolved dialectic of either being a non-racial flesh, or a transparent flesh made up of the different races and cultures therein contained. Third, while the doctrine at times emphasizes the necessity for a historical, embodied, reality of anti-racist existence, some of the rhetoric brackets historical transformation of violence and racism as a primarily spiritual or eschatological ideal, instead instructing patient endurance of evil circumstances.[11]

The Mystical Body is so "spiritual" that it becomes invisible.[12] It reinforces the belief that Christians can be *in* the flesh but not *of* the

---

[10] Pope Pius XII, *Mystici Corporis Christi* 5 (Vatican City: Libreria Editrice Vaticana, 1943), https://www.vatican.va/content/pius-xii/en/encyclicals/documents/hf_p-xii_enc_29061943_mystici-corporis-christi.html.

[11] S. Kyle Johnson, "Racism and the Mystical Body of Christ," 2019, https://www.academia.edu/40560920/Racism_and_the_Mystical_Body_of_Christ.

[12] M. Shawn Copeland has formulated a concept of the Mystical Body that avoids the racist pitfalls described here. Arguing that "the flesh of the church is marked (as was [Christ's] flesh) by race, sex, gender, sexuality, and culture," Copeland manages to unite the particular, historical Christ with his mystical body. (M. Shawn Copeland, *Enfleshing Freedom: Body, Race, and Being* [Minneapolis: Fortress Press, 2010], 5.)

flesh. Even in its insistence that it unites all people into one, it creates a blank space that whites can claim as their own. It refuses to "see color."

In Richard Dyer's book *White*, he argues that European Christians constructed "whiteness" as a spirit that is also "in but not of the body."[13] In earlier centuries, a false science that claimed to study other races' bodies allowed whites to avoid biological self-awareness that might have made them realize they were "like non-whites, no more than their bodies"[14] When, in the late nineteenth and twentieth centuries, whites did apply science to themselves, they attempted to prove their biological superiority with the study of genes—which, like "spirit," cannot be perceived with the physical eye. Thus, whiteness could continue to be an invisible, yet somehow real, concept.[15]

In a paradoxical fashion, the invisibility of "whiteness" manages to also render individual Blacks invisible. Ralph Ellison described his own invisibility as a product of white vision:

> That invisibility to which I refer occurs because of a particular disposition of the eyes of those with whom I come in contact. A matter of the construction of their *inner* eyes, those eyes with which they look through their physical eyes upon reality.[16]

Fanon expressed his similar reaction to white vision as "a zone of nonbeing, an extraordinarily sterile and arid region."[17] He described it not as a feeling of inferiority, but as "a feeling of not existing."[18]

---

[13] Richard Dyer, *White: Essays on Race and Culture* (New York: Routledge, 1997), 14.

[14] Dyer, *White*, 23.

[15] Dyer indicates that the concept of whiteness gains its authority through its disembodiment. Whiteness, he says, functions precisely because of its invisibility. And so, in today's racialized world, an idea that has no basis in the physical world—whiteness—has become the standard against which we are all measured. *White* equals superiority, morality, intelligence, culture, while *Black* equals inferiority, evil, ignorance, and the primitive. Whiteness is not an actual skin color; it is not a genetic race; and yet it insists that it is *just human*. It defines all else that falls shorts of whiteness as nonhuman.

[16] Ralph Ellison, *The Invisible Man* (New York: Vintage, 1989), 3.

[17] Frantz Fanon, *Black Skin, White Masks*, trans. Charles Lam Markmann (New York: Grove Press, 1967), 10.

[18] Fanon, *Black Skin, White Masks*, 118.

As a Black man, how do I make sense of this invisibility I too experience? Fanon and Ignatius of Loyola all offer me answers. In Western society there is a resistance to seeing unity among many that was applied to the body in our midst. Instead of viewing the body as a Gestalt,[19] something that exists as a meaningful unity, science tends to regard it as a complex mechanism made up of discrete parts.[20]

This concept of the importance of being seen means we have little access to our own physical realities. Instead, the body becomes a surface to be written on by others.[21] The skin becomes that which contains the body, giving it a precise boundary that sets it apart from a socially mapped space. For very young children, this setting-apart from other bodies is the beginning of identity formation.[22] For the Black child,[23] this is also the stage when race first enters his experience, fragmenting him from the reality of his biological sufficiency. In the mirror of white people's regard, he learns that his body is problematic. As W. E. B. DuBois put it in *The Souls of Blackfolk*, "How does it feel to be a problem? To have your very body and the bodies of your children to be assumed to be criminal, violent, malignant."

Foundational to racism is the concept that people of different skin colors have fundamental differences, not only physically but also characteristically and morally. In order to create the illusion of white superiority, the idea that Black people are frightening, hypersexual,

---

[19] Though Jacques Lacan is important here as well to understand the body. For him, the body remained a sacred place to be oneself, as he challenged us to engage with the symbol of the body. The advent of the scientific age changed the way we think of the human body.

[20] The human infant, according to Lacan, constructs her sense of self from the "mirror" of others' regard. The reflections that others give the infant about her physical identity may not be accurate. As Lacan stated, "The *mirror stage* is a drama whose internal thrust . . . [leads] to the assumption of the armour of an alienating identity, which will mark with its rigid structure the infant's entire mental development."

[21] Jacques Lacan, *Écrits* (Paris: Éditions du Seuil, 1966), 647ff.

[22] Self-awareness, according to Lacan, is in large part illusory, for it is rooted in the image of the body that others reflect back at us.

[23] The child's image of his own body, the foundational site for the development of his sense of self, said Lacan, is shaped by the cultural reflection he receives from other people. The Black child can only see himself as he is seen by the white racist world. Whiteness becomes the master signifier from which Black individuals cannot escape.

and almost animalistic needed to be embedded deeply into people's minds. These racist ideas were used to justify the economic exploitation of Black people and to ease white consciences, but they were based on faulty science, such as eugenics.[24]

False beliefs take on a reality of their own. They grow stronger and more deeply rooted through repetition. When beliefs are repeated enough times, and people hear them enough times, they internalize them. Just as Blacks hear about their inferior status and begin to believe it, whites hear of their superior status and the danger of Black bodies. These beliefs have become ingrained in our minds, but they don't stay there. Racist beliefs—mental constructs—shape physical reality. They shape our society's legislation, education, medical care, and religious institutions. Ironically, the belief that Black bodies are dangerous creates a world where Black bodies are not safe. For the Black child[25] in particular, the body is always associated with some degree of trauma.[26] As Sheshadri-Crooks summarized, "The discourse of whiteness can be said to function as a condition of dominant subjectivity: it inserts the subject into the symbolic order."[27] Instead of shaping a positive quality, an absence results—"the not-realized"[28] and "the unborn."[29]

---

[24] Eugenics—the study of how to arrange human reproduction to increase the occurrence of desirable heritable characteristics—was thought by many whites to be a scientific foundation for white superiority. Eugenics prioritized white people as the ideal race and sought to erase other races. It was the principle behind Hitler's approach to the "Jewish problem." In short, eugenics offered an authoritative scientific language to substantiate whites' bias against those they feared as dangerous. The evidence base for eugenics, of course, was not only poorly constructed but blatantly false. It was not the product of science but rather of racist imagination.

[25] Lacan believed that the "Real" (the underlying historical and physical causality) and the "Symbolic" (the meaning imposed from the outside world) become interwoven, determining each other in a circular causality. Lacan's Real and the Symbolic become a notion in this Black child trauma.

[26] Jacques Lacan, *Seminar: XI* (Paris: Éditions du Seuil, 1975), 26.

[27] Kalpana Sheshadri-Crooks, "The Comedy of Domination: Psychoanalysis and the Conceit of Whiteness," in *The Psychoanalysis of Race*, ed. Christopher Lane (New York: Columbia University Press, 1998), 358.

[28] Thus, the task we face in the work of anti-racism is to reconnect with the body— the body freed from the imaginary constructs of racism. As Lacan said, we have "an appointment with a real that eludes us."

[29] Ibid., p. 32.

Frantz Fanon and the Power of the White Gaze

Frantz Fanon (1924–1961) expanded on the field of post-colonial studies. Fanon was a psychoanalyst who used both his clinical research and lived experience of being a Black man in a racist world to study the effects of racism on individuals. His work has inspired anti-colonial liberation movements.

In Fanon's book *Black Skin, White Masks*, he describes his own experience of the fragmenting mirror of white regard: "I had to meet the white man's eyes. An unfamiliar weight burdened me. In the white world, the man of colour encounters difficulties in the development of his body schema. . . . I was battered down by tom-toms, cannibalism, intellectual deficiency, fetishism, racial defects." Fanon is speaking here of the history of racist thought—a noncorporeal ideology with no factual basis in physical reality—and yet it has an impact on his sense of his own body. "What else could it be for me," he asks, "but an amputation, an excision, a hemorrhage that spattered my whole body with black blood?"[30]

In the same book, Fanon describes another similar incident where his sense of his own body is changed because of a white person's gaze. When a white child points at him and cries, "Look, a Negro!" at first, Fanon laughs. Then, however, he says, "I could no longer laugh, because I already know there were legends, stories, history and above all *historicity*" that were all contained within the child's cry. Once again, an incorporeal body of thought takes on physical weight when it is applied to Fanon's body. "The corporal schema crumbled," he wrote, "its place taken by a racial epidermal schema." He no longer bore his body as an individual identity but he had become "responsible for my body, for my race, for my ancestors."

Black people's internalization of their supposed inferiority is continuously fed by the white gaze. Meanwhile, the detriment of the white gaze touches not only the interior awareness of Black people; it also puts their bodies in physical danger. The white gaze incorporates a long story within itself, one that reaches back centuries through colonialism and slavery to create a narrative that insists Black bodies are dangerous objects. At some level, when white people see a Black

---

[30] Fanon, *Black Skin, White Masks*, 85.

person they understand themselves to be endangered and in need of further violence to keep the Black threat at bay. Whites, said Fanon, "have woven me out of a thousand details, anecdotes, stories."[31] Using Laconian language, David Marriott commented that "racist society projects onto the black body feelings and values . . . whose *signification* is one of disfiguration, in which the very surface of the body, its skin, becomes a metonym for a certain *historicity of hatred*."[32]

It is this same ancient narrative—the "historicity of hatred"—behind white eyes that led to slavery's brutality, with its routine beating, whipping, shackling, hanging, burning, mutilation, branding, rape, and imprisonment.[33] This narrative was also present after slavery came to an end, when nearly two thousand Black people were killed by white supremacist terrorism during the Reconstruction years from 1865 to 1876, and it was still there during the Jim Crow era, when another four to five thousand Blacks were lynched.[34]

Today's white people did not construct the centuries-old story that Black bodies are both inferior and dangerous, but whether whites like it or not, they have inherited it. It is as present in their minds as the contrary story that they "don't see color." In moments of stress, the older, more deeply ingrained story will inevitably rise to the forefront, counteracting any more politically correct ideologies. In the twenty-first century, the narrative behind the white gaze is still so potent that it caused George Floyd's murder, as well as the deaths of many other Black men and women, at the hands of police officers.

When a jury convicted police officer Derek Chauvin of Floyd's murder, they broke through a rigid policy of finding white police innocent in the deaths of Black men. In many earlier trials, the courts' decisions went the other way. In 2014, for example, Eric Garner died after being held in a chokehold by officer Daniel Pantaleo; no criminal charges were brought against Pantaleo. Later that same year, police

---

[31] Fanon, *Black Skin, White Masks*, 111.

[32] David Marriott, "The Racialized Body," in *The Cambridge Companion to the Body in Literature* (Cambridge, UK: Cambridge University Press, 2015), 164; emphasis in original.

[33] Wilbert Ellis Moore, *American Negro Slavery and Abolition: A Sociological Study* (North Stratford, NH: Ayer Publishing, 1980), 114.

[34] Alex Fox, "Nearly 2,000 Black Americans Were Lynched During Reconstruction," *Smithsonian Magazine* (June 18, 2020), https://www.smithsonianmag.com/smart-news/nearly-2000-black-americans-were-lynched-during-reconstruction-180975120/.

officer Darren Wilson fatally shot Michael Brown; no charges were brought against Wilson. In 2015, police officer Ray Tensing shot Samuel DuBose in the head; charges were brought against Tensing, but eventually, a deadlocked jury led to a mistrial. Later in 2015, Sandra Bland was arrested for failing to signal a lane change and three days later was found dead in her jail cell; Brian Encinia, the state trooper who pulled her over, was accused of lying and indicted on perjury, but the charge was later dropped. The next year, in 2016, after officer Jeronimo Yanez shot Philando Castile seven times, Yanez was tried on charges of second-degree manslaughter, but a jury acquitted him. The police officers who killed Terrence Crutcher later that year were also acquitted. A grand jury voted to not file charges against Daniel Prude's killers in 2021, and Breonna Taylor's killers also escaped legal changes.

In all these cases, the police and the courts looked at Black bodies and used the lens of Fanon's "historico-racial schema." In Judith Butler's view, in all these situations, "it is necessary to read not only for the 'event' of violence, but for the racist schema that orchestrates and interprets the event, which splits the violent intention off from the body who wields it and attributes it to the body who receives it."[35]

In these situations, where Black bodies perceived as dangerous then become the recipients of violence, Black are *seen*, but they are not seen accurately. They are seen only through the warped lens of racism, and, like children in centuries past, they are seen but not heard. Their voices have been silenced by chokeholds, by gunshot, by death. "To speak," wrote Fanon, "is to exist absolutely for the other,"[36] but racism denies Blacks the right to speak. This silencing is not only exterior. It also causes deep inner damage. As Fanon wrote,

> [when] Blacks make contact with the white world a certain sensitizing action takes place. If the psychic structure is fragile, we observe a collapse of the ego. The black man stops behaving as an *actional* person. His actions are destined for "the Other" (in the guise of the white man), since only "the Other" can enhance his status and give him self-esteem at the ethical level.

[35] Judith Butler, "Endangered/Endangering: Schematic Racism and White Paranoia," in *The Judith Butler Reader*, ed. Sara Salih with Judith Butler (New York: Blackwell Publishing, 2004), 210.
[36] Fanon, *Black Skin, White Masks*, 17.

When set against such scrutiny, judgment, and belittlement by the white world, Blacks begin to either fill the stereotypical roles they've been given, or they try to "live for the Other," becoming "more white" and living for the approval and comfort of white people.

According to Fanon, "the black man is a toy in the hands of the white man."[37] By this he means that when the Black man is seen, he is seen only as an object, something nearly inanimate, not human, something without a voice. The toy cannot operate on its own; it must have an owner who has dominance and gives life to the toy, in a similar way that Blacks can only be visible through the white gaze. Fanon describes this experience as "crushing objecthood." The Black man is depersonalized to the point that violence and discrimination against him is justified. Racism is not an ethereal ideology floating harmlessly in the mind. The violence of racism, Fanon wrote, is interiorized in "muscular spasms." Racism is visceral. It is embodied. It is visible. It will continue to exist until we can find a new way to see.

The Ignatian Vision

The sixteenth-century founder of the Jesuits, Ignatius of Loyola, offers us that new way of seeing. As Jesuit author David Fleming explains:

> It's often said, "I'll believe it when I see it." But Ignatius of Loyola reverses the saying: "When I believe it, I'll see it." He observed that our vision largely controls our perception. If we think the world is a bleak place, full of evil, greedy, selfish people who have no love for God or each other, that's what we will see when we look around. If we think that our world is full of goodness and opportunity, a place that God created and sustains and loves, that is what we'll find. Ignatius thought that the right vision lies at the heart of our relationship with God.[38]

The Spiritual Exercises that Ignatius wrote for his followers give us a roadmap for "right vision." Although in many ways the Exercises guide us to an individual, interior experience of self-examination, Ignatius leads us to examine our own reactions and perceptions in a

---

[37] Fanon, 119.
[38] David L. Fleming, SJ, *What Is Ignatian Spirituality?* (Chicago: Loyola, 2011), 1.

way that opens us up to the world around us. We begin to see with new eyes.

The lens through which we now see is the lens of divine incarnation. As Jesuit Father Pedro Arrupe reminded us, Jesus Christ is "the Eternal King of the Exercises, the Incarnate Son of God, . . . the key of our spirituality."[39] In the four "weeks" of the Exercises, we are led deeper and deeper into the Incarnation, thus experiencing embodiment as the very point at which we connect with the divine. We come to realize that the visual, tangible body is holy.

Ignatius's Gaze

In the First Week, we become aware of the ways sin has separated us from the health-restoring vision of the Divine Presence in our world. At the same time that we realize the ways sin has warped our perceptions, we also find ourselves surrounded by divine love. Love empowers us to move now into a new experience of the meaning of the Incarnation. As Jesuit author William Barry put it: "Ignatius presupposes that at every moment of our existence God is . . . trying to draw us into an awareness, a consciousness of the reality of who we are in God's sight."[40] While Fanon defines meaning in the intersection between flesh and others' vision, Ignatius points to a reality where our bodies participate in our communion with God and one another. Unlike the destructive "white vision," divine vision affirms and empowers. It generates relationship rather than division.

In the Second Week of the Spiritual Exercises, we continue to affirm the reality of the body through the use of our senses, particularly our vision. "*See* Jesus going about his life," Ignatius advises; in other words, use mental imagery to create a felt experience of the physicality of Jesus's life. This facilitates an understanding that *every* body (not just Christ's body) is also a "temple." Skin and bones, nerves and muscles, heart and intestines: all are drawn together into the site of divine indwelling. When St. Paul declared that our bodies are temples of the Holy Spirit (1 Cor 6:19), he was expressing the same

---

[39] Pedro Arrupe, "Fifty Years as a Jesuit," in *Essential Writings*, ed. Kevin Burke (Maryknoll, NY: Orbis Books, 2004), 72.

[40] William A. Barry, SJ, "What Are Spiritual Exercises?," in *An Ignatian Spirituality Reader*, ed. George W. Traub, SJ (Chicago: Loyola Press, 2008), 123.

understanding that Ignatius had: we are embodied beings. Each of us gives flesh to the Divine Presence.

Next, in the Third Week of the Exercises, we are present with the body of Jesus as he goes to his death. We see him taunted, beaten, dying, and our awareness of his physical agony arouses and sensitizes our vision to see the oppression and suffering of Black bodies in our world today. We see that people of color are policed and incarcerated differently from others; we see the correlations between skin tone and neighborhoods where government and institutions invest their money; we see the discrepancies in public education and employment opportunities that people of color face. We *see bodies*, bodies with different skin colors, and in seeing, we realize the disenfranchisement and marginalization that Black bodies endure. We see Christ embodied *here*, in the bodies of the oppressed.

Finally, in the Fourth Week of the Spiritual Exercises, we are invited into a new understanding of embodiment as we see the Risen Christ. It might be tempting to think that with the ascension, Christ was released from his body, ushering in a new, more "spiritual" era—but the message brought to Christ's followers after his ascension was, "Why do you stand looking up toward heaven?" (Acts 1:11). This is a reminder to us to shift our gaze. Christ's presence is not to be found floating in the sky, nor is it experienced in the intangible gossamers of the celestial realms. Instead, we see it here, on earth, embodied. The realm of God is incarnated and visible. As we contemplate the mystery of Christ's resurrection, we find ourselves perceiving the reality of divine embodiment everywhere we turn, but we see it especially in one another. The human body is designed to reveal the divine. As Jesuit poet Gerard Manley Hopkins wrote, "God rests in [humanity] as in a place, a *locus*, bed, vessel, expressly made to receive [God] as a case hollowed to fit it, as the hand in the glove or the milk in the breast."[41]

Ignatius guides us firmly away from the error of clothing ourselves in the invisibility of a mysticism that is not tangibly embodied. His incarnational vision insists that we see not only the historical reality of Jesus but also the larger, more comprehensive historical milieu, including Black flesh and blood that have suffered under the oppres-

---

[41] Gerard Manley Hopkins, *The Sermons and Devotional Writing of Gerard Manley Hopkins*, ed. Christopher Devlin (Oxford: Oxford University Press, 1959), 195.

sion of racism. To make that history invisible is, in effect, to deny the humanity of Jesus (like the Docetists), or to separate his divinity from his humanity (like the Nestorians). We must not forget, Ignatius insists, that both the humanity of Christ and the image of God in all humanity are the visible revelations of God among us. As the Gospel of John tells us, "The Word became flesh and lived among us" (1:14), "the image of the invisible God" (Col 1:15). We are called away from the nonvisible function of a purely interior spirituality. Faith in Christ must be embodied. It must be *seen*.

Ignatius also guides us away from another spiritual error: confusing embodiment with materialism. The physical world is a source of goodness and divine revelation, but when we view it as something to be acquired, something to be grasped for our own advantage, then we fall into what Ignatius referred to as *disordered affections*.[42] Racism first arose when whites looked at Africans and saw not the image of God but rather, a possible means for economic gain. Materialism objectifies reality; it sees only what will inflate our egoic sense of ourselves. Meanwhile, if we look at the incarnation of Christ, we see that embodiment is also an act of giving. In the progress through the four weeks of the Spiritual Exercises, we watch as Jesus gives up his divine rights in order to become human (Phil 2:7), in order to give himself in love for us through his life and death (Eph 5:2). Ignatius calls us to follow Jesus's example.

But how are we to *see* the historical Jesus, as Ignatius calls us to do, when he lived some two thousand years ago? How can we escape the invisible spirituality of whiteness and practice a faith that is grounded in seeing physical bodies? Ignatius would tell us that the answer lies in the powers of our imagination.[43]

---

[42] The Ignatian concept of "disordered affections" describes the way in which our selfish desires can warp things that in and of themselves were intended to be divine gifts good. When we allow our attachments to become "disordered"—out of balance, unhealthy—then things that God created to be good can become instead things that pull us away from God. When our desire for God is overpowered by our desire for other things, our affections are out of order. Freedom from disordered affections is essential to following Jesus, Ignatius believed, and he designed the Spiritual Exercises to help us gain that freedom.

[43] The Lacanian understanding of the imagination and the Ignatian understanding are quite different. A Laconian approach would say that fantasy constructs the framework that arranges how we see reality, and thus how we interact with reality. In this sense, the imagination creates something that is more "real" than reality. While

The Imagination and the Real

For Fanon, however, the imaginary is often pathological. It is what gives a narrative to racism; it "makes sense" of racism. The race fantasy has told a story for centuries, and we have all lived within that story. The fantasy is built on racial otherness, and from it springs a series of stereotypical associations (Blacks as criminal and dangerous, for example, while whites are the paradigm of humanity). This narrative both casts blame, creating nightmare scenarios that must be avoided, and at the same time underscores whites' own imagined sense of cultural superiority.[44]

Ignatius believed that the imagination was a powerful tool that could enable us to not only *think about* the life of Jesus, but to enter into it experientially; to actually *live* with Jesus. Again and again, Ignatius tells us to *see* Jesus, *see* Mary, *see* the various characters in the gospel stories. The foundation of the Exercises is the human body, and we are called to encounter it through the vehicle of our imagination.[45] Instead of creating fantasies designed to offer libidinal satisfaction, Ignatius's imagination allows us to move from the interior experience of Christ into a new form of lived exterior experience. It breaks through the egoic imaginary constructions. "The white man is sealed in his whiteness. The black man in his blackness," wrote Fanon[46]—but the Ignatian imagination allows us to see past the distorting filter of racism.[47]

Ignatius's embodied spirituality means that when we see others, we see both their physical reality *and* we see the presence of the di-

---

Ignatius would also have agreed with that statement, he was thinking of a sanctified imagination, something that could be used as a lens into a real too great for our naked eye to perceive.

[44] The imaginary creates radical alienation; it distorts our relationship with our own bodies. Lacan wrote that if "the Imaginary, the Symbolic and the Real are an unholy trinity whose members could as easily be called Fraud, Absence and Impossibility," then the Imaginary, a realm of inherently deceptive surface appearances, is "Fraud."

[45] This is a sanctified, clarified version of Lacan's imagination.

[46] Fanon, *Black Skin, White Masks*, 11.

[47] "The relation of the imaginary and the real, and in the constitution of the world such as results from it," wrote Lacan, "everything relies on the position of the subject." Ignatius's sanctified imagination shifts our position. Instead of continuing to live and act within the nightmare of racism, we take our place at the Cross with Jesus. From there, we can begin to *see* the Real.

vine.[48] We can no longer look with the eyes of materialism, objectifying other human beings, nor can we blind ourselves with the fantasy of an invisible spirituality that counteracts tangible reality. An intimate experience of God and practical, embodied interaction with others cannot be dualistically separated; they are united, just as the divinity and humanity of Christ are united. The imagination empowers this flow from interior to exterior, from self-awareness to practical service. The Ignatian form of spirituality is enfleshed within the sensory world. It sees no disjunction between God and "reality." We see what is Real in those around us—including the fantasy of race that continues to oppress and harm—and we proclaim the incarnation of God through our vision, as well as through our service, our activity in society, in politics, and in economics.

Walter Burghardt wrote, "I am not naked spirit; I am spirit incarnate; in a genuine sense, I *am* flesh."[49] Our bodies are where we meet others, and they are where we meet God. We cannot claim to see each other, we cannot claim to see God, and we cannot claim to see the Real until we truly see bodies.

Conclusion

"The eye is not merely a mirror, but a correcting mirror," Fanon wrote.

> The eye should make it possible for us to correct cultural errors. I do not say the eyes, I say the eye, and there is no mystery about what that eye refers to; not to the crevice in the skull but to that very uniform light that wells out of the reds of Van Gogh, that glides through a concerto of Tchaikovsky, that fastens itself desperately to Schiller's *Ode to Joy*.[50]

---

[48] For Ignatius, the Real is not the opposite of the imaginary, nor is it synonymous with what we usually consider "reality" (that which is contingent on our sense perception). Instead, it is something greater than either. "There is no absence in the Real," Lacan wrote. "The Real is always in its place." Ignatius offers us an entryway into the Real.

[49] Walter J. Burghardt, SJ, "Contemplation: A Long Loving Look at the Real," in *An Ignatian Spirituality Reader*, ed. George W. Traub, SJ (Chicago: Loyola Press, 2008), 92.

[50] Fanon, *Black Skin, White Masks*, 156–57.

It is this correcting mirror—the eye that glimpses the divine and gives rise to its expression—that Ignatius calls us to see. This is what the Jesuit poet Gerard Manley Hopkins describes in his poem "As Kingfishers Catch Fire":

> I say more: the just man justices:
> Keeps grace: that keeps all his goings graces.
> Acts in God's eye what in God's eye he is—
> Christ—for Christ plays in ten thousand places,
> Lovely in limbs, and lovely in eyes not his
> To the Father through the features of men's faces.[51]

"From time to time you feel like giving up," Fanon admitted. "Expressing the real is an arduous job."[52] But this is the life that Ignatius of Loyola challenges us to live. He invites us to look beyond and past Fanon's white gaze;[53] he asks that instead, we surrender ourselves to what science calls an "emergent process," where disparate parts come together to form something new and unexpected, something that is larger than the sum of its parts.[54]

Fanon's "final prayer" was this: "O my body, make of me always a man who questions!" May we too listen to the questions that the body imposes on us, but may we truly *see bodies*.[55]

---

[51] Gerard Manley Hopkins, *Mortal Beauty, God's Grace*, ed. Catherine Phillips (Oxford: Oxford University Press, 1986).

[52] Fanon, *Black Skin, White Masks*, 116.

[53] Lacan's Symbolic and Imaginary as well.

[54] In emergent processes, new systems emerge, nonlinearly, and a new set of rules or protocols arise that drive all the parts to adopt that new pattern.

[55] May we not seek to escape into either racist or spiritual fantasies, but may we truly *see bodies*, and in seeing them, see Christ.

PART III

Contemplating God's Laboring and Loving in the World

Love ought to manifest itself more in deeds than by words.

Ignatius of Loyola: Spiritual Exercises and Selected Works,
ed. George Ganss, SJ (Mahwah, NJ: Paulist Press, 1991),
no. 230, p. 176.

12

The Making and Unmaking of White Ignatian Formation

Matthew J. Cressler

I.

It is safe to say that Ignatian spirituality shaped my religious life before I was ever aware of it. Both my mother and father make silent retreats every year. They have for three decades. This practice, among other things, led my mother to pursue a master of theological studies and then, more to the point, to enter a spiritual director formation program. (She has been executive director of Ignatius House Jesuit Retreat Center in Atlanta, Georgia, since 2009.) I made my first retreat as a college freshman and have made over a dozen since. Each one (trans)formed me in fundamental ways.

All but one of the retreats I've made over the years have been three-day "preached retreats," which translate and abbreviate Ignatius of Loyola's Spiritual Exercises into a weekend experience. This is by far the most common way people are introduced to Ignatian spirituality. And again, this Jesuit silent retreat model transformed me. It so moved me that I brought it back to St. Bonaventure University when I returned from that very first retreat. I condensed my three days of silence down to an overnight experience for the Franciscan contemplative community of which I was a member. (Insert Franciscans versus Jesuits joke here.) A decade later I began attending annual retreats with my father. We made retreat together once again in the spring of 2021, almost twenty years after our first.

It is important for me to name how formative this tradition has been in my spiritual life because I want to invite us into some critical self-reflection. What comes next is tough, but it does come from a place of love. None of those preached retreats—not a single one—asked me to confront the sin of racism in my life or in the world around me. Sure, "social sin" might be mentioned in the abstract but further concrete reflection was left to the discretion of individual retreatants. White retreatants are rarely if ever asked to confront white supremacy as part of their meditation on sin. And so I want to open this essay by asking us to consider: Can one fully engage the Exercises in a racist society without being asked to confront that racism head on?

Patrick Saint-Jean, SJ, doesn't think so. In *The Spiritual Work of Racial Justice: A Month of Meditations with Ignatius of Loyola*, he challenges us to imagine Christ as a person of color. He knows some might object and say that "Jesus transcends race." And he notes that on one level "this is true (just as the statement 'All lives matter' is true)." But this misses the point. It "misses the reality of Jesus' life in a particular place and time."[1] The Spiritual Exercises encourage us "to use our imaginations," Saint-Jean explains, "to enter as completely as we can into Jesus' human experience. If we imagine Jesus as being white, we will miss out on who he really was." We live in a world defined by race and racism. Our Ignatian tradition is inevitably shaped by those surroundings. When we imagine Jesus as white we effectively connect "Jesus to the powerful rather than the oppressed and marginalized," as he certainly was in first-century Palestine. In doing so, "we are even allowing *Christ* to be synonymous with *white supremacy*."[2] It is not a matter of *whether* the Exercises should confront racism. The question, instead, is whether we will proceed in ignorance or confront those circumstances head on.

The Jesuits who convened at General Congregation 36 posed an important question: *"Why don't the Spiritual Exercises change us as much as we would like?"*[3] Lay people shaped by Ignatian spirituality must

---

[1] Patrick Saint-Jean, SJ, *The Spiritual Work of Racial Justice: A Month of Meditations with Ignatius of Loyola* (Vestal, NY: Anamchara Books, 2021), 111.

[2] Saint-Jean, *Spiritual Work of Racial Justice*, 112.

[3] Saint-Jean, 9.

ask this of ourselves as well. *Why don't our experiences of silence change us as much as we would like?* These questions are ultimately a matter of historical inquiry. Our spiritual lives are structured by our social, political, historical, and cultural context. In order to understand why the Exercises don't change us as much as we would like—indeed, why they may actively reinforce an unjust status quo—we must understand how the Ignatian tradition is encountered in particular places and times. As I will show below, when it comes to white Catholics in the United States, it is impossible to understand what it means to be *religious* apart from what it means to be *white.*

II.

In the forum "Writing Catholic History After the Sex Abuse Crisis," historian John Seitz reflects on a common question people exclaim when faced with the fact of predator priests. "What kind of person could do such a thing?!" The question is usually an instinctive expression of disgust and outrage. But Seitz argues that it is also an important historical question. "No longer rhetorical lament or protest," he writes, "and no longer the sole province of psychologists, the question in historians' hands can be literal and specific: how are priestly lives made and unmade in particular places and times?"[4]

I suggest we make a similar move when we approach Ignatian spirituality in a society defined by racism.[5] When we reckon with the long history and ongoing reality of white supremacy in the US Catholic Church—with white Catholics of all stripes who enslaved Africans, who fought for the Confederate States of America, who wrecked Native lives in residential schools, who engaged in open

---

[4] John C. Seitz, "The Lives of Priests," *American Catholic Studies* 127, no. 2 (Summer 2016): 18.

[5] I will not belabor this point. If readers would like to read more on the persistence and pervasiveness of racism today, I highly recommend reading Eduardo Bonilla-Silva, *Racism Without Racists: Color-blind Racism and the Persistence of Racial Inequality in America* (Lanham, MD: Rowman and Littlefield, 2003); Michelle Alexander, *The New Jim Crow: Mass Incarceration in the Age of Colorblindness* (New York: The New Press, 2010); Bryan Stevenson, *Just Mercy: A Story of Justice and Redemption* (New York: Spiegel and Grau, 2014); Ta-Nehisi Coates, *Between the World and Me* (New York: Spiegel and Grau, 2015); Patrisse Khan-Cullors and asha bandele, *When They Call You A Terrorist: A Black Lives Matter Memoir* (New York: St. Martin's Griffin, 2017).

warfare against Black communities, who quashed Black vocations and tormented postulants, who massively resisted desegregation—when we come face to face with this catalogue of Catholic horrors we, too, must cry out: What kind of people could do this?! How could Catholics commit such atrocities?![6]

These questions assume a special significance for those who've experienced the power of the Spiritual Exercises firsthand. The Jesuits who enslaved human beings, who broke up their families and auctioned them off to the highest bidder, *made the Exercises.*[7] So too did the Jesuits who sexually abused Native children in communities across the country.[8] Our instinctive response is to shout, How?! How

---

[6] A select bibliography of the horrors of US Catholic racism and colonialism would include: Justin D. Poché, "The Catholic Citizens' Council: Religion and White Resistance in Louisiana," *U.S. Catholic Historian* 24, no. 4 (2006): 47–68; Michael Pasquier, " 'Though Their Skin Remains Brown, I Hope Their Souls Will Soon Be White': Slavery, French Missionaries, and the Roman Catholic Priesthood in the American South, 1789–1865," *Church History* 77, no. 2 (2008): 337–70; Maura Jane Farrelly, "American Slavery, American Freedom, American Catholicism," *Early American Studies* 10, no. 1 (2010): 69–100; Mark Newman, *Desegregating Dixie: The Catholic Church in the South and Desegregation, 1945–1992* (Jackson, MS: University of Mississippi Press, 2018); Katherine Moran, *The Imperial Church: Catholic Founding Fathers and United States Empire* (Ithaca, NY: Cornell University Press, 2020); Gracjan Kraszewski, "Devout Catholics, Devoted Confederates: The Evolution of Southern Catholic Bishops from Reluctant Secessionists to Ardent Confederates," *The Catholic Historical Review* 106, no. 1 (2020): 77–106; Kathleen Holscher, "Graves in Canada Reflect Catholic Logic of Indigenous Vanishment," *National Catholic Reporter* (June 22, 2021), https://www.ncronline.org/news/accountability/canadian-native-childrens-graves-reflect-history-indigenous-vanishment; Shannen Dee Williams, *Subversive Habits: Black Catholic Nuns in the Long African American Freedom Struggle* (Durham, NC: Duke University Press, 2022).

[7] For reporting and scholarship on Jesuit slaveholding, see Thomas Murphy, *Jesuit Slaveholding in Maryland* (New York: Routledge, 2001); Kelly L. Schmidt, "Enslaved Faith Communities in the Jesuits' Missouri Mission," *U.S. Catholic Historian* 37, no. 2 (Spring 2019): 49–81; Kelly L. Schmidt, " 'Without Slaves and Without Assassins,' Antebellum Cincinnati, Transnational Jesuits, and the Challenges of Race and Slavery," *U.S. Catholic Historian* 39, no. 2 (Spring 2021): 1–26; Rachel L. Swarns, *The 272: The Families Who Were Enslaved and Sold to Build the American Catholic Church* (New York: Random House, 2023).

[8] For reporting and scholarship on Jesuit sexual abuse in Native communities, see Emily Schwing, Aaron Sankin, and Michael Corey, "These Priests Abused in Native Villages for Years. They Retired on Gonzaga's Campus," *Reveal* (December 17, 2018), https://revealnews.org/article/these-priests-abused-in-native-villages-for-years-they-retired-on-gonzagas-campus/; Jack Lee Downey, "Colonialism Is Abuse: Reconsidering Triumphalist Narratives in Catholic Studies," *American Catholic Studies* 130, no. 2 (Summer 2019): 16–20.

could they commit such brutal acts of violence, dehumanize and destroy lives on such a scale if they've been formed by Ignatian spirituality?!

There is a moral imperative behind these questions. The Exercises are often approached as though they operate independent of history and culture—especially in the context of a three-day preached retreat. Times may change, but the path Ignatius laid out five hundred years ago endures. Take the Exercises to heart, we are told, and you will find out for yourself that it still works! Jesuit historian Raymond Schroth, SJ, names this as a distinguishing feature of the Society of Jesus. Jesuits identify with their founder by repeating "the most formative experience of their founder's life, and, through God's grace, thus undergo[ing] a transformation or conversion similar to his."[9] There is truth to this, of course. Nevertheless, this ahistorical approach to the Ignatian tradition poses dangers for us today if left unexamined.

People have made the Spiritual Exercises comfortably alongside settler colonialism and genocide, human trafficking and enslavement, masculinist domination and sexual abuse and conspiratorial cover up for half a millennium. I don't say this to be controversial so much as to say aloud an historical truth we'd rather not name. To be clear, this doesn't mean there is some inherent or causal connection. These horrors extend beyond and exist without the Exercises. And, of course, there are countless women and men formed in the tradition who have fought and continue to fight against social evils of all kinds. But if we tried to dismiss all instances when the Exercises occurred in conjunction with violence we would end up dismissing much of Jesuit history. More to the point, such an ahistorical dismissiveness would only keep us in willful ignorance of what Thomas Merton once called the "seeds of destruction" sown in our midst.

I suggest, instead, that we expand on the question posed above. How are religious lives made and unmade in relationship with the Spiritual Exercises in particular places and times? To answer this question, we must examine the ideas, institutions, relationships, and social forces that structure our experience of the Exercises. We must think critically about *formation*.

[9] Raymond A. Schroth, SJ, *The American Jesuits: A History* (New York: New York University Press, 2007), 7–8.

III.

I imagine that thinking of religious life as a matter of "formation" comes as second nature to most readers. The word might call to mind a discrete phase of vocational life—the five stages of Jesuit formation—or make one think of religious education as a matter of "faith formation." In both instances the term offers insights into the making of religious lives, especially in a Catholic context. It is worth pausing to reflect on the term itself. To "form" means to give shape; to mold; "to model by instruction and discipline."[10] "Formation" is best thought of as a kind of education. It implies both physicality and relationality. To be formed is to be shaped by someone. It calls to mind a sculptor who molds clay into art. We are formed into particular kinds of spiritual selves. As we will see, we are also formed into particular kinds of racialized selves. (White people are formed to "not see" themselves as racialized at all, for instance.)

Thinking about religious life as a matter of formation challenges many commonly held assumptions. In our secular modern age, religion is often imagined to be, more than anything else, ideas individuals hold about the gods, the universe, and the afterlife. This contemporary common sense locates religion in the privacy of one's heart.[11] Formation implies an altogether different framework. Here, religious lives are forged through instruction and discipline that involves a variety of factors and forces. It includes training the body by performing rituals again and again (and again). It involves being taught by—to a certain extent, being in obedience to—religious authorities who transmit tradition from one generation to the next. It is rooted in a community and dependent upon relationships, not simply a matter of individual agreement with certain intellectual propositions.[12] Religious formation is never untethered from history,

---

[10] Merriam-Webster.com Dictionary, s.v. "form," accessed August 23, 2023, https://www.merriam-webster.com/dictionary/form.

[11] For a compelling analysis and critique of the idea that "religion" is, first and foremost, the sincerely held, and, thus, ultimately unknowable and unassailable, beliefs of the human heart, see Adam B. Seligman, Robert P. Weller, Michael J. Puett, and Bennett Simon, *Ritual and Its Consequences: An Essay on the Limits of Sincerity* (Oxford: Oxford University Press, 2008). See also Charles McCrary, *Sincerely Held: American Secularism and Its Believers* (Chicago: University of Chicago Press, 2022).

[12] I have written about Catholic education as "religious formation" more expansively in my book *Authentically Black and Truly Catholic: The Rise of Black Catholicism*

never free from the powers that be. Quite the opposite. Ever-shifting circumstances—the social, political, economic, and cultural forces that shape the world around us—are necessary ingredients in the process.[13]

When we think of religious life in this way it becomes clear that we cannot separate "religion" from categories like class, gender, sexuality, and race. If religious lives are formed through embodied practices and daily disciplines, they will be shaped by the historical and cultural contexts in which our bodies move. To focus on race, there is a synergy between this notion of religious formation and what scholars call "racial formation." "Race"—the pernicious idea that the human species can be subdivided into groups that are fundamentally distinct from one another—is not *real* in any biological sense. We are all members of one human race. However, as an idea, race has been foundational for the making of our world. At its most basic, race is a category that separates Us from Them. It justifies exploitation and violence. It insists that They are not Us, and, therefore, We may do with Them as We please. Religious studies scholar Malory Nye put it succinctly: "the term race is a means of exerting power."[14] Sociologists Michael Omi and Howard Winant coined the term "racial

in the Great Migrations (New York: New York University Press, 2017). See especially "Chapter 2: Becoming Catholic: Education, Evangelization, and Conversion."

[13] My understanding of religious formation draws deeply on the work of anthropologist Talal Asad, who, in writing about medieval Christian thought, argues that "it is not mere symbols that implant true Christian dispositions, but power—ranging all the way from laws (imperial and ecclesiastical) and other sanctions (hellfire, death, salvation, good repute, peace) to the disciplinary activities of social institutions (family, school, city, church) and of human bodies (fasting, prayer, obedience, penance)." "It was not the mind that moved spontaneously to religious truth," he insists, "but power that created the conditions for experiencing that truth." Talal Asad, *Genealogies of Religion: Discipline and Reasons of Power in Christianity and Islam* (Baltimore: Johns Hopkins University Press, 1993), 35.

[14] Malory Nye, "Race and Religion: Postcolonial Formations of Whiteness," *Method and Theory in the Study of Religion* (2018): 11. There are innumerable texts to which one could turn to understand "race" as a category and how it operates in history. Some of the most formative for me include: W. E. B. Du Bois, "The Souls of White Folk," in *Darkwater: Voices from Within the Veil* (New York: Washington Square Press, [1920] 2004): 21–37; Barnor Hesse, "Racialized Modernity: An Analytics of White Mythologies," *Ethnic and Racial Studies* 30, no. 4 (July 2007): 643–63; Karen E. Fields and Barbara J. Fields, *Racecraft: The Soul of Inequality in American Life* (New York: Verso Books, 2012); Sylvester A. Johnson, *African American Religions, 1500–2000: Colonialism, Freedom, and Democracy* (Cambridge: Cambridge University Press, 2015); Judith Weisenfeld, *New*

formation" to illuminate how race works in this regard. Race is not static or stable over time. Instead, "social, economic and political forces determine the content and importance of racial categories."[15] Like religious lives, racial categories are forged in the ever-shifting circumstances of the world.

Whether we're talking about religious formation or racial formation, both highlight how power is instrumental in the making of human lives and the worlds we inhabit. Here, "power" is not necessarily a good or bad thing. It simply is. Much like an exercitant is formed in the Ignatian tradition through physical, intellectual, and spiritual disciplines under the guidance of a director, so too things are racialized in specific historical conditions for certain political purposes. In both instances, the term *formation* emphasizes that these things do not exist in a vacuum, they do not spring into existence fully formed. When we're talking about the making and unmaking of religious lives, race is one of the many factors involved in that process. If we imagine religion can be somehow isolated from race— that real religion is "color-blind"—we run the risk of religion itself becoming a kind of racial formation. To put it bluntly, if we assume we can engage in "race-neutral" religious formation, all we will end up doing is reinforcing our complicity in a white status quo.

IV.

What does it look like when religion becomes a kind of racial formation? We can talk about this concretely in history. We tend to assume religion and race are separate categories, ideas we can keep apart from each other easily. But personal experience and history testify against this assumption. A few years ago I found myself in conversation with a white deacon before the start of a silent retreat. When he asked that innocuous icebreaker—So, what do you do?— I told him. "I teach African American religion and Catholicism." This

World A-Coming: Black Religion and Racial Identity during the Great Migration (New York: New York University Press, 2016).

[15] Michael Omi and Howard Winant, *Racial Formation in the United States: From the 1960s to the 1980s* (New York: Routledge, 1986), 61. See also Daniel Martinez HoSang, Oneka LaBennett, and Laura Pulido, eds., *Racial Formation in the Twenty-First Century* (Berkeley, CA: University of California Press, 2012).

was simply a statement of fact. His response was telling, though. This sixty-something-year-old white man replied that, when his Polish family immigrated in the 1800s, they "had it rough." They had been unwelcome. "Just like the Irish." He shared with me how he once proudly told an African American, "we don't owe you a dime. Not one dime." He said all this in response to my saying the words "African American" out loud and alongside "Catholicism."

I'm sure many readers can recall moments like this, instances when the sheer presence or mere mention of someone non-white instigated a discomfiting, even hostile, reply. This personal story illustrates a tendency that courses through US Catholic history. The problem of "color-blindness" in the Ignatian tradition is part and parcel of a much larger problem within white Catholicism itself. While we might like to think of religion and race as separate, my research has shown that white Catholics often make no such distinction in their own lives. In the 1960s, civil rights activists in Chicago fought to desegregate schools and neighborhoods in their city. When the archbishop expressed support and proposed parallel plans for parochial school desegregation (albeit modest ones), he was met with massive resistance from white Catholics across the archdiocese. White Catholics wrote hundreds of outraged letters, took to the streets in protest, and even engaged in acts of violence.[16]

Crucially for us here, these white Catholics did not separate their whiteness from their Catholicness. On the contrary, they regularly described themselves as "real good and sincere Catholics" in the same sentences in which they reinforced white supremacy. "Are you trying to push the white people out of the Catholic Church?" one letter writer asked in 1966. "We were born and raised in Chicago as Catholics. I go to communion almost every morning." "But," they insisted, "I will not attend Mass with any Negroes."[17] That same year, Mr. George J. Burns declared, "we are the parents of seven children in Catholic Schools from kindergarten to a senior in college and we

---

[16] I engage this research in depth in " 'Real Good and Sincere Catholics': White Catholicism and Massive Resistance to Desegregation in Chicago, 1965–1968," *Religion and American Culture* 30, no. 2 (2020): 273–306.

[17] Anonymous to Archbishop John Cody (undated 1966), John Cardinal Cody Papers Collection, Archdiocesan Archives of Chicago, "Race Mail," EXEC/C0670/19#9. (I abbreviate this collection as simply "Race Mail" below.)

are endeavoring to raise our boys and girls to be good catholics and certainly not with the intent of their later integrating and marrying people of a different color."[18] In 1968, Mrs. Florence Fako described herself "as a devout and practicing Roman Catholic" who wished "to protest most strongly your proposed busing of negro children to parochial schools in the city and the suburbs." She acknowledged that "all men are equal in God's eyes," at least in theory, then added that "each one of us must *earn* the respect of our fellow man. This, Cardinal, the vast majority of negroes have not done."[19]

White Catholic resistance to racial justice has a lot to teach us about Catholic history. I have argued that we need to consider letters like these essential sources for understanding white Catholicism as a racial formation.[20] We need to shift the way we think about religion and race in order to recognize how, quite often, the very Catholicness of white Catholics—since I am a white Catholic myself, I should say *our* institutions, *our* ideas, *our* actions, *our* bodies, *our* relationships, *our* lives—is shaped by their whiteness.[21] This approach invites us into a fuller understanding of the lives of those who received communion every morning, prayed novenas every night, aspired to raise good Catholic children, expressed outrage at even the notion of equal-

---

[18] Mr. George J. Burns to Archbishop John P. Cody (July 12, 1966), "Race Mail," EXEC/C0670/18#17.

[19] Mrs. Florence Fako to John Cardinal Cody (January 30, 1968), "Race Mail," EXEC/C0670/20#3.

[20] In this I follow in the footsteps and join numerous theologians and religious studies scholars, including Charles H. Long, *Significations: Signs, Symbols, and Images in the Interpretation of Religion* (Aurora, CO: The Davies Group, Publishers, 1986); M. Shawn Copeland, *Enfleshing Freedom: Body, Race, and Being* (Minneapolis: Fortress Press, 2009); Christopher M. Driscoll, *White Lies: Race and Uncertainty in the Twilight of American Religion* (New York: Routledge, 2016); Johnson, *African American Religions* (2015); Weisenfeld, *New World A-Coming* (2016); Laura McTighe, ed., "Roundtable: 'Religio-Racial Identity' as Challenge and Critique," *Journal of the American Academy of Religion* 88, no. 2 (June 2020): 299–459.

[21] I am by no means the only scholar arguing that white Catholics must acknowledge and reckon with the ways their whiteness shapes their Catholicism. Other examples of this include Katie Walker Grimes, *Christ Divided: Antiblackness as Corporate Vice* (Minneapolis: Fortress Press, 2017); Jeannine Hill Fletcher, *The Sin of White Supremacy: Christianity, Racism, and Religious Diversity in America* (Maryknoll, NY: Orbis Books, 2017); Daniel P. Horan, OFM, *A White Catholic's Guide to Racism and Privilege* (Notre Dame, IN: Ave Maria Press, 2021); Maureen H. O'Connell, *Undoing the Knots: Five Generations of American Catholic Anti-Blackness* (Boston: Beacon Press, 2021).

ity for Black people, used racist epithets against their non-white neighbors, and fought to maintain segregated suburbs. It helps us understand why my simply saying "I teach African American religion and Catholicism" proved so threatening to that deacon. It compels us to appreciate how religion and race are intimately bound up with each other.

The inseparability of whiteness and Catholicism for white Catholics is especially evident when it is left unnamed. White people tend to assume that they are the norm—that they embody the normal, universal experience of what it means to be human.[22] As a result, white people typically resist the notion that they (or their religion) has anything to do with race. Instead, they understand their religion as simply the normal, universal way of being religious. This is why it is important to read between the lines and pay close attention to those unsettling and uncomfortable moments, like my dinner with the deacon. Many white Catholics presume they represent "real" and "authentic" Catholicism. Most truly cannot fathom the existence of non-white Catholics, or else they assume that non-white ways of being Catholic (i.e., Black, Latinx, Asian, etc.) are culturally specific in contrast to the universal, "true" Catholicism of European immigrants and their descendants.

This comes through quite clearly in my own historical research. And it is especially clear when white Catholics were confronted with the lived reality of Black Catholicism. Many white Catholics forcefully objected to Black Catholic liturgical innovations that emerged in the years after the Second Vatican Council. For example, one woman criticized what she called the church's "catering to African bongo-bongo to be used in the Masses—catering to Negro priest Clarence Rivers who is writing Masses with Negro-beat." Father Rivers was a transformative musician, liturgist, and theologian who spearheaded the liturgical revolution in the 1960s and 1970s. Meanwhile, this white woman wondered "what the Hell is happening to my Church?" This is a moment that calls on us to pause and pay attention to language. Note the ownership this white Catholic took over *her* church. "No

---

[22] See Toni Morrison, *Playing in the Dark: Whiteness and the Literary Imagination* (New York: Vintage Books, 1992); Nell Irving Painter, *The History of White People* (New York: W. W. Norton, 2010); George Yancy, *Look, a White!: Philosophical Essays on Whiteness* (Philadelphia: Temple University Press, 2012).

wonder," she concluded, "Catholics are leaving the Church. Stop this goddam [sic] catering to Negroes!"[23]

When letter writers like this woman identified themselves as "Catholic," they claimed that word for white people. Mr. Stanley Werdell, writing in 1965, declared that he was "past sixty years of age, born of and raised by Roman Catholic parents" and had "never been ashamed of my religion until our Nuns and Priests commenced to engage in the so-called 'Civil Rights' demonstrations." He signed as "A very disillusioned Catholic."[24] Mary Wollenberg reported that, "as a staunch Roman Catholic for twenty-three years and having attended Catholic schools for sixteen years, I have never been so shocked, horrified, embarrassed and disgusted by the conduct of a group of nuns at a recent civil rights demonstration."[25] Edward Armruster, writing from a US Air Force base in Florida in 1966, wrote, "I have been a Catholic for all my 34 years and consider myself a good Catholic." "Personally I cannot see Priests and nuns participating in these civil rights movements," he reflected. It is "a disgrace."[26] Again and again letter writers opened their letters by claiming "good Catholic" status before proceeding to defend their anti-civil-rights, anti-integration, and anti-Black opinions. Each time they did this, they implied that *real* Catholics supported the reigning racist order.

Let's return to the Spiritual Exercises. One of the primary tools Ignatius offered to guide exercitants closer to Christ was "contemplation." In this context, contemplation "springs from our emotions and imaginations." It is an invitation to imagine ourselves as characters in the drama of the gospels.[27] By necessity, contemplation draws on our lives, on our experience of the world around us. It is, by definition, shaped by the historical and cultural circumstances in which we find ourselves. This is not a problem. The Exercises are designed

[23] Mrs. Irene Dolan to Archbishop John Cody (July 17, 1966), "Race Mail," EXEC/C0670/18#16.

[24] Stanley Werdell to Marillac Social Center (June 18, 1965), "Race Mail," EXEC/C0670/18#6.

[25] Mary Wollenberg to Bishop Cletus O'Donnell (June 16, 1965), "Race Mail," EXEC/C0670/18#6.

[26] Edward D. Armbruster to Archbishop John Cody (August 10, 1966), "Race Mail," EXEC/C0670/19#7.

[27] Saint-Jean, *Spiritual Work of Racial Justice*, 14.

precisely to help us "overcome ourselves"—as a Jesuit might say, to be freed from the disordered attachments that keep us from a more intimate relationship with our Creator. However, when the social forces that shape our imaginations—that inevitably infuse our contemplation—are left unexamined, our imaginations can end up reinforcing the present order of our world. Ignatian spirituality aspires to form us not into the world as it *is*, but rather to transform us into the world as it *ought to be*. When the white supremacy that shapes our imaginations is left unattended and unchallenged, religious formation itself is racialized. Thousands of white people—like the white deacon from my story—walk away from preached retreats each year with their uncritical, "color-blind" views affirmed.

V.

It doesn't have to be this way. A confrontation with color-blindness and white supremacy can be an integral part of faith formation. *It must be if we hope to be changed!* Christopher Pramuk's *Hope Sings, So Beautiful: Graced Encounters across the Color Line* offers one model for what that might look like. Pramuk asks readers to consider questions like: "To whom do we belong and are we responsible? Who is the 'God' in whom we place our trust, and what does this God ask of us in building a world of greater justice, compassion, and solidarity? . . . *for what do we dare to hope?*"[28] If religious and racial formation have forged the broken world we live in, perhaps a different kind of formation is required to repair it. This is not my attempt to make prayer a panacea, to imply that we can pray racism away. It is to say that if, in particular times and places, religious lives are made in ways that maintain white supremacy, they can be unmade too. They can be made anew. Bodies can be retrained. Minds reeducated. Communities reconciled. Relationships repaired. But it will not happen spontaneously through the same color-blind that have reigned for centuries.

This rings a cord, of course, with Ignatian spirituality. The Spiritual Exercises were designed to produce this kind of lasting transformation, to change people who would then to go forth and change the

---

[28] Christopher Pramuk, *Hope Sings, So Beautiful: Graced Encounters across the Color Line* (Collegeville, MN: Liturgical Press, 2013).

world by being companions of Jesus. Jesuits were not meant to be contemplatives cloistered in a monastery. They were meant to be "contemplatives in action," those who overcame attachment to self and, in doing so, moved beyond the self to serve others as Christ once did.[29] There is a deep irony, then, in anyone who would approach the tradition as if it were blind to the conditions of the world, as if it operated free and independently of racism (or, for that matter, classism, sexism, homophobia, or transphobia).

Thomas Merton, that great twentieth-century contemplative, wrote incisively against this inclination in *Seeds of Destruction*. "The contemplative life," he insisted, "is not, and cannot be, a mere withdrawal, a pure negation, a turning of one's back on the world with its sufferings, its crises, its confusions and its errors." Merton recognized that there comes a time when a monk's "very silence and 'not knowing' may constitute a form of complicity. The mere fact of 'ignoring' what goes on can become a political decision." The result, he proclaimed, is "that the monk in his liturgy, in his study or in his contemplation is actually participating in those things he congratulates himself on having renounced."[30]

Those of us formed by Ignatian spirituality run the same risk when we ignore the powers and principalities that structure our world. To pretend to be color-blind when the material consequences of white supremacy pile up around us is, in the words of Merton, "to prolong the reign of untruth, greed, cruelty and arrogance in the world of men [sic]."[31] Proceeding with the pretense of color-blind Christianity in the face of all evidence to the contrary is to insist on one's innocence amid the devastation of our broken world.[32] To quote another great

---

[29] J. Michelle Molina's work proved incredibly useful for thinking through the questions at stake here. See especially Molina, "Chapter 1: The Jesuit Spiritual Exercises: To Conquer Oneself, To Conquer the World," in *To Overcome Oneself: The Jesuit Ethic and Spirit of Global Expansion, 1520–1767* (Berkeley, CA: University of California Press, 2013), 24–49.

[30] Thomas Merton, *Seeds of Destruction* (New York: Farrar, Straus and Giroux, 1964), xi–xii.

[31] Merton, *Seeds*, xii-xiii.

[32] Though much of it centers the stories of white evangelicals, there is great work being done today that critiques the idea and ideology of color-blind Christianity. See Jeannine Hill Fletcher, *The Sin of White Supremacy: Christianity, Racism, and Religious Diversity in America* (Maryknoll, NY: Orbis Books, 2017); Jemar Tisby, *The Color of*

twentieth-century thinker, one Merton admired deeply, "it is not permissible that the authors of devastation be innocent. It is the innocence that constitutes the crime."[33] By this, James Baldwin meant that his white countrymen were not simply committing the crime of anti-Black racism but committing an even more heinous one: feigning ignorance and pleading innocence as the dead and destroyed piled up around them.

The solution is not to "politicize" contemplative life in some crass partisan sense, but to recognize and embrace the fact that to be a contemplative in action is to be situated in the particularity of history. (Though, it must be said that imagining that a contemporary Christian can live a "color-blind," "apolitical" life is its own kind of political statement.) Christianity is a tradition "centered on an historical event which has changed the meaning of history," on the Word made flesh in the form of a poor Palestinian man born under the boot of imperial power and executed for sedition.[34] Religious life cannot be "a retreat into abstract eternity," Merton warned. "The adversary is not time, not history, but the evil will and the accumulated inheritance of past untruth and sin."[35] When we consider the long history of European Christian colonialism, of Catholic enslavement, of Jesuit violence, there is certainly enough accumulated inheritance there to be confronted.

We find ourselves faced with a moral imperative. Recognizing and denouncing the evils of white supremacy and racism must be an essential element of our religious formation. As Patrick Saint-Jean

---

Compromise: The Truth about the American Church's Complicity in Racism (Grand Rapids, MI: Zondervan, 2020); Robert P. Jones, *White Too Long: The Legacy of White Supremacy in American Christianity* (New York: Simon and Schuster, 2020); Jesse Curtis, *The Myth of Colorblind Christians: Evangelicals and White Supremacy in the Civil Rights Era* (New York: New York University Press, 2021); Anthea Butler, *White Evangelical Racism: The Politics of Morality in America* (Chapel Hill, NC: University of North Carolina Press, 2021).

[33] James Baldwin, *The Fire Next Time* (New York: Vintage International, [1963] 1992), 5–6.

[34] Merton, xii. For one of the most compelling imaginings of Christ as embodied by those marginalized among us, I recommend viewing Rev. Osagyefo Sekou, "The Liberation Theology of Ferguson," Candler School of Theology Dean's Lecture (April 8, 2015), https://vimeo.com/125610838.

[35] Merton, *Seeds*, xiii.

puts it, "antiracism is not an optional aspect of the spiritual life . . . it is essential to becoming all that God calls us to be." As with religious formation, this is not something we ultimately achieve with finality. It is "an ongoing process for our entire life . . . a constant quest for grace to see each other as Christ sees us."[36] There is no avoiding it. The question is simply whether or not we're willing to be complicit in the unjust order that reigns today.

[36] Saint-Jean, *Spiritual Work of Racial Justice*, 12.

$$= 13 =$$

The God of Us All
Praying with Black Spirituality

Justin White

"What does it mean to be Black and Catholic? It means that I come to my Church fully functioning. That doesn't frighten you, does it? I come to my Church fully functioning. I bring myself; my black self, all that I am, all that I have, all that I hope to become. I bring my whole history, my traditions, my experience, my culture, my African-American song and dance and gesture and movement and teaching and preaching and healing and responsibility—as gifts to the Church."

Sr. Thea Bowman's Address to the US Bishops' Conference,
June 1989

History of the Retreat

The Jesuit Antiracism Sodality (JARS) started designing and planning the retreat "The God of Us All: Praying with Black Spirituality" in August 2020 with the active engagement, input, and accompaniment from the Black Jesuits of the United States. In June 2021, nineteen people (Jesuit and lay) gathered for the inaugural retreat experience in Bay St. Louis, Mississippi.

Logistics of the Retreat

Directors for this retreat are individuals who have been formed in both Black and Ignatian spirituality. Our days together begin and end in communal prayer, including daily Mass, to highlight the daily graces that frame this sacred time of reflection and prayer. Throughout the retreat, Black sacred song, optional films, and other supplemental prayer resources illustrating the Black experience, enrich the graces of each day and serve as guideposts to the grace.

Returning to the words of Sr. Thea Bowman, what does it look and feel like to be "fully functioning" in one's whole self? What does it look and feel like to have the complexity of past and present experiences and identities commingle? What does it look and feel like to return to the presence of an expansive God? I was unaware that these were questions my Black body and soul held, but my time as a retreatant and then a facilitator on the "God of Us All: Praying with Black Spirituality" retreat team helped me to unearth their answers.

Becoming Empowered in God's Presence

In the summer of 2021, my good friend and Jesuit priest Sean Toole, SJ, invited me to attend this eight-day in-person, directed retreat, themed around Black Catholic spirituality. I responded with hesitancy and because he was my good friend, I told him bluntly that I did not want to attend something *performative*. I did not want to serve as a *"POC evaluator"* on this inaugural retreat. My identity as a Black, Jesuit educator is one that brings me great pride, but it can also be a lonely identity—a commodified identity. The hesitation I felt was a manifestation of the trauma within my body. The onslaught of videos, images, headlines of Black and Brown bodies slain, coupled with DEI training and workshops that caused more harm than good left me guarded. Sean listened to my concerns, validated them, and told me that my only role would be to "go and be with God." I trusted him, I trusted God.

On the first night we were asked to share with the group why we came on the retreat. I was prepared to give an answer that spoke to how my external work with racial justice brought me to the gathering. However, when I stood up the words, "I'm here for healing," escaped from the prison of my unaddressed desolation. I sat down shocked at my unfettered vulnerability. The next morning, I thought it was best that I kept in check the feeling that *leapt forth* the previous night. I told myself before I left my room for morning prayer that there was no way I'd receive healing in eight days, but maybe I'd receive some balm. Little did I know that the song that would be played for morning prayer was a song that would directly confront my limited belief in God's goodness . . . a song that would give space for my grieving heart . . . a song that would help usher in my fully functioning self . . . a song that proclaimed that "There Is a Balm in Gilead."

To say that this was the *noisiest* silent retreat I've ever attended would be an understatement. Three times a day we gathered as a community to commune with the Black spirituals, the Sacred Songs, through the divine, musical direction of Meyer Chambers. The songs resonated through my body and their words took up residence. Songs that I knew returned home to me, and songs that I did not know were invited to the table to share their truth. Each day retreat leaders testified to the grace of the day and connected it to an Ancestor—those living and those a part of the communion of saints. Sr. Thea Bowman, Amelia Boynton Robinson, James Baldwin, Sr. Mary Antona Ebo, Bryan Stevenson, Maya Angelou, Mamie and Emmett Till, and Fr. Augustus Tolton went from people I *read* or *knew* about— to brothers and sisters I was journeying with. I was a part of their stories, and they were a part of mine.

Having Eric T. Styes, a young, Black man, as my spiritual director provided me a sense of peace, safety, and encouragement as we traveled through the movements of the Spiritual Exercises. The vulnerability that leapt forth that first night, danced, cried, and laughed as he and I talked.

Each day retreatants were offered a space for optional faith sharing. I listened to my fellow retreatants and was amazed at how, when a space for true racial reconciliation is granted, healing in other areas of one's life can appear. At night we watched documentaries and/or movies that further highlighted the Ancestor and the grace of the day. There was no passive consumption of words and the images on the screen, but I could feel, see, and hear in the room the deep digestion and integration of the Ancestors' stories and lives.

Was I healed of all my strife, weariness, and uncertainty in eight days? No. Did I feel a deep sense of healing, hope, and a newfound purpose? Yes.

I wrote the following in my journal:

First retreat in the Ignatian tradition where the power of my Blackness is not a subsection in my journal, but instead the main meditation. That tremendous shift has allowed me to go deeper into the mystery of myself and the mystery of God. A deeper sense of consolation, a deeper understanding of mercy, and fuller experiences of Grace followed because of it.

Gratitude

> "Blessed are Jack and Justin. You are God's Mary and Martha. Attentive to detail, thoughtful in your care, presence over all else. You embody the gifts each of these women brought to creating sacred space for others. I see you."
> With permission to share from the journal of Elise Gower

> "Thus you will know them by their fruits."
> Matthew 7:20

In the summer of 2022, myself and Jack McLinden, SJ served as the retreat directors for the second year of the "God of Us All" retreat. Jack was one of the first people I met during the retreat in 2021, and I felt a kinship with him within a few moments. That's another thing that providing a space for true racial reconciliation does—it creates avenues for soul-to-soul interactions. We welcomed returning spiritual directors and embraced new spiritual directors into the fold. It felt like a family reunion.

Our retreatants represented a diverse tapestry of our church and Jesuit apostolates. Our community was built by the presence of an Episcopal priest and chaplain at a Jesuit university, a religious sister of the Sacred Heart of Jesus and professor at a Jesuit university, an elder of the African Methodist Episcopal (AME) Church and director of an office of anti-racism, three lay women working in Jesuit ministries, three ordained Jesuits, and one Jesuit in formation. These vocational titles served as only a glimpse into the richness of the perspectives, joys, traumas, and truths that each person offered at the altar of our vulnerability and connectedness.

Once again, we journeyed through the history of Black spirituality. We deeply honored and deeply lamented the survival of horror-filled plantation fields. We drew courage and fortitude from the resounding faith of those during the civil rights movement. We faced the sober reality that neglect and marginalization continues within and through our church. I watched as the Sacred Songs visited old friends and ascended the porch steps of new friends. I watched and listened to how the heavy air and history of the looming trees of Bay St. Louis, Mississippi, intermingled with our own breath and groundedness. I watched and listened to healing leaping forth from others' hearts. I watched and listened as we became kindred spirits.

I, we, were no longer *becoming* empowered in God's presence, I, we, just were.

Resonating with the words of Sr. Thea Bowman, this is what it looks and feels like to "come to my Church fully functioning." This is what God wants for me—healing, reconciliation, peace, community, power in my identity, and most importantly . . . a deep, resounding joy. I feel bold enough to say that this is what God wants for *all of us*.

14

The God of Us All
Examen Reflection

Elise Gower

The place in which we gather is not only about the time and space we occupy; it is also a joining of the collective contribution to that which shapes us—people, circumstance, history, perspective. My reflections on my retreat experience in Bay St. Louis, Mississippi, do not belong solely to me. I offer a sacred land acknowledgment for the grounds on which we gathered. These grounds carry stories, known and unknown, honored and dishonored. My story does not exist without others'. I honor the collective contribution to my learning and growth. The people and voices that cultivated this holy experience are captured in my journal, but not accurately credited. These insights are the fruit of God's holy weaving in prayer, scripture, witness, and the communal voice of those with whom I journeyed.

I prepared for retreat with a preconceived understanding of the "God of Us All." My white assumptions projected multiple meanings from this title. Each idea was wrapped in my own centrality, not God's. I imagined a space where people of color could access God in the same way I have been afforded access in the church. Privilege, yes, but more specifically, a narrow understanding of God, as if the divine necessitates a gateway or point of access. James Baldwin, our Day 6 retreat witness, described the embodiment of our individual and collective histories, "We carry our history with us. We are our history." My own presuppositions brought forth into retreat the history I carry. I encountered this truth in the silence of retreat. I was daunted by the truth of the silence. And, it is in the silence, that I encountered the "God of Us All."

Retreatants were invited to pray a daily guided Examen. Though a familiar practice, I wasn't prepared for this experience. In its five-step structure, I'm sometimes inattentive to the first two—(1) becoming centered and aware of God's presence, and (2) gratitude. This time, they unsettled me. I felt unhinged. I could no longer find comfort in the images of God I knew. I was disoriented by what was once familiar. I craved expansion and newness. Gratitude emerged from my ability to be spiritually whole in my whiteness, not despite it.

Become Centered and Aware of God's Presence

"There is no such thing as a silent retreat. We just stop talking." Fr. Joseph Brown, SJ, framed retreat in this way. This revelation repeatedly resurfaced. As I aimed to become centered, I was overcome by how naturally I center myself. Sitting in the chapel praying with a multiracial community, *made in God's image* shook me. It wasn't a question of God's creativity and intentionality, but of my own. *God made in my image.* For so long, I've subconsciously clung to images of God I now recognize as disordered attachments. Interpretations of my acquired history; a history stripped of truth, centering white. *The wrong version of history had become a part of my relationship with God. Hadn't I overcome these ideas through my racial justice work?* As I sat imagining the God I've so-long accepted, I couldn't fathom sharing that God with my fellow retreatants. This was not the God of Us All. It was my God; the intentionally shaped, white-designed God. No wonder I presumed access was needed. I sat in the chapel feeling naked, revealed. In the community with whom I gathered, I encountered a God that no longer fit the descriptions given to me; a God I had yet to conceive of.

To become aware of God's presence, I needed to decenter my guilt and shame. The day's grace—*to know interiorly the deep love God has for us all*—awakened in me an ever-changing God. I was being moved to *receive* God, not *find* God. To *encounter* God on the continuum

Resmaa Menakem describes in *My Grandmother's Hands: Racialized Trauma and the Pathway to Mending Our Hearts and Bodies*:

> In today's America, we tend to think of healing as something binary: either we're broken or we've healed from that broken-ness. But that's not how healing operates, and it's almost never how human growth works. More often, healing and growth take place on a continuum, with innumerable points between utter brokenness and total health.[1]

God, the Continuum, was calling.

Gratitude

There is an overt white need to create and define anti-racism work. I anticipated the retreat content with expectations and goals. Leaning into the need for control, I began to force the experience. My spiritual director countered a question I had been ruminating over, "How has your prayer been impacting you?" Instead, she offered, "How are *you* impacting your prayer?"

My mind and body were in conflict—an unforeseen grace. What I knew and what I was experiencing were not aligned. The Spirit was alive in the music we prayed; even more so in the stories the lyrics told. The witness of the ancestors was communicated through these spirituals. There is a synchronicity in the spirituals and Spiritual Exercises. Stories of lamentation, invitation, and transcendence. We were invited to know these stories through our bodies and with our voices. Prayer was moving me in ways my "reverent" (robotic) white Christianity could not make sense of. I was physically encountering God. Our individual prayer was connected through a communal recognition and receiving of one another's physical embodiment of the sacred. It was a full-body experience that took me out of my head. Black spirituality exposed a more full, truer sense of the Divine. I heard my director's reflection, "No one leaves church singing the sermon." I left the chapel singing about the God of us all.

---

[1] Resmaa Menakem, *My Grandmother's Hands: Racialized Trauma and the Pathway to Mending Our Hearts and Bodies* (Las Vegas: Central Recovery Press, 2017), 12.

Composition of place was critical to understanding the history of our retreat location. The trees shading the grounds were the same lynching trees in which Christ, in Black bodies, was crucified. There was an evident, racial divide in one another's experience of these trees. Our histories knew these trees differently. As I heard and felt the anguish of black retreatants navigating the presence of the trees, I began to walk among them differently. My spiritual journey was intersecting with a history I began to own. As I noted in my journal, *my learning can lead to healing if I open myself to the true cross it sets forth.*

The history of the William J. Kelly Retreat Center in Bay St. Louis, Mississippi, is described on its website:

> St. Augustine's was founded by Divine Word Missionaries in Greenville, Mississippi in 1920 and moved to Bay St. Louis in 1923. It was the first Catholic Seminary in the United States opened for the education of Black men for the Catholic priesthood. In the 1960s almost all African American priests in the United States had been trained at St. Augustine's. Today, More than two-thirds of all African American bishops in the USA are graduates of St. Augustine's Seminary.

For days, I sat in the chapel confused by the white Jesus hanging on the cross. *How could this image so aggressively misrepresent Jesus?* Over time, I realized it was an exact representation of the Jesus I had been given—the same white Jesus missionaries proclaimed to the Black men being formed at St. Augustine's.

The African American spiritual lyric, "Woke up this mornin' with my mind stayed on Jesus," challenged this. I felt God's invitation to confront the false images of Jesus I've held. To imagine Jesus in the scenes of history, and to be curious about Jesus in the scenes of today: the scenes of America. To examine myself in relationship to Jesus. *In Christ we find the fullness of divinity; in Christ we find the fullness of humanity.* God, the Continuum, in my life *and* the world around me. At this intersection, I most authentically discover God.

In the fullness of our being, we are called to be active participants in Christ's rising. *This* is an anti-racist invitation. It is a spiritual invitation to move forward without a predetermined destination. It's a commitment to the collective transformation of conscience so that we may receive God at work in each of us. It is an openness to the healing continuum.

$$\underset{=\!=\!=}{15}\underset{=\!=\!=}{}$$

Truth, Healing, and the Journey through Indigenous Catholic Boarding School History

Maka Black Elk

Over the last several years, more and more people have been made aware of the bitter and cruel history of the Indian boarding school systems in the United States and Canada. Policies pursued by both nations, informed by the prevailing attitudes of the time that Indigenous people were inferior in all ways, set up schools run both by governments and by Christian entities that sought to, in the words of Captain Richard Henry Pratt, one of the architects of this system, "kill the Indian, and save the man."

I am an alumni and work at Maȟpiya Luta | Red Cloud, the only K-12 Jesuit school in the county on an Indian reservation. Before Maȟpiya Luta was the school we are today, we were once Holy Rosary Mission, one of the hundreds of boarding schools that sought to extinguish Indigenous culture, spirituality, and language. Today I lead the effort of our Jesuit school to examine that history, be unflinchingly honest about that history, and do what we can in order to help generations of our community heal from the wounds caused. It is difficult, and painful, though ultimately healing, work.

What is a Truth, Healing, and Reconciliation process? There is hardly one answer to this question, but in general, it is something that we, whether we are individuals, families, organizations, or even whole nations, can go through when we seek to repair and heal from

221

the great harm that was caused. It reminds me of the First Week of the Spiritual Exercises, when you take time to acknowledge your sinfulness and the bounty of God's immense forgiveness.

We do this first by recognizing the truth and examining it closely. We're working to gather the stories of those who experienced the boarding school years directly. These stories are full of both tragedy and beauty, such as when one elder described his elementary classroom experience of speaking his native language and being punished for doing so, or of the young woman who found herself being supported and educated and spoken to in her own language by a learned Jesuit priest.

We're examining our records and archives to share and highlight the stories they tell and make them accessible to more people. Records also matter because it can mean everything to the boarder and their family to see their story acknowledged in historic records and learn more about their own time there. Seeing letters written by family members can bring healing to those who never saw them before.

The healing that is needed is deep. The wounds spread far beyond those who experienced the boarding school system directly. Those traumas that they experienced have been passed on from generation to generation in what we now recognize as historical trauma. An Indigenous scholar, Dr. Maria Yellow Horse Brave Heart, described this as the "cumulative emotional and psychological wounding" across generations.

It brings up immense challenges that our community faces. One exemplified by a very simple truth.

God made me an Indigenous person. Part of a community with deep spiritual and sacred ties to Mother Earth. Part of a community that exemplifies in our own traditions that God truly is in all things. Care for our common home was paramount to much of our worldview and core to our spiritual beliefs. In Lakȟóta we have an expression we use in prayer that is similar in practice to how many Christians use "Amen." We say, "Mitakuye Oyasin," meaning "all our relations." It means we're all related. When we pray, we are reminded that we pray for everyone, we are connected to all things, and that we are one of many.

For many people, it might seem deeply incompatible to see me and recognize that I am an Indigenous person who is also Catholic.

I understand the sentiment. How can one be a part of a faith that historically inflicted so much pain and wielded immense power over your community? Who even viewed your people as inferior, in need of a patronizing salvation, and who seems to time and time again fail to hold itself accountable to that history or repeat it in many ways even to this day?

I understand that contradiction and live it out in my own life.

I can recognize for myself that the historical Catholic Church and the faith itself aren't always the same thing. The reality is that the church should never have run these schools even according to the tenets of the faith itself. This was beautifully illustrated by the Canadian theologian Brett Salkeld who wrote that the Indigenous boarding schools were a violation of two core beliefs in the Catholic faith: that the family is sacred and that we are a church of no singular culture.

It is in this context that Pope Francis made his pilgrimage of penance to Canada, which marks a pivotal moment in the Catholic Church and Indigenous peoples' journey towards potential reconciliation. This was one of the ninety-four Calls to Action outlined by the Canadian Truth and Reconciliation Commission in the wake of their seven-year effort to document, inform, and seek justice for First Nations, Inuit, and Metis peoples across Canada. The visit from Pope Francis on Canadian soil to apologize for the residential school system marks another step in what is insisted upon by Indigenous peoples and the pope himself to be an ongoing journey toward healing. In his apology, Pope Francis declared "that is only the first step, the starting point" for a long road toward creating a right relationship.

The actual work of reconciliation will not be in the pope's hands. Through issuing his apology, Pope Francis has called upon the whole Body of Christ to now take the steps necessary to face our history as a church in North America and seek to right our relationship with Indigenous peoples.

It is no individual today who is responsible for or should hold guilt for the sins of the Church's past. We are, however, collectively responsible for how we repair relationships moving forward. To do so is to affirm the God-given dignity of Indigenous peoples and call us to a deeper relationship in order to create a new future together.

Healing is incredibly difficult work.

We have learned much about healing, what it is and isn't, and what we're capable of, responsible for, and the limitations we have both as individuals and as a member of this Church through the Jesuits.

Healing is ultimately a personal journey. We cannot make anyone heal, and in this way there really isn't such a thing as collective healing. We are, however, responsible for providing the things that people need in order to heal. To help them along their journey. This is why apology does indeed matter. There was immense criticism and anger towards Pope Francis and the greater Catholic Church upon his apology in Canada. There were many who felt it wasn't enough, that it was too little too late, or that there is nothing the Church could ever do to truly atone. That may be true for many people. And yet, there were also hundreds if not thousands of Indigenous people who needed that apology. Who wanted that apology. And who are one step closer to healing because of it.

The more recent move of the church to openly repudiate the Doctrine of Discovery has also furthered the relationship and conversation Indigenous people are having with the Catholic faith and the institutional church. We saw a similar reaction to the one given when Pope Francis apologized. Many Indigenous people felt that the repudiation didn't go far enough and was weak in the overall message. Other Indigenous people were inspired, comforted, and emboldened in their belief that this was another helpful and important step in the right direction. Thus, once again, healing came to some but not all. More can be done to support the healing of all those who continue to struggle with it in their lives.

Healing has other barriers as well. In this work we learned about three barriers that instruct us in this process. First, healing can only happen when we desire it. Two, we must believe healing is possible. And finally, we must believe we are worthy of healing.

The Jesuits and the greater Catholic Church ought to consider themselves in light of this whole truth, that they were historic perpetrators of great harm to a people that still exist to this day. What does it mean to heal while in the seat of perpetrator or inheritor of perpetrator harms? I think the Spiritual Exercises could be extrapolated further, beyond the individual journey, and expressed in a communal journey of healing and reconciliation. While we do not yet know what this looks like in detail, we can say the shape of that path is already drawn for us.

Discernment serves an important role here. Ignatian spirituality asks us to pay attention to the ways in which God is leading us and calling us, and ways in which we might turn away from God and become more distant from his love and purpose for us. Some questions about relationship and healing moving forward are going to be profoundly difficult to answer. But God is waiting for us in every situation to follow his lead. We must each discern how we move forward toward right relationship and new beginnings as we overcome our historical bonds of pain.

Moving forward from here, understand where you might be on the road to healing. Ask yourself, do I want to heal, do I believe healing is possible, and am I worthy of healing? Love is at the center of each of those questions. I believe God is at the center of each of those questions. When we ask those questions, I imagine God whispering in our ears as a comforting friend, "Yes."

Contributors

Maka Black Elk (Oglala Lakota) is from the Pine Ridge Indian Reservation in Southwestern South Dakota. He is an educator and teacher and has served in various roles throughout his time at Maȟpiya Luta | Red Cloud school, including as their former director for truth and healing. He advocates for reconciliation and racial healing, particularly between Indigenous communities and the Catholic Church.

Laurie Cassidy, PhD, currently teaches in the Christian Spirituality Program at Creighton University and was associate professor in the religious studies department at Marywood University in Scranton, Pennsylvania. An award-winning author and editor, her latest book, *Desire, Darkness, and Hope: Theology in a Time of Impasse,* was edited with M. Shawn Copeland. Cassidy has been engaged in the ministry of spiritual direction for over thirty years, giving directed retreats around the United States. Raised in Massachusetts, she now makes her home in the foothills of the Rocky Mountains, traditional homeland of the Ute in Colorado.

Matthew J. Cressler, PhD, is a scholar of religion, race, and culture. He is the author of *Authentically Black and Truly Catholic: The Rise of Black Catholicism in the Great Migration* and numerous peer-reviewed articles on Catholic and African American religious histories, clerical sexual abuse, horror, comics, and more. He has written for *America, The Atlantic, National Catholic Reporter, Religion News Service, The Revealer, Slate, U.S. Catholic,* and *Zócalo Public Square.* Together with Adelle M. Banks, he co-reported the *Religion News Service* series "Beyond the Most Segregated Hour," which won a Wilbur Award from the Religion Communicators Council.

Paulina Delgadillo is a first in the family, first-generation undocumented student interested in uplifting undocumented voices and co-creating spaces of accompaniment for those searching to dive deeper into their faith and spirituality, emphasizing the importance of living *en lo cotidiano*. She is a current graduate student pursuing a master's degree in pastoral ministry from Catholic Theological Union through the Pathways Program. This program creates living-learning community for young adults who are passionate about co-creating the church of tomorrow. She holds a BA in natural science and a BA in theology from Dominican University.

Elise Gower (she/her) is the associate director of Contemplative Leaders in Action (CLA). She holds a BA in religious studies from Marywood University and an MS in elementary education from the University of Scranton. Elise is personally and professionally committed to fostering intentional community around the tradition and values of Ignatian spirituality. Her career has been focused in ministry, community engagement, and leadership development. She has extensive experience working with the Jesuits in higher education and the USA East Province. Elise is drawn to the art of sacred storytelling. She is committed to individual and collective anti-racism work and fostering connections between spirituality and LGBTQ+ identity. Elise proudly calls Baltimore, Maryland home.

Armando Guerrero Estrada is a PhD candidate in theology and education at Boston College. As a DACA recipient and a first-generation college student, he is passionate about fostering *acompañamiento* and *protagonismo* among Hispanic youth and young adults. He currently serves as the director of the PASOS Network at Dominican University, and he teaches in the theology department. Armando holds a master of theological studies from Vanderbilt University's Divinity School, where he also earned graduate certificates in Latin American studies and religion and the arts in contemporary culture, with an emphasis on US Hispanic literature, and was awarded the J.D. Owen Prize in Biblical Studies and the Academic Achievement Award. He holds a BA in theology and philosophical studies from St. Joseph College and a BA in Spanish from Lamar University.

Jeannine Hill Fletcher, ThD, is a constructive theologian writing at the intersection of Catholic systematic theology and issues of diversity (including gender, race, and religious diversity). She is the author of *The Sin of White Supremacy: Christianity, Racism, and Religious Diversity in America* (Orbis Books, 2017). As professor of theology at Fordham University, Bronx, New York, she also serves on the board of the Northwest Bronx Community and Clergy Coalition, an intergenerational, multiracial, multireligious grassroots organization that addresses social justice issues in New York City and beyond. Her current project is titled *Grace of the Ghosts: A Theology of Institutional Accountability.*

Ken Homan, SJ, is a Jesuit of the Upper Midwest Province. He is a historian of US labor and Catholicism, with special focus on St. Louis, where he grew up. Ken additionally works in community organizing and Ignatian education.

Alex Mikulich, PhD, is author of *Unlearning White Supremacy: A Spirituality for Racial Liberation* (Orbis Books, 2022). He won a 2023 ACTA Foundation grant to pilot an adult education anti-racism program in Catholic parishes. Alex offers decolonial anti-racism facilitation and educational programming through his Other Ways Collaborative, LLC. He has served as an invited affiliate member of the Black Catholic Theological Symposium since 2008. He brings over twenty years of experience in Jesuit institutions, including training in the Spiritual Exercises of St. Ignatius.

María Teresa Morgan, DMin, is associate professor of theology at Saint John Vianney College Seminary, where she also coordinates the Humanities Program. She is a resident columnist and member of the editorial board of *ElIgnaciano.com*, the online quarterly publication of the Pedro Arrupe Institute. Dr. Morgan has authored over twenty articles. Her chapter "The Sentinel" is included in *Desire, Darkness, and Hope: Theology in a Time of Impasse; Engaging the Thought of Constance FitzGerald, OCD*. The book is the recipient of a 2022 award by the Catholic Media Association. She and her husband Robert reside in Miami, Florida.

Marilyn L. Nash (she/her) is a white, cisgender, LGBQ woman, educator, writer, spiritual director, and facilitator committed to the liberative power of Creative Love. Marilyn teaches Ignatian spirituality at Seattle University and manages a consulting practice, A Change of Being, through which she offers retreats, coaches individuals, and advises various mission-based schools and nonprofits to encourage personal and collective spiritual discernment that accounts for our current social context and the distortion of White supremacy culture and racism. She holds a bachelor of social work from Millersville University, a master's of transformative spirituality with a specialization in spiritual direction, and a post-master's certificate in pastoral leadership through Seattle University. She finds joy in being an auntie on both coasts, while living and cold-water plunging in the Pacific Northwest on the ancestral homelands of the Coast Salish people.

Maureen H. O'Connell, PhD, spent eight years in the department of theology at Fordham University in New York City before returning home to Philadelphia to chair the department of religion at LaSalle University, where she is also an associate professor of theology. She authored *Compassion: Loving Our Neighbor in an Age of Globalization* (Orbis Books, 2009) and *If These Walls Could Talk: Community Muralism and the Beauty of Justice* (Liturgical Press, 2012), which explores the arts as source of ethical wisdom and catalyst for moral action and won the College Theology Book of the Year Award in 2012, as well as the Catholic Press Association's first place for books in theology in 2012. Her current research project explores racial identity formation, racism, and racial justice on Catholic college campuses. She serves on the board of the Society for the Arts in Religious and Theological Studies and is the vice president of the College Theology Society.

Hung T. Pham, SJ, PhD, a Jesuit priest, currently serves as the provincial assistant for formation of the Central South Province (UCS) of the Society of Jesus. In this role, he accompanies young Jesuits—brothers, scholastics, and priests in their spiritual and pastoral formation. Prior to this assignment, he spent seven years teaching Ignatian spirituality at the Jesuit School of Theology of Santa Clara University in Berkeley, California. A Jesuit for thirty years, he has written, lectured, and led seminars on different Ignatian themes and topics as well as directed numerous Ignatian workshops and retreats in Belize, Canada, Singapore, South Africa, Spain, Thailand, and Vietnam.

Christopher Pramuk, PhD, is the chair of Ignatian Thought and Imagination and professor of theology at Regis University. He is the author of seven books, including *Hope Sings, So Beautiful: Graced Encounters across the Color Line* (Liturgical Press, 2013), and two award-winning studies of the famed Trappist monk and spiritual writer Thomas Merton. His most recent book, *The Artist Alive: Explorations in Music, Art, and Theology* (Anselm Academic, 2019), is the fruition of many years of using the arts with young people in the theology classroom, and he is currently completing a book with iconographer Fr. William Hart McNichols.

Andrew Prevot, PhD, holds the Amaturo Chair in Catholic Studies in the department of Theology and Religious Studies at Georgetown University. He researches and teaches in the areas of spiritual, philosophical, and political theology. He is the author of three books: *The Mysticism of Ordinary Life: Theology, Philosophy, and Feminism* (Oxford University Press, 2023); *Theology and Race: Black and Womanist Traditions in the United States* (Brill, 2018); and *Thinking Prayer: Theology and Spirituality amid the Crises of Modernity* (University of Notre Dame Press, 2015). He is the coeditor of *Anti-Blackness and Christian Ethics* (Orbis Books, 2017) and the author of numerous journal articles and book chapters.

Patrick Saint-Jean, SJ, PysD, is a member of the USA Midwest Province of the Society of Jesus—the Jesuits. He is a trained psychoanalyst, clinical psychologist, and associate professor of psychology at Creighton University, Omaha. Dr. Saint-Jean is a prolific writer on race, racism, and Ignatian spirituality. He has written several books; his most recent one is *The Spirituality of Transformation, Joy, and Justice: The Ignatian Way for Everyone* (Broadleaf, 2023).

Justin T. White, a native of Philadelphia, earned his BA in sociology from Loyola University Maryland in 2009. He then spent eight years as a theology teacher at Cristo Rey Jesuit High School in Baltimore and directed the school's community service program as a component of campus ministry. Since 2017, he has worked at Loyola Blakefield in the areas of campus ministry, community service, diversity, inclusion and equity, teaching theology and psychology, and admissions. In May 2022 he earned a master's in school counseling from his alma mater and began serving as a middle school counselor at Loyola Blakefield. Equity work and its intersection with education, spirituality, and mental health are areas of great personal and professional interest. In his free time, Justin enjoys fellowship with family and friends, Marvel and Star Wars, kayaking, and reading works about liberation.